PERESTROIKA ANNUAL

In this series:

PERESTROIKA ANNUAL
VOLUME 1

PERESTROIKA ANNUAL

Volume 2

Editor-in-Chief
Professor Abel G. Aganbegyan

BRASSEY'S (US), Inc.

Washington · New York · London · Oxford · Moscow
Beijing · Frankfurt · São Paulo · Sydney · Tokyo · Toronto

A Brassey's (US) Book

Copyright © 1989 Vadim A. Medvedev, Alexander A. Bessmertnykh, Vladimir N. Kudryavtsev, Georgi Kh. Shakhnazarov, Julian V. Bromlei, Nikolai N. Chetverikov, Abel G. Aganbegyan, Ivan D. Ivanov, Gavriil Kh. Popov, Roald Z. Sagdeev, Vladislav Teryaev, Mikhail P. Kulakov, Mark A. Zakharov, Valentin G. Rasputin, Lev Yashin.

English translation © 1989 Futura Publications

Published simultaneously in Great Britain in 1989 by
Futura Publications, a Division of
Macdonald & Co (Publishers) Ltd
London & Sydney

All rights reserved. No part of this publication may be reproduced, stored in a retrieval system or transmitted in any form or by any means; electronic, electrostatic, magnetic tape, mechanical, photocopying, recording or otherwise, without permission in writing from the publishers.

ISBN 0-08-037455-7

Printed and bound in Great Britain by
BPCC Hazell Books Ltd
Member of BPCC Ltd
Aylesbury, Bucks, England

Brassey's (US), Inc.
A Division of Macmillan, Inc.
New York

Editorial Offices
Brassey's (US), Inc.
8000 Westpark Drive, 4th Floor
McLean, VA 22102

Order Department
Macmillan Publishing Co.
Front and Brown Streets
Riverside, NJ 08075

ISSN 0958-3939

Brassey's (US), Inc., books are available at special discounts for bulk purchases for sales promotions, fund-raising, or educational use through the Special Sales Directo Macmillan Publishing Company, 866 Third Avenue, New York, New York 10022.

10 9 8 7 6 5 4 3 2 1

Published in the United States of America

Foreword

ROBERT MAXWELL

It is a source of great personal pleasure for me to write the foreword for this volume – the second in the Perestroika series. Perestroika I enjoyed a justifiable success and I am pleased to build on it with this book.

In the closing years of the twentieth century there can have been few words which have so comprehensibly entered the political lexicon throughout the world. At first we all tended to be unsure of the full scope of this concept. As time has progressed we have learnt that it is more far-reaching and revolutionary, in the full meaning of the word, than we had originally expected.

The restructuring of the Soviet economy has already produced results which have impinged on all strata of Soviet society. In my own visit to the Soviet Union this year there was barely a conversation which did not refer to the changes brought about by Perestroika and every reference was in a positive sense. This is not to imply that all Perestroika's goals have already been achieved. It is clearly only the beginning of a process that will inevitably be long and difficult. With its long term aims this series of books is ideally suited to follow Perestroika's progress.

In this volume we do so by widening the range of topics covered still further with articles dealing not only with politics and economics but also, amongst others, ecology and football. This in itself is an index of the diversity of fields affected by Perestroika.

I should like to emphasise that this volume again reflects Perestroika as seen from the inside. It contains the views of distinguished Soviet citizens as they have chosen to express

FOREWORD

them. My role has been to make their thinking available to a wide readership in the West.

I have devoted a great deal of my working effort over the past forty years to the improvement of communications and understanding between the peoples of the world. I can think of no more worthwhile endeavour in this regard than to give as wide a circulation as possible to Soviet views on another momentous year in the progress of Perestroika.

November 1989

Robert Maxwell
Publisher

Contents

Foreword ROBERT MAXWELL	v
Introduction: The Language of Perestroika	1
A Who's Who of Perestroika	7

Social and Political Problems

The Ideology of Perestroika VADIM A. MEDVEDEV	23
Foreign Policy – a New Course ALEXANDER A. BESSMERTNYKH	43
Political Reform in the USSR: the First Stage VLADIMIR N. KUDRYAVTSEV	67
The New Thinking: Principal Ideas and Guidelines GEORGI KH. SHAKHNAZAROV	81
Ethnic Relations and Perestroika JULIAN V. BROMLEI	101
A Secret no Longer NIKOLAI N. CHETVERIKOV	123

The Economy

Profitable for Us and for Our Partner ABEL G. AGANBEGYAN AND IVAN D. IVANOV	143
Perestroika and the Managers GAVRIIL KH. POPOV	161

CONTENTS

Science

Where Did We Lose Momentum? 183
ROALD Z. SAGDEEV

The Whole World Gave Us a Helping Hand:
The Phase of Isolation 197
VLADISLAV GO TERYAEV

Religion

An Open Door 213
MIKHAIL P. KULAKOV

Culture

Nostalgia for Meyerhold 233
MARK A. ZAKHAROV

Ecology

Hopes and Despair, and Hopes... 255
VALENTIN G. RASPUTIN

Sport

Football Requires Competence 277
LEV YASHIN

Public Opinion Polls 291

Armenia: Lessons for All 295

A Chronology of Perestroika 299

Bibliography 305

Index 309

Introduction: The Language of Perestroika

The Committee for Constitutional Supervision. During the period of stagnation this was an informal group which monitored adherence to the constitution. It was persecuted by the Soviet authorities as a criminal association. At present, it is a Committee established by the Congress of People's Deputies to broaden the process of democratization in the USSR by monitoring the governmental bodies' and other organizations' observance of the Constitution.
Free enterprise zones. Special areas of the territory of the USSR which are being formed as a part of the restructuring of foreign economic activity. They are to receive favoured treatment to encourage joint ventures, the import of capital, trade and other forms of direct links between Soviet and foreign firms.
The ecology of culture. An informal trend which originated in Soviet culture, science and technology during the last decade. It utilizes both intellectual and emotional means to instil a feeling of harmony between man and nature in every member of society.
A farmer's houshold (a farm). Earlier in the USSR this was a scornful term that referred to individual farms in capitalist countries. It is now a form of contract in Soviet agriculture under which a family or a small group of agricultural workers leases a plot of land and the necessary facilities for agricultural work on a long-term basis.
Public opinion. This has previously been a fiction formed in the quiet of the offices of the Party bureaucracy. This is now a phenomenon of public consciousness which reflects the most important aspect of political restructuring in the USSR and a method of studying the views of the masses.
TV-bridge. A form of direct discussion between the TV viewers

INTRODUCTION: THE LANGUAGE OF PERESTROIKA

of the USSR and other countries (the USA, Great Britain, etc.) on contemporary, topical questions. Introduced in the USSR during the last three years.

People's diplomacy. This is a social movement of the population of the USSR and other countries which originated two to three years ago which aims to search for better mutual understanding through an exchange of visits between participating countries.

A beauty contest. A televised show, new to Soviet audiences, staged to identify the most beautiful woman of the year. The charming Julia Soukhanova became the winner of the first beauty contest in the USSR.

Mercy. Until 1985 this was a condescending word used to denote the flabbiness of those strata of society which did not belong to the workers and peasants. Now it has become a norm of human morals which is being restored in the USSR.

General human values. Until recently, these were the norms and criteria to evaluate the individual and society which were rejected by Soviet official bodies and Communist morals as unacceptable alternatives to class morals and values. Now, as we witness the de-ideologization of general human values, they have become a major element in the new political thinking outlined by Mikhail Gorbachev.

Professional sports. For nearly seventy years the USSR denied the existence of professional sports because they were considered to be a phenomenon of bourgeois civilization and alien to Soviet amateur sports. Only in recent years have professional sports been recognized in the USSR as legitimate as amateur sports. Soviet athletes now sign contracts with Western professional teams and play for them.

The Memorial to the Memory of the Victims of Stalinist Repression. An informal association founded a year ago with the aim of immortalizing the memory of the victims of Stalinist repression and preventing a future repetition of the personality cult.

A multitude of property forms. This puts into practice the principle of economic pluralism proclaimed by Mikhail Gorbachev. It officially recognizes the equality of State, cooperative, individual and other forms of property.

INTRODUCTION: THE LANGUAGE OF PERESTROIKA

Leasing. This economic form is based on the transfer of production funds to a work collective through the signing of an economic agreement with the State (as represented by a local Soviet or a state organization), in which both parties have equal rights. Under the agreement the leaseholder becomes, for the stipulated period of time, the legal owner of the means of production, with complete freedom of economic manoeuvre. The leaseholder must only make a fixed payment to the budget or a superior organization. The introduction of the lease system overcomes the alienation of an employee from the public-property status of the means of production, enhances his interest in higher quality work and its final results. In the Soviet Union lease systems in agriculture and some branches of industry have been gaining ground.

Conversion. This is the turning of military production and other military activity over to peaceful lines. Conversion is an important factor in a stronger social orientation of the national economy and, among other things, provides for a new area of international cooperation that is the coordination of individual states' measures in converting military resources to peaceful purposes. The USSR decided to cut military expenditures by 142,110 million rubles for 1989–90 and the production of weapons by 19.5 per cent.

Convertible ruble. This is the status of the USSR's national currency which will be guaranteed by the State and will ensure, in the case of complete convertibility, the free and unlimited exchange of rubles into other currencies and its transfer to other countries for all categories of holders and for all types of international financial operations. Giving such a status to the ruble is a key aspect of Soviet economic restructuring which envisages the formation of a developed Socialist market.

People's Deputy. He or she is a citizen of the USSR who is at least 21 years old, and is elected by secret ballot in a one- or multimandate electoral district, or by a public organization through universal, equal and direct suffrage. The number of candidates for deputies is unlimited, so every participant in a voters' meeting may propose any candidacies, including his or her own. Any number of candidates may be included on the ballot. Preparations for the election of People's Deputies are made openly and in an atmosphere of glasnost. The elections of People's Deputies of the USSR in March to May 1989 saw a true battle between 9,505 candidates who ran for 2,250 mandates.

Popular front. This is a historically established form of organization of the broad popular masses to protect democratization and the interests of the working people. At present some regions of the USSR (the Russian Federation (RSFSR), the Baltic republics, etc.) are witnessing the formation of popular fronts which act as public movements for the defence of perestroika and for the strengthening of the national sovereignty of the republics. A popular front is based on a wide pluralistic platform and acts outside the framework of traditional public formations.

New agrarian policy. This denotes a resolute shift to an agro-industrial complex centred on a diversity of forms of property, the use and disposal of this property, and an equality of economic conditions for all types of agricultural households. This implies the granting of full independence to agriculture's main production element, the decentralization of the APK (Agro-Industrial Complex), a social orientation of investment policies, the priority development of processing sectors of the APK, the strengthening of its material and technological base, and the acceptance of new principles in the purchase of agricultural produce which is geared to regional and local self-government.

New foreign economic policy. This provides for the integration of the Soviet national economy into the world economic system on the basis of an economic approach to the managing of foreign trade relations, decentralization, a multitude of forms of external ties, including direct ties; the establishment of a new world economic order that ensures the equal economic security of all states; the search for a just settlement of the debt problem, and a gradual switch to a convertible ruble.

Organized crime. This is a form of criminal activity characterized by a striving for a monopoly in certain areas of criminal activity (drug trafficking, large-scale extortion, etc.) through the establishment of specific criminal structures often connected with corrupt layers of the State apparatus and public organizations. The existence of organized crime in the USSR was recognized during the period of glasnost. Recently there has been an increase in the rate of organized crime, in part due to an increase in cooperative activities. Legislative and practical measures are being taken to combat it.

Special rule. This is provided for by the Constitution of the USSR which specifies special forms of rule exercised by the State bodies of the USSR and constituent republics for the protection of the USSR and the security of its citizens. It can be enacted by the Presidium of the USSR Supreme Soviet. On January 20 1989, special rule was enacted in the Nagorny Karabakh Autonomous Region of the Azerbaijan SSR because of the continuous ethnic tension in that area. A Committee for Special Rule was formed. The Committee is directly subordinate to the USSR's highest bodies of State power and administration and enjoys the full powers of the Soviet of People's Deputies of an autonomous republic and its executive committee.

A rule-of-law state (law-governed state). This is a state which ensures the supremacy of law in all spheres of the life of society, where the mechanism of Socialist law-enforcement operates on the basis of well-developed people's power. The construction of a rule-of-law state is a major element in the safeguarding of perestroika and is now under way in the USSR. It is based on a broad legal reform which is aimed at consolidated rule and drastically enhancing the role of the Soviet laws that regulate all important aspects of social relations according to the principle: everything is allowed which is not specifically banned by the law.

The reform of economic management. This is a scientifically based, integrated programme for improving the system of control over processes that take place in the country's economy. The radical economic reform envisages a large-scale democratization of the management of the national economy, the greater independence of enterprises, the conversion of them to complete cost-accounting, self-financing and self-management, qualitative reorganization of the planning and control system, structural and investment policies, a real shift from mainly administrative methods of management to economic ones, and a broader system of money-commodity relations. The fulfilment of this programme will make it possible to reveal the potential of Socialism, make the economy more dynamic, adaptable and responsive to scientific-technological progress, further democratize industrial life and relations, comprehensively promote the creative potential of masses and bring into play the human factor.

Soviet manager. He is a leader, a highly skilled specialist in business administration who is guided in his work by the laws and methods of management, the peculiarities of economic and organizational systems, Soviet economic legislation and international practice in foreign economic relations. The training and proper use of competent managers in the national economy constitute an important element in the reorganization of economic management, intensifying economic development and integrating the USSR economy into the world economic system.

Joint ventures on the territory of the USSR (mixed enterprises). These are enterprises established for industrial, scientific and technological, and other types of economic activity involving at least one Soviet enterprise (organization) and at least one foreign firm which are legal entities. Partners in joint ventures base their relationship on agreements and operate in accordance with Soviet legislation and their charter. The basic capital of the joint ventures is formed by contributions from the partners to the enterprise's charter fund. The profits are distributed in proportion to this basic capital. The controlling body of a joint venture is its board, whose members are appointed by the partners. The Directorate runs the daily activities of the venture and has both Soviet and foreign members. All hard currency expenditure should be covered by the revenues received from the sale of the joint venture's products in foreign markets.

Financial normalization of the economy. This comprises a series of measures necessary for pursuing an active financial policy which is required by the pressure of the existing situation on the national economy. The measures are primarily aimed at eliminating the State budget deficit, ensuring a balanced commodities offer and solvent demand, and provide for a wide range of short- and long-term measures to ensure a link between earned wages and the final results. Some extraordinary administrative measures are also envisaged.

A Who's Who of Perestroika

What's the price of independence?

In large Russian families, particularly those living in villages, all brothers usually practised one craft, but, as a rule, only the most capable or talented one, the 'possessor of God's gift', made it. Today, however, three brothers in the Starodubtsev family living in Tula region have made their mark one after another, coming to head collective and state farms. Vladimir Starodubtsev got the worst farm, unprofitable, with a dearth of services and amenities, with worn-out machinery. But Vladimir carried on quite undaunted, introducing new economic techniques that gave his farmers an economic interest in expanding productivity, a large degree of freedom and material incentives. He got the farm off the ground. Within two years the farm was no longer a crippled business, and still another two years later it was spoken of as a leader.

What Vladimir introduced was a prototype of the family-lease system. Having made his farmers independent, the chairman decided to win some independence for himself, or rather for the farm personnel. The district Communist Party committee did not like the idea, nor did the regional one. In the late 1970s, when the country was mired in the bog of stagnation, they raised a hue and cry, and Vladimir was framed and jailed. But finally the truth triumphed. Today Vladimir is free, and director of the same farm again (the fortunes of his farm declined once again while he was in gaol). With him at the helm, his farm got on its feet once more, developing into a powerful agrobusiness. Perestroika needs people of Starodubtsev's type in the countryside, those who are ready to stand up for the man of the soil, who are caring and considerate. Giving high grades to Vladimir's courage, his constituency returned him to the Soviet parliament.

Who invented *Homo sovieticus?*

Human history recedes into hoary antiquity. Textbooks tell us that our predecessors were *Homo erectus* and *Homo sapiens*. But some ten years ago the Soviet press began to run articles claiming a need to prove the existence of a new species of *Homo sapiens: Homo sovieticus*. One of the first scholars to analyse *Homo sovieticus* was Ivan Frolov. A philosopher by training who went through college after World War II and realized that no original approach to orthodox Marxist philosophy stood a realistic chance of succeeding, Frolov became interested in philosophic issues of natural sciences as a whole, and biology in particular. One of the more professional Soviet philosophers, he sought to have his say even on the Procrustean bed of traditional Marxism-Leninism and to inject new life into the drudgery of interpreting Marx, Engels and Lenin and quoting from them endlessly. Having defended his doctoral thesis, Frolov worked at the Soviet Academy of Sciences' Institute of Philosophy, and when the position of editor-in-chief at the *Voprosy Filosofii (Philosophical Issues)* journal became vacant, he headed the first theoretical journal of Soviet philosophers. At the time perestroika was already dawning, and Frolov's life took a sharp turn as he got a chance to fulfil himself. He organized an institute to investigate human problems in their totality and came to head a philosophic society. The country's new leaders gave top marks to Frolov's ideas concerning the social orientation of perestroika. Frolov became the CPSU General Secretary's aide. But despite his meteoric rise, Frolov is as democratic as ever, and he can often be found taking part in numerous philosophic debates.

On the crest of glasnost

Glasnost has become one of the hallmarks or even birthmarks of perestroika. But what is it? First and foremost, glasnost means providing for the people to use their constitutional freedom of speech and of the press. In contrast to the past, virtually no socially significant event in the Soviet Union can go unnoticed now or be drowned in a flood of cliché-ridden articles or programmes. The press has regained its good reputation. If asked which publication is the most popular today, 99 per cent of respondents would say, 'the *Ogonyok* magazine'.

True, over the last three years the magazine has regained the popularity it had during the early post-revolutionary years, largely due to the efforts of its editor-in-chief Vitali Korotich. Starting out as a journalist in the Ukraine, he made the *Molod Ukrainy* magazine an interesting publication that raised socially poignant issues. During the early days of perestroika he became editor-in-chief of the *Ogonyok* magazine. Glasnost, glasnost and nothing but glasnost is the creed of Korotich and his magazine.

This creed helped him to stand up under pressure from opponents of perestroika when Korotich publicly accused several top Party officials of corruption at the 19th Party conference. He also came under pressure from the criminal elements because his magazine published very tough articles on racketeering, organized crime, the mafia, drug-addiction and prostitution, but this pressure did not make a dent in his civic commitment.

Today *Ogonyok* is a standard-bearer in the fight against Stalinism. The magazine took the lead in the establishment of the Memorial to the Memory of the Victims of Stalinist Repression.

Diplomacy

The Soviet diplomatic corps consists of two groups of staff: professional diplomats trained at the Moscow State Institute of International Relations and Party functionaries appointed to work as diplomats.

Yuli Vorontsov belongs to the former category. Born in 1929, he was too young to join the military and fight in World War II. But he had his share of wartime troubles, and even as a young man he developed the pacifist creed he has been following throughout his life. He was deeply impressed by the terse lines of the official reports about diplomatic talks during the war and the early post-war years. He firmly decided to serve his country as a diplomat, not a soldier, entered the Institute of International Relations in 1947, when the cold war was still in its infancy, and graduated with honours. Having shown himself to be a promising diplomat when he was still at school, he worked his way up from the very bottom, at the Soviet Foreign Ministry, starting out as an adviser at the Second European Department of the Ministry. During the subsequent fourteen years he rose in the Soviet UN mission, becoming an attaché, third secretary, first secretary, mission adviser, and deputy chief of a department in the Foreign Ministry.

At thirty-seven, Vorontsov was already minister resident at the Soviet embassy in the USA, a responsible post indeed. In 1977 he rose to the top of the foreign service ladder, becoming Soviet Ambassador Extraordinary and Plenipotentiary in India and later in France. At every stage of his diplomatic career Yuli Vorontsov showed himself a consummate diplomat and negotiator. He is no respecter of status, his main goal being to safeguard his country's interests. Since the very beginning of the Afghan venture, that low tide mark of the period of stagnation, Yuli Vorontsov advocated diplomatic methods and forms of settling the Afghan problem, but his voice was not heeded. Not until he was appointed first deputy Minister of Foreign Affairs of the Soviet Union in 1986 did he begin to promote his creed at diplomatic summits; since 1988 he has also been Soviet Ambassador in Afghanistan and completed the Soviet withdrawal. So at the peak of his diplomatic career he had to unravel one of the thorniest political problems in the international arena.

Wonder-boy musician

At the age of ten, Evgeni Kisin played Bach's E minor Piano Concerto no. 1 with an orchestra for the first time, and then Mozart's Concerto no. 20 in E minor. He gave his first solo concert at eleven at the Concert Hall of the All-Union House of Composers, and at twelve made his début at the Great Hall of the Moscow Conservatory where he played two Chopin concertos with the orchestra of the Moscow Philharmonic under Dmitri Kitaenko. The recital was such a resounding success that shortly thereafter his name became known internationally. Since that time Evgeni has performed regularly to become, at seventeen, one of the best known pianists in the world. He has often played in solo concerts and with leading orchestras and directors in West Germany, Britain, France, Japan, Hungary, Yugoslavia,

West Berlin, Italy, Spain, Israel, Austria, Switzerland, etc. His concerts are always successful and draw capacity crowds.

In 1986 Evgeni was awarded Japan's best-concert-of-the-year Crystal Prize at Osaka's famous Japanese Hall (Symphony Hall).

Where does the attraction of the young talent's style lie? Why is he invited to come back to any country where he performs? The way we see it, his assets are romanticism, an unusual penetration into the heart of music, a wonderful sincerity, a natural, elevated and poetic quality, plus an accomplished technique and great range that allow him to play works of different styles and by various composers.

Dissident becomes a People's Deputy

For some twenty years Western radio stations and publications have invariably listed Roy Medvedev among Soviet dissidents. Having developed a philosophy of his own, he was one of the first major scholars to investigate Stalinism as a socio-political phenomenon of the twentieth century. His first findings were published in the West in individual articles and a book, *Let History Judge*, which he began in 1962. In the 1970s the book was translated in twelve Western countries. The Khrushchev thaw came to an end in 1965, and several years later Roy Medvedev was expelled from the Communist Party and quit his job. For all these troubles, the scholar refused to go down on his knees. Attempts by journalists and some officials to link him with various dissident groups failed, as Medvedev's theories have always been rooted in Scientific Socialism, which Medvedev believes has been distorted in the USSR. Today virtually every Soviet newspaper would subscribe to this thesis, but during the years of stagnation it was the heresy to end all heresies. Medvedev's life story before he began to be associated with dissent is quite typical of his generation.

He was born in the city of Tbilisi in 1925 into the family of a Red Army commissar who was purged in Stalin's time and died in a camp in Kolyma. He lived with his mother and twin brother in Tbilisi, and finished school in 1943. He worked at defence factories on the Transcaucasian front. In 1946–51 he was a student at the department of philosophy of Leningrad University. In 1951–7, he was principal of a village school, and in 1956–61, an editor and deputy editor-in-chief with Prosveshchenie Publishers. He joined the Communist Party in 1959.

He has written the following books that were published in the West: *On Socialist Democracy* (1972); *Leninism and Western Socialism* (1980); *The Difficult Spring of 1918* (1976); *The October Revolution* (1977); *Khrushchev* (1981); *China and Superpowers* (1984); *Problems of the Literary Biography of Mikhail Sholokhov* (1977); *A Question of Madness?* (co-authored with his brother Zhores Medvedev, 1970); *Philip Mironov and the Russian Civil War* (co-authored with S. P. Starikov, 1977); *Nikolai Bukharin – The Last Years* (1978). The majority of his books are now in print in the USSR.

Elected a People's Deputy in 1989, he now stands a very good chance of fulfilling his political creed.

The difficulty of being loved

Perestroika is said to have let the genies of chronic problems out of the bottle, and one of the evil spirits is worsening ethnic relations. The first acute ethnic crisis erupted in the Nagorny Karabakh Autonomous Region when the Armenian majority of the region's population demanded officially that the region be made part of the Armenian SSR. The Armenian SSR's Supreme Soviet supported the demand, but Azerbaijan and the USSR Supreme Soviet disagreed, and the conflict reached a stalemate. In this difficult period Moscow sent Arkady Volsky to the region as head of the Committee for Special Administration of the NKAR. His tact, unfailing tolerance, compassion and an ability to find a compromise won him the empathy of the area's population, and he was elected a People's Deputy from Nagorny Karabakh.

Born in 1932, Volsky is Russian. He joined the Communist Party in 1958. He graduated from the Moscow Steel Institute and took his first job in 1955 as a foreman at the Moscow I. A. Likhachev Automobile Factory and rose to factory secretary of the Party committee. From 1969 he headed a sub-department, then was a deputy director and full director at the engineering department of the CPSU Central Committee.

In 1983–5 he was an aide of the CPSU Central Committee's General Secretary. Since 1985 he has been director of a CPSU Central Committee department and combines this job with that of representative of the CPSU Central Committee and of the USSR Supreme Soviet Presidium in Nagorny Karabakh. He has repeatedly spoken at the USSR Supreme Soviet in defence of the interests of Nagorny Karabakh.

The chequered career of Gavriil Ilizarov

One would be hard put to point to another doctor in the history of Soviet medicine who has been as selfless and as vilified by the medical establishment as Gavriil Ilizarov. Officials of the Soviet Health Ministry and the Academy of Medical Sciences rejected the new methods of the treatment of the locomotor system; indeed, they dismissed the doctor as a quack. But all hardships notwithstanding, Ilizarov has made it to the top of his profession, becoming a famous surgeon in this country.

He graduated from the Simferopol Institute of Medicine and was sent to work as head doctor at the village of Dolgovka in Siberia. Later he was a flight surgeon on an AN–2 plane at the regional hospital in the city of Kurgan.

He comes from the Tat ethnic group living in Transcaucasia, and is from the village of Khusary. His parents were illiterate and Gavriil was the eldest of their six children. He went to school at eleven and received a doctor's diploma in 1945, the last year of World War II. It took him a long time to try to defend his Candidate of Science thesis, but when he did, he skipped the Candidate of Science level and was awarded a Doctor of Science degree.

Ilizarov's are novel techniques in the theory and practice of world orthopaedics and traumatology, and he holds 122 patents for his inventions.

Today he is director of the Kurgan Research Institute of Experimental and Clinical Orthopaedics and Traumatology, one of the biggest in this country. He has a large therapy unit, an experimental animal clinic, a workshop manufacturing advanced prostheses, and an outpatient hospital.

During the last five years Italy set up an association to study and use Ilizarov's methods with offices in Spain and France. Thousands of leading medics from Western Europe, Africa and Latin America have been trained at this association's international school.

Ilizarov's intraosseous osteosynthesis apparatus is constantly updated.

The Kurgan Institute's pilot factory that produces his apparatus delivers to every area in the Soviet Union and sixty foreign countries.

Be vigilant!

'Be vigilant!' Repeating this exhortation twice, Telman Gdlyan finished his speech at a sanctioned meeting in Luzhniki Park in Moscow on 7 June, 1989, on the completion of the Congress of People's Deputies. Isn't it a bit of a paradox? It's peacetime now, you know, and hadn't the Congress given all power to the Soviets? So what did Gdlyan, a People's Deputy, mean?

Gdlyan believes his mission is to fight corruption and the mafia in different strata of Soviet society. Five years ago when he was an unknown investigator employed at the Soviet Prosecutor's Office and working on especially important cases, he was placed at the head of a group of investigators to unravel the so-called Uzbek case. His group exposed the embezzlement of 2 billion rubles from state funds.

The investigation led to the arrest of the Uzbek Communist Party's Central Committee secretaries; regional committees' secretaries; chairmen of the republic's Council of Ministers and presidium of the Supreme Soviet; and the Uzbek and USSR Ministers of the Interior. The investigators cracked a mafia grouping under Rashidov, the Uzbek Communist Party Central Committee's first secretary. The criminal ring was found to have connections in Moscow. Brezhnev's son-in-law Churbanov was arrested and went to gaol. The Minister for Internal Affairs, Shchyolokov, killed himself. The criminals returned 40 million rubles to the state treasury of their own accord. For five years Gdlyan was the golden boy of the central press, who called him a hero and fighter of organized crime. But, proverbially, life is full of ups and downs. In May 1989, the CPSU Central

Committee secretary Egor Ligachev filed a suit against Gdlyan and his deputy Ivanov. According to Gdlyan, Ligachev did so because the Uzbek affair developed into the case of the 'Kremlin' bribe-takers. He made their names public; allegedly, they are: Grishin, Aliev, Romanov, Kunaev, Solomentsev, all former CPSU Central Committee Politburo members. Presumably the truth will triumph in the already-declared war of Gdlyan versus Ligachev. For this purpose, the Congress of People's Deputies set up a special probe into the Gdlyan case.

Why, she can't sing at all!

The Central Recording Studio in Moscow has a commission consisting of the most famous Soviet composers. They select and evaluate singers and songwriters. Twenty years ago it auditioned a girl nobody knew who sang her own songs. Her name was Alla Pugacheva. The audition over, the commission said with one voice that Alla Pugacheva could not sing pop songs at all. But before the next three years were out, young people in the Soviet Union and Socialist countries were singing her songs, and by the mid-1970s the more lyrical ones were even accepted by the older generation. Probably the best vehicle for her talent was Pugacheva's work with the composer Raymond Pauls. She has won numerous prizes at competitions in the Soviet Union and abroad and has released a huge number of records, singing other songwriters' songs as well as her own. All her new songs are recorded immediately and sell like hot cakes. Alla has become the star of stars in Soviet pop music, but star fever has not affected her much. She continues to work hard: she has created new groups and even a theatre. Her contribution to perestroika was the creation of an international show business. What is the secret of the undying popularity of the rock-singer? Ask Alla.

Help people and be kind

This was Nikolai Kasyan's motto during the election race for the Congress of People's Deputies when Kasyan was on the ballot for the Soviet Charity Foundation. In the old days such people were called folk doctors, but in the Soviet period they have been brought to court for treating people with folk medicines. His father was a famous healer, and throughout his childhood Nikolai saw crippled and suffering people in their house. After the army, he was severely ill with tuberculosis. The doctors gave him up as hopeless, and his mother was the only person who didn't throw in the towel. She found an old woman who brewed potions, and these potions, together with her kindness and compassion, not only got Nikolai on his feet, but also made him strong enough to work fifteen to eighteen hours a day. Kasyan receives several hundred sick people daily, but, with tens of thousands of people with damaged locomotor systems in this country, this is clearly a drop in the ocean. Instead of spinal surgery, Kasyan offers manual therapy, an exceedingly humane treatment. The traditional techniques are extremely painful, and though spinal surgery brings partial recovery, the patient remains an invalid. True, we cannot dispose of surgery altogether, but most operations would not be necessary if we could train enough good manual therapy doctors in this country. This is Kasyan's battle-cry, and he has been making efforts for many years to have a manual therapy centre opened in the village of Kobelyaki, Poltava region, his home village.

This year he secured the consent of Health Minister Chazov to have a 120-bed hospital built in three years. This is quite a breakthrough after years of neglect or downright harassment. But he has not been recognized officially yet, and Kasyan aims at getting folk medicine and non-traditional treatment recognized. He dreams of establishing a folk medicine centre and a department of folk medicine at the Academy of Medical Sciences. Voting for him, his constituency actually voted for compassion and charity.

Scientist becomes a government member

In recent times the Soviet media have been more outspoken in discussing the crisis in the country's economy and analysing the legacy of the preceding decades. Soviet press, radio and television are constantly speaking about regional cost-accounting, self-financing, self-recoupment, lease-holding and negotiated prices, in the way they spoke quite recently about the team contract, the 1979 economic reforms, new forms for the assessment of economic activities, and the first and second models of cost-accounting. And still earlier the topics were: the efficiency, if any, of the 1965 economic reform, councils of the people's economy, etc. Yet there is a larger, more fundamental, issue behind this ragbag of economic terms. It is not the need to have a market, as many believe, it is ownership relations. Today we sorely need to revise these relations. The collectively owned means of production are actually no one's means of production, or rather they belong to the administrative apparatus. The rest of the people are no more than hired labour. This situation is what gives rise to the deformation of our political system when executive bodies ride roughshod over the whole system of state power and the Soviets. So speaking about the reform of the country's political system, we cannot restrict it to reforming the electoral procedure. It is not enough to elect one or several deputies to effect these transformations. The crux of the matter is the functions the deputies will be entrusted with and whether they will have real power and a right to decide on the use of capital investments and financial and material resources. In other words, a real political democracy should stand on the firm foundation of economic independence or economic protection, says Leonid Abalkin, one of the pioneers of the restructuring of the Soviet economic system.

For the first time in Soviet history a major scientist (Abalkin is an Academy member) has become a deputy Prime Minister. His first steps in his new job show that he means business and is all set to bring economic reform to a successful completion.

Social and Political Problems

Vadim A. Medvedev

Vadim Medvedev was born on 29 March 1929 in the Yaroslavl region. He graduated from Leningrad State University and holds the degree of Doctor of Science in Economics. In 1951 he became a teacher, and later a senior teacher at Leningrad State University. From 1956 to 1961 he worked as an associate professor at the Leningrad Institute of Railway Transport Engineers and in 1961 became head of the Department of Political Economy at the Leningrad Institute of Technology.

In 1968 Medvedev became a secretary of the Leningrad City Party Committee; in 1970 he was appointed Deputy Head of the Propaganda Department of the CPSU Central Committee and in 1978 he became Rector of the Academy of Social Sciences under the CPSU Central Committee. In 1983 he was appointed Head of the Science and Educational Establishments Department of the CPSU Central Committee, and in March 1986 he became a secretary of the CPSU Central Committee, also occupying the post of a Department Head at the CPSU Central Committee. In October 1988 he became a Politburo member.

He is Chairman of the Ideological Commission of the CPSU Central Committee, a People's Deputy of the USSR and a corresponding member of the USSR Academy of Sciences.

The Ideology of Perestroika

VADIM A. MEDVEDEV

Perestroika has become a fact of our life. One of the most important developments occurring in the less than five years since its inception is that the situation in society has changed from stagnation to motion. The formation of a law-governed state has begun, and economic reform is under way.

Public consciousness is discarding the ideological dogmas that over the decades have bolstered the mechanism of authoritarian power and the administrative-command system of governance. Socialist pluralism, which was only recently considered to be a dreadful ideological bogey, is becoming a firmly-set notion. The public mentality is increasingly politicized, and social activity is growing. A qualitatively new type of public opinion is taking shape as a powerful ideological, political, social and psychological factor in the life of the country.

The renovation of ideology so that it will be centred on the individual and his needs and will bring into play the democratic potential of society through freedom of speech and information (glasnost) considerably stimulates the process of change. This ideology, which is formulated by the Party, gains strength in practical experience and develops by absorbing the ideas of many people, public organizations and movements.

At the same time, the revolutionary character of the renovation process assumes complicated, contradictory and at times conflicting forms. A range of acute economic, social, ethnic and other problems which were hushed up for decades have now surfaced. The nation has not yet overcome the grave economic crisis which became obvious in the early 1980s. In conditions of democratization and glasnost people are irritated by the tensions on the market and housing shortages. Miscalculations and shortcomings occurring in the course of perestroika itself are an additional cause of public discontent.

In a word, the first stage has not been an easy period. But the country's leadership and society as a whole are confident that the path is charted correctly and that it is possible to cope with all problems and move on to new horizons of social development.

I

There have been two crucial events in the political reform of this country. First was the 19th Party Conference, which theoretically substantiated and identified the main directions of work to overcome the alienation of the individual from the government and to build a law-governed state. Second, the USSR Congress of People's Deputies, the first practical step in this endeavour.

The essence of the process which is now beginning is, above all, that society's political institutions have been set in motion and their relationships and hierarchy are assuming new outlines.

This concerns the legislative branch, which is emerging from its former submissive situation.

This concerns the executive branch, which is becoming, as the process of the formation of the government demonstrated vividly, strictly answerable to the legislature.

And this concerns the central element of the historically formed and long functioning political system, the Party.

The role and place of the Party in the democratic mechanism of government, the distribution of functions between the Party, the legislature and the executive and economic bodies is a central issue in the ideology of perestroika and the practice of renewal. It is a focus of all the substantive changes in society's life.

Some see the process as the Party's dramatic farewell to power, to real possibilities of influencing politics, the course followed by society.

If we assume that the Party is a 'general manager', that societal processes should be controlled with command-and-administer methods and orders, then the ongoing changes are indeed dramatic.

As a matter of fact, however, the issue is not of the Party

giving up its role in social-political life. What is at issue is the performance of this function through its policy, the ideological and political activities in the masses, through Party members working for state and public organizations. It is by shedding the burden of economic routine, of what should never be within the purview of a political organization, that the Party can fully concentrate on the development and implementation of its policy and ideology.

Basically, one of the root-causes of the present situation is that for many years the Party 'pulled the blanket' of social-control functions and responsibilities over itself. The practice forced it to build up a cumbersome parallel apparatus and spawn bureaucracy. The entire responsibility for current affairs rested with the Party. Any drawback, any mistake was seen as a near collapse of the Party's policy, its fault, or even a defect of Socialism. And no amount of selfless work by Communists in elected positions or the Party apparatus could change this impression.

Today the CPSU is renouncing this approach. Without giving up its position as a political force and a political vanguard of society, it delegates executive powers to those whose function it is to apply them: the Soviets, the economic entities and so on.

The transfer of power to representative organs and the division of functions are some of the more important areas of reform. This certainly requires that the Party acquire a new quality, an ability to act in new conditions, reorganize itself quicker, and set the tone for other voluntary organizations.

A society which is undergoing renewal needs a party which does not shun renewal. This formula reflects the thrust of the current change.

What is the meaning of this formula?

First, it is a dramatic democratization of intraparty life to make the Party an example of democratic development. It is the creation of an atmosphere of free discussion of problems and comparison of views, advancement of alternatives, guarantees for the minority to be heard and to defend its position, provided that everybody submits unquestionably to Party discipline and decisions. In one word, it is the creation of all conditions in the

Party that would ensure the maximum realization of its potentialities, optimal decision-making, and promotion of the most able and authoritative people.

Second, there is a need for a drastic change in relations between the Party and the entire system of voluntary organizations and movements. The Party is part of our society, and if it wants to express and meet the public's needs as fully as possible, to respond accurately to swiftly changing needs of different layers of society, it needs an ongoing dialogue with trade unions, women's, youth and other organizations.

The Party is forging new relations with numerous voluntary organizations that ride the wave of perestroika. Stability has not yet set in. There are misunderstandings on both sides. Yet it is clear that regardless of their heterogeneity, ideological and political as well, these movements are a product of democratic transformations, and it would be wrong to repudiate them. The art of politics is an art of a broad discussion, of involving all interested forces in a social process, of reaching a consensus acceptable to society.

Third, it is the people's democratic control over the Party, in particular, through elections of its members to organs of power and volunteer organizations.

The Party embarked on this road with its eyes open. It is not easy, there is virtually no time left for adaptation. But we are certain that the Party has enough democratic potential to reorganize itself and be successful as society's political vanguard, an integrating force of social interests.

Perestroika was initiated by the CPSU. Having as its members representatives of all social layers, all nationalities, it is objectively the most powerful factor for consolidation of our society. It is above departmental preferences.

The Party is the only social structure that cements society at a time when the transfer of power to Soviets of all levels has just started.

This does not at all mean that a multiparty system to Socialism is contra-indicated. The thing is what opportunities a society can offer its members to express and compare their views, the views of social groups, to take them into account, and to ensure real participation of the masses in the exercise of political power. One has to take into account historical practice, traditions, conditions and needs of social progress.

Today, when many ties that were based on administer-and-command methods are disrupted, the Party's unique role is emphasized by existing conditions. Attempts to weaken the Party, to counter it with other political forces, mean a threat to the force that consolidates society, a threat to perestroika and society as a whole.

True, a democratic society is unthinkable without a collision of opinions and dissenting views of individuals or groups. The precept that Socialism is the creativity of the masses does not imply some faceless masses of individuals, but people who belong to different social, national or professional communities and express their interests.

So, what is at issue is a form of government that would absorb the plurality of opinions, that, more importantly, had to do this. In our view, this is the only way of overcoming alienation and placing our political system on a solid foundation of democracy, ensuring the country's social-democratic progress, and mobilizing society's spiritual and intellectual potential.

One of the reasons for the protracted disregard for democracy and negation of a legitimate character of pluralism under Socialism is the prevalence, for many years, of rather distorted notions of society's social structure and the exaggerated notion of its homogeneity. Stubborn attempts were made to squeeze multifaceted and contradictory economic, social and spiritual interests into the mould of one single interest, with an unfounded emphasis laid on trends towards social homogeneity or the merging of nations. These views failed the test of reality.

To feel the whole range of public, group and individual interests, to help satisfy them, while removing possible contradictions and offering a balance of interests, a political system should be flexible, decentralized and differentiated.

I am certain that this is the approach that can help solve the most complicated problems in our interethnic relations.

The CPSU has developed a platform on the nationalities problem in today's conditions. It has set itself the task of aligning the nationalities policy with new realities and needs, the heightened national consciousness. We are guided by the desire to identify the criteria that should determine the building of the Union of Soviet Republics, to provide all conditions for the free development of nations.

It should be said that the removal of the distorting influence of the administer-and-command system on all aspects of interethnic relations is a complex, painful process of the new ideology extricating itself from the thicket of old dogmas.

The official concept did not recognize contradictions and conflicts in Soviet society, its nations and nationalities. It ignored the national-regional diversity of social and cultural processes, the rich forms of real development and interaction between peoples, and the fact that interethnic relations are a consequence of social and political processes.

The atmosphere of democratization and openness stimulated a process of the tempestuous development of national self-awareness of great and small peoples. We regard the process as a testimony to the fact that our multiethnic Socialist society has reached another rung on the ladder of spiritual maturity.

Yet it is impossible not to see that the growth of national self-awareness is often accompanied by national egoism. Ethnic prejudices that sometimes generate widespread emotions are on the rise. The recent events in Union republics bear special testimony to Mikhail Gorbachev's words that political extremism of the nationalistic kind is particularly intolerable and dangerous in conditions of perestroika, for it hampers the normal development of the democratic process and damages our national cause.

The increased ethnic factor in the process of perestroika leads to a special emphasis on ethnic problems in the political reform of Soviet society. On the one hand, Union and autonomous republics, and all national communities, should have greater autonomy, and on the other, they should be more responsible for meeting the Union's interests. Our aim is to create a political system which would take into account society's existing structure, the many and diverse interests and expectations of all social groups and national communities.

The Party emphasizes the democratic means of overcoming contradictions. Attempts to use violence are fraught with the escalation of tension. Confrontation and extremism cannot solve existing problems. They are a way of self-destruction, not creativity.

The interests of nations and nationalities can be harmonized only by way of large-scale discussion, a search for a consensus based on autonomy, responsibility and mutual help.

II

Major revolutionary changes in a political system cannot be stable without profound economic changes. A radical economic reform is not concerned with higher production efficiency alone. It is concerned with providing a material basis for the democratization of society. As such, it is an inalienable part of our ideology of perestroika.

Arguments as to what should come first – economic or political change – appear to be of little importance. As Lenin said, 'Taken separately, no kind of democracy will bring Socialism. But in actual life democracy can never be "taken separately", it will be "taken together" with other things, it will exert its influence on economic life as well, will stimulate *its* transformation; and in its turn it will be influenced by economic development, and so on. This is the dialectics of living history' (V. I. Lenin, *The State and Revolution*, vol. 25, pp. 425–53).

Those who follow closely the development of changes in our society will remember that they started with the idea of using scientific and technical progress, of making a breakthrough in this area.

It turned out however that it was impossible to break the iron vice of the administer-and-command system, which impedes economic progress, without political reform. Subsequent critical thinking led us further, to the understanding of the need for the reorganization of property relations. Otherwise it would be impossible to solve the key problem: to overcome man's alienation from common property, to rebuild the economic mechanism and the management structure. Without drastic changes in production relations, new economic management techniques are rejected as something alien.

Two sets of vested interests are impeding economic reform.

One exists in the higher economic echelons that are concerned about losing the levers of control and letting the process become unmanageable. The other one exists at the lower level: there is a fear of losing their low but guaranteed wages and salaries that are unaffected by performance. The vicious circle can be broken only by a reform of property relations, by admitting a variety of forms of property.

The Party has opted for this approach, banking not on one or two 'advanced' or 'most Socialistic' forms but on the entire set of equal forms of property.

Unfortunately, for a long time the criterion of 'Socialism' in terms of property in this country has been the degree of state control. In practice, that meant a lack of responsibility for property, the formal unification of socialization, conditions and contents of work; this led to a reduction of cooperative and individual forms of economy to a disenchantment with incentives, to wage levelling, and indifference as regards one's quantity and quality of work.

The drive toward many forms of Socialist property and economy is an organic part of the technological diversity inherent in modern production. It is in full accord with the democratic nature of the economy, its logic which fills all existing niches and makes them function.

A radical renewal of property relations means the creation of flexible and effective relations that use public property to enable each form to prove its efficiency and right to life. There is no place here for stereotypes or prejudices. The only condition of this renewal is the lack of exploitation and alienation from the means of production. All national property is and should be at the disposal of the Union, the republics, the autonomous and local Soviets.

Perestroika has opened wide opportunities for cooperatives, lease contracts, various other contracts, household production, and individual labour activity. Joint-stock companies are in no way contrary to Socialist economic principles. Some enterprises issue shares to accumulate the funds of their employees and use them to develop production, and increase their interest in the results of work. This share-generated income is basically an earned income and a peculiar form of the produce of personal property.

This is certainly not a smooth process. But it is already clear that this approach can identity new motive forces and put to use an enormous mass of intiative.

The ethical side of the problem, the humanitarian aspect of economic reform, is also important. A person who becomes a master of his work changes his psychology, his attitude towards work; conscientious work, high skills and knowledge come to the foreground. Favourable conditions are created for the eradication of wage levelling and a sense of dependence.

This is of course not a conflict-free process. New conditions will probably lead to a greater differentiation of incomes. This is an acute social-economic problem. But we shall continue to mark time if we do not overcome the wage-levelling sentiment. Socialism rejects demagogic appeals for equal incomes for everybody. Equal poverty means no incentives for economic progress and, eventually, a negative influence on the development of individuals. Our principle is: 'From each according to his ability, to each according to his work.' Being loyal to its Socialist objectives, our society will continue to provide social protection to low-paid groups, pensioners and youth. This is the will of the Congress of People's Deputies.

An active use of commodity-money relations, the market, is a most important element of economic reform. It was very much developed under capitalism. But strictly speaking, capitalism cannot claim priority or a monopoly on commodity-money relations.

The market-place is a major achievement of human civilization, an important instrument of harmonizing production and social needs, of control over the quality of goods and production costs in very different economic systems, including Socialism.

Socialism uses many other economic forms inherited from the past: e.g. money, leasing, profit, banks, though all of these instruments under Socialism stimulate different economic relations.

It would be naïve to resort to market-place romanticism and to believe that market relations can provide all the answers to all questions automatically. Yet attempts to do without a market in a Socialist planned economy inevitably lead to extra-economic coercion, to the predominance of the producer over the consumer, the growth of monopoly and inflation of the bureaucratic apparatus.

True, we encounter difficulties in applying the economic instruments that are new to our life; they encounter a social-psychological barrier because for a long time a 'commodity-free' society has been our Socialist ideal, and the word 'market' was a political judgment. We have not yet mastered the market mechanism. There are substantial price distortions. Trade in the means of production is sluggish. Economic difficulties are compounded by disturbances in the consumer market-place, monetary problems, state finances and credits. No system of economic regulations can operate without a stable currency. We are for making it convertible in the future.

These are large-scale problems. But there is no way back to the administrative system. By developing many and varied forms of property, cost-accounting, markets and self-government, we are to democratize further all aspects of the economy, to remove any monopoly and restrictions on initiative and creativity. We regard a far-reaching reorganization of property relations and the diversity and equality of all of its forms as a guarantee of the renewal of Socialism and the consolidation of a law-governed state.

III

A central place in the ideology of perestroika is reserved for the removal of man's alienation from his culture. Otherwise, it would be impossible to awaken the individual, to involve him in spiritual processes. Without this, perestroika is impossible.

In V. I. Lenin's words, for a state to become 'a completely Socialist country' (*Collected Works*, vol. 33, p. 475), Russia would need to undergo an enormous cultural upheaval. Culture should be interpreted as a very broad notion embracing man's attitude toward the world, society and himself: from elementary literacy, the care of nature and historical monuments, and simple ethical rules to the loftiest possible spiritual values, political culture, the advanced organization of work and life, and the latest advances of science and technology.

In applying these demanding criteria to the country's cultural achievements, one should be realistic about the results of our development in this area. Yes, the level of education has been substantially raised during the years of Soviet power, the USSR has become a country of major artistic achievements, of powerful scientific potential. But let us be frank: the country lost many opportunities.

They are due to the 'residual' principle of allocations for culture, to the use of administrative methods in a sphere which is least amenable to levelling and orders, to the desire to apply hidebound ideological measures to cultural achievements and values.

As a result, our rich cultural life became a victim. It was impoverished and reduced to some mediocre notions, it lost all ties with the heritage of the past and world traditions.

Perestroika meant a fresh look on culture and its significance for society's progress. It meant a refusal to oppose the class approach to the universal human approach, a denial of a confrontational vision of traditions and innovation, with traditions invariably regarded as conservative; the emergence of new traditions meant the death of old ones.

Perestroika meant a fresh look at the role of a creative person, talent, intellectual work as a whole, their recognition as highly valuable social capital, a powerful driving force of eternal significance.

Among the major transformations experienced by culture is the publication of the works of authors who had to emigrate for various reasons.

For the Party, perestroika means a radical departure from the command style, the imposition of subjective and often incompetent views on what is good or bad in culture, what should or should not be represented by the arts.

Without giving up its active role in society's spiritual life, the Party strives to influence it by other means: by providing complete information, convincing arguments, by critically overcoming biased assessments and conclusions, and providing thorough explanations and persuasion.

On the whole, the destruction of the administer-and-command system annihilates the erstwhile interpretation of ideology as a means of supporting already adopted decisions, transmitting directives and commands from top to bottom, with unanimity being the main objective.

In the environment of pluralism, glasnost and increasing self-government, no important decision in the economy, social development or scientific and technological progress can be adopted without or against public opinion. Life keeps reminding us of this literally every day. Proof is supplied by the tumultuous and justified response of the public to environmental issues, price reforms, the development of cooperatives and, of course, the experience of the election campaign.

All of this invokes the need for open, imaginative, people-oriented ideological work that would be based on a reliable feedback mechanism which reflects the people's views, its collective mind. This means that the familiar monologue is being replaced by an extensive equal dialogue with the public. This means that the winning over to our side of the public, an active shaping of public opinion, explanation and persuasion are becoming an organic part of and a major component of managing social processes.

A new quality of ideological activity emerges as a response to a new ideological need. The process is not easy, for it involves a collision between the old and the new.

There is an urgent need for reorganization of the Party. The environment of discussions, pluralistic views and arguments has given birth to new voluntary organizations and movements. They are a product of pluralism, and rallies are their natural element. The Party's experience is not very rich. It is saddled with the command practice of the Stalinist period and the uniform 'barracks' experience of the stagnation period. This is why a considerable number of Party functionaries find it difficult to master new approaches that meet today's requirements, to master the skill of working in any, even an unsympathetic, environment.

The difficulty of mastering new methods of management, the presence of old habits affect the country's discussion of the problem of the mass media.

THE IDEOLOGY OF PERESTROIKA

They became a vanguard of renewal from the very beginning of perestroika. They should be credited with removing the obstacles of the past, developing glasnost, society's increasing openness and assertion of Socialist plurality of opinions. At the same time, our society has never had such polarized views on their activity. There are even calls to establish rigid controls over the mass media.

The Party believes that the diversity of opinions, openness and the raising of acute problems are an achievement of perestroika and an instrument of its further progress. It would be inconceivable to restrict glasnost now that perestroika has entered what we believe is its most important stage. This is simply unacceptable for our society; this is impossible for the process of democratization is increasingly irreversible.

Furthermore, the sharp criticism in the press, the contradictory nature of publications, reflect the acute situation in the country and the degree of social tension. In this sense the mass media cannot overdo themselves or forget the objective state of affairs.

Yet we should not forget that the mass media are going through the same processes as the country and all of its social-political institutions: the school of democracy, the mastering of a new and more responsible social role.

The process has involved many costs. People are worried by claims of some publications to absolute truth, their partisanship, expressions of group egoism, attempts to shed many valuable spiritual experiences together with all that is outdated.

The Party and society would like to see the press, radio and television not only reflecting but shaping, skilfully, actively and purposefully, public opinion in favour of perestroika, democratization and glasnost.

We are not in a unique situation: the erstwhile command-and-adminster methods are outruled and there is still insufficient experience of management through political and legal means.

What solutions do we envisage?

First, we need legal norms. Great hopes are pinned, in this area, on the Law on the Press and Mass Media. This law is to determine the general framework for the freedom of the press and establish the legal norms which will specify the relations between the press, the state, public organizations and the individual.

At the same time, a rule-of-law state should be characterized by the increased responsibility of each journalist for the content and orientation of his publications – the greater the public impact of the oral and written word, the sharper, more substantiated and responsible this word should be.

And finally, publishers and Party organizations are not facing new tasks in directing the mass media. By supporting everything that is viable, valuable, aimed at moving perestroika forward they are called to exercise their influence not through strong words, bans or excommunication, but through sound arguments, a search for the truth, meticulous exposition and explication.

IV

It is well known that at the outset of all mankind's great social changes were new ideas which emerged from a revision and re-evaluation of old views. Perestroika is no exception. A formidable mass of ideas has been revised and re-evaluated. The intellectual potential, which has been rapidly increasing during the last five years, is now quite notable.

Perestroika's major victory is its new political thinking, which is a system of views on world affairs, it is based on the supremacy of a general, human approach over a class approach, on an understanding that the modern world is an interdependent and interrelated entity, on the renunciation of the use of force for the solution of disputes, the freedom of choice as a universal principle, and a dynamic interaction in the resolution of the global problems facing mankind.

Perestroika enabled us to view Socialism's place in the world process differently – in the context of the wealth of mankind's roads and forms, of which Socialism is only one possible choice among many other multi-coloured and various forms.

As a matter of fact, since the time of the October revolution, Socialism has been for us a 'bulwark', or a 'camp' that confronted another, the capitalist 'camp'. Today we have sufficient reason to believe that the image of Socialism and capitalism as systems allegedly doomed to a 'power' confrontation and capable of isolated, parallel, development is outdated. Inevitably, both systems interact. Such an interaction goes hand-in-hand with competition, which tests the basic values of each system and reveals their capabilities to deal not only with the system's own problems, but to a growing extent with general human problems.

The realities and challenges of the modern world required a profound and complete revaluation of our ideas pertaining to the entire concept of Socialism.

Now we realize much better that the late 1920s and 1930s shaped a doctrine which was intended to service ideologically the administrative-and-command system that was being formed. Superficially it was dressed in Marxist–Leninist terminology, but in its substance it was a retreat from creative Marxism and Leninism.

Today, as we stand on the solid ground of reality, we are cleansing our concept of Socialism of erroneous views and dogmatic schemes. As a result of this, things which were considered unacceptable only yesterday are, today, important preconditions for and tools of economic and social activity.

Of course, these changes are difficult for the masses to accept. They imply the collapse of seemingly eternal truths, and sharp conflicts of views and positions. Yet, without a new understanding and approaches, it is inconceivable to deal with a task of immense importance; the elaboration of a modern concept of Socialism which can accommodate the realities of the late twentieth to the early twenty-first centuries.

The problem has another aspect. For a long time we viewed the Socialist ideal as a sort of building which was finished to the last detail – with balconies, porticoes and columns. We even had clearly marked levels, or 'stages of social maturity' that had their own timetables and corresponding technical, economic and sociological indices which were to be reached by specific times.

Now we have to change our ideas of Socialist society drastically. As Vladimir Lenin said, we cannot know the future in all its details. Our present concept of Socialism cannot be compared with a finished building, but rather only with the frame of its main structure. The rest is to be added in the process of work, in our case – perestroika. Perestroika itself breaks all attempts to give it a preset rigidity and shows that life is much richer than the most audacious schemes and designs.

What are the components and basis of the modern concept of Socialism? First of all there are the fundamental ideas of Marxist philosophy which reflect, in a most general form, the key features of a new social system. Added to this is Lenin's understanding of Socialism – the result of the application of Socialist ideas to the practical work for the revolutionary transformation of society in our country and the generalization of the first experience in dealing with the tasks of the transition period.

Yes, we return to Lenin's concept and revive many of the principles and specific approaches to Socialist construction which were developed by him. In no way does this imply a mechanical return and repetition. First, we cannot ignore the fact that Lenin's own views underwent an evolution, for example, on the eve of 1921 during the transition from a war Communism to the NEP. Second, almost two-thirds of a century separate us from Lenin, and this was a time filled with much profound change and rich experience of social development.

Drastic changes have taken place in the development of science and technology, material production, the means of human communication and, what is most important, in the development of man himself.

Hence there is a need to comprehend Lenin's concept of Socialism in the light of modern conditions, experience and tasks.

For this reason the return to Lenin is primarily a rehabilitation of Lenin's dialectics, Lenin's methods of analysis for the practical resolution of problems, Lenin's realism in assessing social phenomena, his ability to see the world in motion and his commitment to the truth, no matter how bitter it might be.

It is natural, however, that as we try to combine theoretical considerations with practical work on the deep transformations which are under way in the country, we are eager to draw as many lessons from the five years of perestroika as possible, to analyse and comprehend the emerging trends and processes. All the more so as they progress with controversy, through struggle, by over-riding conservative forces and traditions.

THE IDEOLOGY OF PERESTROIKA

When speaking about the most important sources for the modern concept of Socialism, we should also mention the collective experience gained by the Socialist countries. We consistently follow Lenin's idea that wholesome Socialism can be constructed only by a series of attempts, each being more or less one-sided, and by international efforts.

Gone are the times when such diversity was looked upon with dogmatic, sectarian suspicion. We proceed from the fact that the diversity of forms, methods and approaches in Socialist construction enriches everybody, demonstrates the might of Socialism and the universality of a Socialist path (i.e. the possibility of applying it to different conditions). It is important not to oppose the multifaceted experience of Socialist construction in different countries, to study it thoroughly and incorporate it into the modern concept of Socialism.

Finally, there is another task of paramount importance – to comprehend fully the meaning of Lenin's words that Marxism 'took in and processed everything that was valuable in the more than two-millenium history of human thought and culture.' Life has refuted any claims to create a perfect social system separated from world civilization and culture. Practice has shown that the paths of social progress in different social systems cross, and to ignore this would be the worst case of political doctrinism and a violation of common sense. Nihilism toward the progressive achievements of the countries which have a different socio-political and economic orientation would run counter to the Marxist–Leninist tradition, no matter whether this concerns scientific and technological advances or some forms of social life, experience in the resolution of social problems, democracy, etc.

With regard to the main criterion of Socialism, it should be said that it lies in the humanism of society and its priority orientation toward man. It is an integrated index of the present formula of Socialism which we would like to deliver:

- the economy should be based on all the achievements of scientific and technological progress; it should also be dynamic and geared to meeting the needs of society;
- social justice should combine social guarantees and strict observance of the principle of distribution according to work,

the eradication of all forms of wage-levelling and social parasitism;
- the sphere of political administration should include people's power, the full realization of human rights and freedoms, law, openness and glasnost;
- the sphere of culture and morals should include the crowning achievements of world civilization which are put to the service of man;
- the sphere of ethnic relations should ensure the full equality of all nations and nationalities, the relations between people being in the spirit of internationalism and brotherhood.

The humanistic nature of a renewed Socialist society goes hand-in-hand with the nature of its relations with the outside world, which are based on the unconditional recognition of the sovereign right of every nation to determine its own destiny, a striving for strengthening peace and international cooperation and the establishment of normal civilized relations beween all states and nations.

We are sure that this Socialism can make a tremendous constructive contribution to the development of the human community and the solution of world problems.

Like other processes of historical magnitude, perestroika least of all resembles a triumphant ascent. It involves clashes of interests, overcoming many difficulties and, at times, even the dramatic deterioration in situations. We have made our choice conscientiously, however, and can see the main goal through all obstacles: our society has embarked on the right road, and the one-way traffic along this road is becoming irreversible.

Alexander A. Bessmertnykh

He was born into a Russian family in 1933. In 1957 he graduated from the Moscow State Institute of International Relations of the USSR Ministry of Foreign Affairs.

From 1960 to 1966 Alexander Bessmertnykh worked at the UN Secretariat in New York. He was a councillor (from 1971 to 1977) and a councillor-minister (from 1977 to 1983) at the USSR Embassy to the United States in Washington. In 1983 he was appointed chief of the USA Department of the USSR Ministry of Foreign Affairs and a member of its Collegium.

In 1986 he became Deputy Foreign Minister of the USSR, and in 1988 First Deputy Foreign Minister of the USSR. He has the diplomatic rank of Ambassador Extraordinary and Plenipotentiary.

Foreign Policy – a New Course

ALEXANDER A. BESSMERTNYKH

Four centuries ago Niccolò Machiavelli observed a most basic feature of the behaviour of individuals and hence nations: 'People nearly always go along established routes and imitate others in their actions.' Such a reliance on 'beaten tracks' has created a powerful and durable set of traditional views on the fundamentals of foreign policy and diplomacy, a peculiar code of conduct and manners in the international arena.

Nations, borders and leaders changed; policy tools were perfected, yet many things seemed immutable: that the success of nation-states is brought by victories, on battlefields; victories are gained through amassing weapons and combat troops; any weakening of the enemy is for the benefit of your country's security; concealing one's true intentions and plans from 'the enemy' is a noble art of fighting men and rulers; matching the interests of nation-states is temporary and unstable, which is shown by the débris of alliances, unions and ententes filling the pages of history . . . The sacred notion of 'power' was basic to the philosophy of politics.

When in the mid-1980s the Soviet Union advanced the concept of a new thinking in foreign policy, many in the West did not immediately grasp its meaning. The initial response was stereotyped: any new leadership, no matter in what country, prefers to say it will act in a new way, since no administration can completely satisfy everybody. Not a big deal – we've heard it before. Others have grasped the meaning of the new phenomena only partially. I remember the US Secretary of State, George Shultz, observing during a break in diplomatic conversations in Moscow with the Soviet Foreign Minister Eduard Shevardnadze: 'The United States has benefited from new thinking in politics for the past two hundred years already.' It is true that the American Revolution of the eighteenth century brought in many fresh ideas; yet, it left intact the basic postulates of the past. What President George Washington said in the US Congress in 1790, i.e. 'getting ready for a war is one of the most effective means of creating peace', is still found in a somewhat modified form in statements and doctrines of US politicians. Thus, the 'new thinking' is more than a declaration of novel approaches or an interpretation of reality.

Our critics claim specifically that by adopting the new thinking the Soviet Union in a way has dissociated itself from the politics of the past, totally rejecting the traditional elements in politics. This is a fairly serious reproach which needs to be addressed.

No doubt, any epoch carries a feeling of its uniqueness. Yet this uniqueness is permeated with living threads linking a given historical stage with the preceeding one and, at the same time, with the subsequent course of events. By singling out one, even the most prominent, facet of a given period out of the sum of its features, we do not get the closest to the true picture. And yet each epoch has something of its own that leaves a deep imprint on the memories of contemporaries and on the minds of later generations. Each nation has its own high and low points.

Looking back, one sees that the history of Russia, and of any other country for that matter, is first and foremost a kind of catalogue of the most outstanding events which give identity to the period. One speaks about such periods as feudal struggles, the establishment of centralized state power, the times of trouble, the seventeenth century before Peter I, Peter's reforms, the period of peasant emancipation, the February revolution, the October revolution, etc. Not every century has been lucky enough to witness many outbursts of development. Some of them passed by as a grey uneventful spiritless evolution (although this view may be a mistake due to our distance from these events).

The twentieth century cannot complain of being a routine period lacking in events. It began with massive upheavals, national and global in scale.

The new thinking does not negate all that was positive in the past, since a nation's foreign policy even after the deepest qualitative changes in the country, or around it, cannot be totally new in everything. Its aims, interests, methods, concepts, theoretical premises or tools may change. But permanent factors remain, such as, say, history, which, like gravity, holds the keys to its politics; or geography, forever linking a country with specific neighbours, continents or seas.

Therefore the core feature of the new thinking is not necessarily a departure from everything habitual and traditional, but finding essentially new solutions in a changing environment, creating conceptions radically changing our views on the ways of humanity's survival and development in unprecedented circumstances of the nuclear era and space age.

At the same time, seeing world developments from the perspective of the new thinking, one should by no means negate or underestimate the actual balance of forces or the laws operating on the existing system of states. Entirely new relations between nations will be built step by step with a better balance between the new thinking and the foreign policy interests of different countries.

Meanwhile the new thinking is corrected and verified by the experience derived from real-life policy. Changing the way of thinking for the sake of the reconstruction of foreign and domestic policies is among the fundamental phenomena which have emerged in the latter half of this century, first in the Soviet Union, and are now extending gradually into other countries and regions. In this sense, perestroika is contagious, and its transnational character is becoming ever more evident, although it goes without saying that it is not carried out everywhere purposefully or in a uniform way.

The new thinking in Soviet foreign policy has as its origin the revolution of restructuring that has been going on in the Soviet Union since 1985. As with domestic policy, its initial impulse was the objective need of Soviet society for a critical self-analysis, for an honest scrutiny of the complicated system of causal relations which brought about difficulties in the social, economic and political development of Socialism. At the same time, as a special sphere, government foreign policy has its own specific features.

However, in terms of method to concentrate on these features only would not be fully justifiable, given all the risks involved in a 'pure' laboratory-type analysis.

I

The most general parameters of the new thinking in the formulation and implementation of foreign policy were defined at the April Plenary Session of the Party's Central Committee and at the 27th Party Congress. The period until the 19th Party Conference (1988) saw the deepening of the philosophical-conceptual foundations of the new foreign policy, of working out its principles and mechanisms of implementation.

Restructuring of the social and economic structure of Soviet society and the search for the optimal solutions for accumulated complicated problems put the task of providing favourable external conditions for perestroika on the agenda. Thus, the new thinking in domestic policy largely coincided in time with the development of new principles in foreign policy. The need for a realistic rethinking of the world situation, the status of the USSR in the world, its relations with Socialist and capitalist countries, with the developing world, i.e. of the whole complex of world ties and problems, was defined in a bold and innovative speech by Mr Gorbachev in the Ministry for Foreign Affairs of the USSR on 23 May 1986 (it was published in a compressed form in the *Bulletin of the USSR MFF* of 5 August 1987). Mr Gorbachev said that we cannot maintain our positions in the international arena without accelerating the country's economic and social development. At the same time the key to success in foreign policy affairs is in a healthy society and economy. We need, as was noted, 'a really dynamic, effective, assertive diplomacy'. For this, the new thinking should also prevail in diplomacy, which should 'energetically get rid of the stereotypes and clichés of the past'. Mr Gorbachev set concrete tasks for the Soviet diplomatic service, which formed the basis of our foreign policy planning for the future.

The foreign policy conception based on the new political thinking started with a *critical understanding* of the past, which, alongside the rejection of all that is truly obsolete (but not the whole previous experience), involved lessons for the future. This painful and not very simple process still goes on. There are quite a few 'blank spots' in our practice and history, many examples of the adoption of decisions in an undemocratic way, which had serious implications for the country. One should not indulge in an indiscriminate criticism of the foreign policy activity of the Soviet State during the past seventy years. In those stormy decades the basic policy line of Soviet diplomacy was generally pursued in keeping with the general line of ensuring peace and international security. It brought about many major accomplishments, but today is not the time to revel in achievements. We need first and foremost the courage of self-criticism.

E. Shevardnadze, who is now leading the work of the Ministry for Foreign Affairs in analysing the policies of the past and formulating new standpoints in specific policy areas, has further developed important elements of the new conception in a number of his speeches. He identified, as one of the causes of the static thinking of the past, the lack of options in blueprints and solutions, and conservatism in our approach, in contrast to the dynamism of the decision-making process, and in key foreign policy matters, plurality of opinions at all levels, and the rejection of the absolutization of 'the boss is always right' principle.

In this challenging work it was very important to come up with a correct methodology which would help to arrive at the most reasonable conclusions through objective analysis. We began by rejecting a one-sided perception of history, recognizing the need to view historical events from as many sides as posisble, with all the dark and light spots, the positive and negative aspects. This approach helped to avoid the mistake of looking at past events from today's perspectives, as one already knows the consequences of the action taken many years ago. It is clear that a number of errors and mistakes were caused, among other things, by the international situation of yesterday, by the balance of forces in the country's leadership, and by the power structure which prevailed at the moment of decision-taking – in a word, by concrete historical circumstances.

It is from this perspective that we are now studying a number of issues which have a significant impact on post-war history.

Well, how did the 'cold war' start? Can one blame only one side or should one split the blame between all the leading powers whose policy-line in the latter half of the 1940s determined the course of international developments? Are we entirely beyond reproach in the sense that some of our actions in that period, determined by scholastic thinking, by the largely absolutist personal power of J. Stalin, may in some way have hampered development in a different, more favourable direction?

For instance, what psychological and political motives can explain this famous statement of the chairman of Sovnarkom, V. Molotov, on 6 November 1938: 'We will respond to any provocative acts on the part of war-mongers, on the part of aggressors against the Soviet Union – be it in the West or in the East, we will respond to every strike with a double and triple blow on the instigators of war. . . . If somebody would like to test the strength and might of these forces, let them try.'

Unfortunately, two and a half years later they did try. But the question is not so much in that mystical invitation to war as in the infectious persistence of the conviction of the desirability of the 'double and triple blow' in response to each strike. It existed for many more years, even when potential strikes became nuclear in character. This conviction began to weaken somewhat after Khrushchev recognized in 1956 that wars were no longer 'inevitable'.

One can today reflect on the question whether the statement by the same Khruschchev in 1959 rendered some service to the US military industrial complex. 'We have good missiles and in the required numbers. And we are adding more missiles.' This statement may have cooled some reckless generals in the Pentagon, yet in 1962, when the Caribbean crisis broke out, the United States had a manifold superiority over the USSR in the number of strategic nuclear missiles.

It would be interesting, perhaps, to assess the consequences of the statement by the newly elected President J. Kennedy, who said soon after the above-mentioned remark of N. Khrushchev (in May 1961): 'The great battlefields in the defence and propagation of freedom are today . . . Asia, Latin America, and the Middle East, the lands of awakening nations.'

Or take this question: Can one justify the decision to send

FOREIGN POLICY — A NEW COURSE

Soviet troops into Afghanistan? Could it be that another, more democratic, decision-making method or clearer distinctions between the ideological and pragmatic approaches to development in third world countries could have led to different options in Afghanistan?

There is much argument today concerning Soviet foreign policy on the eve of World War II and particularly the talks of V. Molotov with Hitler and Germany's foreign minister Ribbentrop. It is important to understand how the agreements reached were viewed by the Soviet leadership in those troubled years, in terms of ensuring the Soviet Union's security and preventing a war. Their precise and complete content remains the subject of further research. Could there have been other options in the conditions where the USSR as a result of its allies' actions began to feel isolated in the face of a growing German threat?

There are many unanswered questions left concerning the history of our pre-war policy and of much later events. It is important that in-depth studies be made in order to restore truth and not to repeat the past mistakes.

If one is to generalize, the main result of this self-critical analysis is that we have become fully aware of the need to make a *realistic vision of reality* the basis of our policy. It is on realism that the new thinking in foreign policy is based. In fact, most blunders in the many centuries of diplomatic history were due to a lack of realism by military commanders, tsars, presidents and governments in assessing their own and their enemy's capability. Whatever the causes of unrealistic intentions — hate, too much ambition, lack of information or perfidy of the other side, they have always led to major failures or at best to lack of success.

In the case of Soviet foreign policy, a strictly realistic vision was at times hampered by the lack of discrimination between the ideological and the state approaches in a given situation. At the dawn of Soviet diplomacy, V. I. Lenin warned about the need to observe the borderline between the 'NKID' (the People's Commissariat for Foreign Affairs) i.e. the state approach, and the 'Comintern' — in today's jargon, the ideological approach. However, this borderline was not always observed in practice. A number of political and diplomatic decisions which had serious consequences for the state interests of the country were adopted for reasons which are only indirectly related to these interests. It can now be recognized that some of our actions in Africa and possibly also in Asia were caused by the impatient desire of some of our influential leaders in charge of ideology to see what did not yet exist. At times we did practise wishful-thinking. Overtly class assessments of events in isolation from the country's national interests shifted the emphasis in policy and sometimes led to a material and military involvement which should never have taken place.

Making realism the basis of policy has inevitably led us to the necessity of defining precisely what *our own interests* are, and analysing the interests of others. Such an attitude does not at all seem unusual, and it seems to fit in with traditional thinking. But the essence of the new thinking in this respect is to bring to the foreground not egoistic, but increasingly altruistic interests. Altruism ceases to be an attribute of the romantic school of diplomacy. It has suddenly become an element of the modern thinking. How did this come about?

First, the fundamental research into models of national interest has brought us to believe that the age-long conviction about the priority of national interests over all others ceases to be indisputable. It has been found that under the circumstances the best way to ensure national survival and prosperity consists in the difficult task of establishing a delicate balance between one's own interests and those of others. This leap of consciousness from the axiom that the *balance of forces* ensures optimal stability to the recognition of the *balance of interests* as the way out of the impasse in which humanity found itself in the late twentieth century is a truly revolutionary one.

Second, we have come to a conclusion on the primacy of universally recognized interests over national, individual or group interests. This idea comes from the awareness that the emerging global problems connected with the danger of a nuclear holocaust, the ecological crisis, etc. can no longer be solved by one state or even an alliance of states. The scale of possible catastrophes calls for joint efforts by everybody. Survival has become a universal human concern.

A creative consideration of universally recognized values has allowed us to look in a new way at the content of *peaceful coexistence*, which in the nuclear age has ceased to be viewed as a special form of class struggle. Peaceful coexistence – and this is one of the conclusions of the new thinking – is becoming the supreme universal principle regulating relations between states. This matter has not, unfortunately, been given due attention by public opinion and experts in the West. Only the most perceptive political analysts have managed to grasp the deeper meaning of the new approach to this fundamental issue shown by the Soviet Union. There were attempts in the West to present this problem as a kind of argument between those in the Soviet Union who admittedly reject class struggle altogether and those who see nothing but this struggle. Such a false perception of the essence of this highly important conception does not apparently help the leaders of some Western countries to use the possibilities provided by this concept for joint actions to secure a durable peaceful period in international relations.

The correct understanding of one's national interests should contribute, in our view, to the policies of the great powers becoming less global with less overextension of foreign policy interests. The rejection of confrontation as a prevailing method of policy should inevitably lead to increasing moderation in determining the scale and priorities of interests. Naturally, national borders are again becoming the limits that should restrict the military activity of all states.

The USSR adheres to this important principle in practice. This was shown by the withdrawal of a significant part of its arms and armaments from the GDR, Hungary, Czechoslovakia and Mongolia, as well as the whole of its contingent from Afghanistan. This is also shown by the lack of any interest in obtaining military bases and strongholds in other territories. This not only builds trust, turning it from an abstract into a concrete political category, but also introduces the necessary coordination and order into diverse interstate relations, significantly narrowing the possibility of conflicts and outbursts of tension.

The formulation of the more coherent conception of the place of national interests in world politics was followed, quite logically, by an important conclusion about the *diversity of the political spectrum of today's world*, where everything is interrelated and interdependent. This being the case, one should recognize not only the common destiny of all countries, big and small, but also the danger of major errors or miscalculations by one of the largest powers. Such an error, through its repercussions, would affect other countries and people. And, *vice versa*, positive constructive actions can trigger a powerful response if this positive action affects vitally important aspects of humanity's life.

One can cite as an example the powerful effect produced in the world by the US–Soviet agreement on the reduction and elimination of medium and shorter range missiles or by the Multilateral Treaty on the Non-Proliferation of Nuclear Weapons. The Soviet unilateral moratorium on underground nuclear testing, which lasted for over one and a half years (although it has not so far brought about any serious response on the part of other nuclear powers, particularly the United States), still brought the problem of the cessation of nuclear tests to the forefront of the political activity of many governments and public organizations, creating a greater basis for a possible consensus. Various proposals and initiatives are by no means accidental, providing options for the solution of this urgent problem. A special role is played among them by the group of countries called 'the Delhi six'.

This international community which emerged toward the end of the century significantly changed the habitual standards which used to determine the closeness of the relations of the USSR with various countries. Present-day experience shows that the global community most actively manifests itself at this stage through regional consensuses: it applies, first and foremost, to developments in Europe. This continent witnessed the merging of three processes – integration in the West, integration in the East, and a growing all-European integration, which is figuratively called the process of building 'the European home'.

The same direction, although with some delay, is being taken by developments in Asia, the Pacific, Africa and Latin America. The recognition of a growing unity of interests of different states together with their greater diversity and with the growing interdependence of the world is an important discovery of the new thinking. Having assimilated this truth, Soviet foreign policy and diplomacy show in many respects creativity, originality, boldness and the constructive nature of the solutions offered. The fact that we belong to one and only one terrestrial civilization means that the way to its survival is through cooperation and interaction, with the establishment of the freedom of choice for all states and systems.

These appear to be the most important principles generated by the new thinking. They make up a fairly coherent and – most importantly – a self-correcting system of views.

Now, a few words about the practical application of this concept, first of all in the settlement of regional conflicts and in the sphere of security, the central sphere of foreign policy activity.

II

One of the merits of the new thinking in foreign policy is that it allows us to generate solutions for seemingly insoluble problems. Rejecting stereotyped and rigid approaches, we say that even deep-seated contradictions can be modified. For this, one has to understand the realities of today and to pursue a practical policy in the spirit of the new thinking.

This also refers to the settlement of regional conflicts, which constitutes the 'horizontal' dimension of international security (as against the 'vertical' one – arms reduction).

The international situation at any given time has not one, but several, hotbeds of tension. Many of them result from contradictions, the roots of which go back centuries. Others are the consequences of major changes resulting from the collapse of the huge colonial empires in the middle of this century. Still others are the results of a cunning pitting of some states against others in keeping with the notorious principle of 'divide and rule'. To find the most acceptable ways of settling all these conflict situations, one should clearly understand their roots.

Until recently, the incorrect interpretation of their causes has been one of the difficulties here. In most cases regional conflict situations were considered to be generated by the confrontation between the USSR and the USA, between East and West, and sometimes between the Warsaw Pact and NATO. The new thinking has among its elements the requirement for a comprehensive analysis of the origins of regional conflicts, which would allow us to see the processes in their social, ethnic, military, political and historical aspects. Very often it is a combination of pretexts that leads to confrontation. It would seem to be wrong to reject the fact that some regional situations originate from the struggle between the two social-economic systems. Likewise, one should not forget that in some cases the continuation of conflicts was supported by third countries, including the great powers. In such regions as the Middle East, the Persian Gulf, South-East Asia, Central America, Latin America and Africa we have been witnessing a direct involvement of the major states.

At the same time, if one is to look at the Middle East conflict, it cannot be explained solely by the involvement of great or not so great powers. The roots of this conflict go back to the historic clash between Israeli expansionism and the interests of the Arabs, primarily of the Palestinian people. To bring the conflict to a long-awaited settlement, it is important that the USSR and the USA, the Western European and other states should see these primary causes and focus on the search for relevant solutions.

As a kind of history lesson, one should critically look at the evolution of the Afghan conflict, which meant for the Soviet Union ten years of active military involvement. It appears that the first stage of the analysis should be concerned with the way the Afghan leadership perceived the April revolution and defined its character. At the same time, one should look at the way these assessments were viewed in Moscow at the time. The combination of these two approaches brought about decisions which are now the subject of debate.

It is to be noted that the Afghan leadership, during the April revolution and long after, believed it was a proletarian revolution. The ideological bias in our perception of those events ('wishful-thinking') did not in its turn allow us to see at once that this conclusion was far-fetched. The Afghan leadership for several years could not determine definitively the character of the April revolution and this ambiguity hampered the determination of the prospects of the development of the situation. It was only toward the end of 1985, when Kabul came to a definitive conclusion that the Afghan Revolution had a national democratic and not any other, more advanced, character, that it became possible to work out practical ways for a political settlement. During the search for an Afghan settlement, a major discovery of the new thinking was born: *the conception of national reconciliation* as a method of settling regional problems. The importance of this concept has now gone beyond Afghanistan and is specified with regard to other regions of the world. In Afghanistan, national reconciliation involves the creation of a coalition government on a sufficiently wide political basis, allowing the participation in the government of opposition forces, irrespective of their attitude to the legitimate government in Kabul.

The history of Soviet involvement in Afghanistan also requires a thorough study of the mechanism of decision-making which made this action possible. It is now reliably known that the decision to send a Soviet military contingent to Afghanistan was taken not on a democratic and open basis, but by a fairly narrow group of the country's leaders. But it is a separate question which should be investigated thoroughly.

The most important thing is that the Soviet leadership became convinced of the necessity of a solely correct decision – to withdraw the troops from Afghanistan. The decision announced in Mr Gorbachev's statement on Afghanistan is a practical manifestation of the new political thinking. The formula of the Afghan settlement has revealed two important elements of the new thinking, which should become part of international experience in these matters.

The first element is the principle of national reconciliation. This principle is already operating in Kampuchea, in Central America and in South Africa. Internal reconciliation acts as the centre of gravity for opposing sides, as a force which reduces tension in the relations between them, makes it possible to solve in a pragmatic way the problems of the further coexistence of different political forces within one single structural framework.

Second, this formula has shown that whatever the causes of conflicts, they cannot be eliminated by military means.

Thus, in the area of regional conflicts, a settlement model

began to form that makes it possible to find optimal solutions, of course taking into account the specific situations.

Soviet foreign policy is making an active contribution to the easing of tensions, to the settlement of regional problems and to all the peace-making processes which serve to calm down explosive situations. It is our conviction that the political orientation of a country is its own internal affair. This approach comprises both the modern political and high moral ideal of conduct. It is extremely important that other countries, particularly those claiming to have 'vital interests' in various zones of the world, adopt this policy, which is the only reasonable one, thus contributing to the reduction and elimination of international tensions.

The concept of the new thinking has had the biggest impact on the key sphere of world politics – *international security*. For the past decades, security – national and international – has dominated in the politicians' perception of the aims and tasks that were set for the foreign policy and military machines of their states. Security interests became all-pervasive, shaping not only the daily activity of the major state institutions but also such areas as science, technology, industry, education, culture, etc. Gradually these interests became sacred and unquestionable. The material and financial provisions for these interests were, therefore, beyond criticism. Military-industrial complexes speeded up the production of armaments of many kinds and types, in particular of the weapons of mass destruction.

And yet this was not the main problem. The real problem involving the transformation of security concerns into a government policy's obsession was that the world found itself confronted with a paradoxical metamorphosis: the all-pervasive obsession with security led to reduced security, to the growth of a real danger for humanity's survival.

If analysts had looked attentively at this phenomenon, they could, at least two decades ago, have come to the conclusion about the interdependence of states that the Soviet leadership began to speak about in the middle of the 1980s. In the past, interdependence manifested itself primarily in a negative way. Building up arms for the sake of national security was not only the policy of states on the other side of the strategic barrier, but also of the states which were outside the zone of immediate confrontation. They speeded up arms production, at times exhausting their generally weak economies.

A dangerous feature of these negative tendencies was that those who determined the military-political strategy were to a great extent ideologically motivated. Both sides, if one is to take the USSR and the USA, were building an ideology of the 'enemy'. The United States was seen as the embodiment of the wicked forces of imperialism, and the Soviet Union was portrayed as 'a Communist empire of evil', conceived and existing solely to achieve the coveted goal of global liquidation of freedom and private property. It was no longer a matter of protection of state interests, which were replaced by 'vital interests', national security interests, which amounted first and foremost to maintaining the social and economic foundations of either system. This is, for example, how the task of the US armed forces was defined in the document 'Long-Range Strategy' worked out by the US Joint Chiefs of Staff in 1945: '. . . the following premises are to serve as the basis of our policy: we cannot allow the survival of a political system opposite to ours. We have no choice but to use Cato's strategy.'

The reference is, of course, to that member of the ancient Roman élite who is remembered for concluding his every speech in the senate with the famous phrase, 'And yet I believe that Carthage must be destroyed.' Not having documents of the Soviet General Staff at hand, I can only speculate that in those documents as well one could perhaps find a large degree of irreconcilable confrontation, although, not reaching the level of hate the Roman Consul felt for the prosperous city many centuries ago and which inspired those who drafted the above-mentioned US document.

The grim combination of the political-ideological intransigence underlying the military-strategic planning of both sides with unprecedented nuclear superarmaments meant that, instead of tablets promising immortality, humanity received a ticket to that greatest catastrophe which was seen as the Apocalypse by the prophet John.

Having become aware of this, the Soviet leadership fundamentally reconsidered the philosophical basis and the system of security. The new concept was first outlined by Mr Gorbachev during his meeting with US President Reagan in Geneva in 1985. It was said then that it was not in our interests to achieve strategic superiority over the US, and that neither was it in the US interests to try to achieve superiority over the USSR. Such a desire would inevitably result in strategic instability, with all its negative consequences for the world's destiny. Furthermore, the Soviet leader said, 'a lesser security for the United States compared with the Soviet Union would not be to our advantage.' It was also said that a nuclear war is unacceptable and cannot be viewed as a policy instrument, even in an extreme situation.

Being aware of the tendency of the US side to see in Soviet initiatives first a propaganda exercise, then a political bluff, and only after that, genuine politics, in order to create an atmosphere of trust for the novelty of the Soviet strategic concept to be more easily perceived, the Soviet Union took a number of concrete steps. It stopped unilaterally all nuclear tests, expressed a readiness to resume the negotiations on a complete ban on all nuclear tests; announced a unilateral moratorium on anti-satellite weapons testing; put forward radical proposals on cutting nuclear arsenals; elaborated proposals on the prevention of transferring the arms race into space.

Mr Gorbachev thus formulated his intention: 'The time has come when, faced with a global nuclear menace, we should learn the great art of living together.'

At the first summit meeting between Mr Gorbachev and President Reagan in Geneva, the concept of the inadmissibility of a nuclear war was initiated only with great difficulty. During many hours of discussions, a formula was worked out which was to become the cornerstone of Soviet–American understanding on security. The instructions which were given to us, the experts, by the Soviet leader were precise and clear. They were the basis for our work. Well after midnight on 21 November 1985, when we had become bogged down in trying to reconcile the drafts, Mr Gorbachev suggested several options for 'diplomatic ways out' which, together with US moves towards the Soviet position, gave the world the following, seemingly very simple, formula: 'A nuclear war must never be started; there will be no winner. Recognizing that any conflict between the

USSR and the United States could have catastrophic consequences, they also underscored the importance of preventing any war between them – nuclear or conventional. They will not strive to achieve military superiority.' The new thinking was for the first time specified in terms of international law in the area of security.

The next important breakthrough in the basic approaches to national security was the conclusion that strategic parity, which today ensures stability in global US–Soviet relations, may become less reliable and more fragile with a continuation of the arms race and the accumulation of nuclear weapons.

To recognize this important thesis, we had again to analyse the past period during which the USSR and the USA produced a total of 45,000 nuclear charges.

Having taken a critical look at the forty years of our participation in the arms race, we came to the conclusion that we had let ourselves succumb to the predominantly military-strategic vision of world developments, the real and imaginary dangers to our country, and the ways of opposing them. Tensions emerging in the world in that period meant almost automatically that we, as well as the West, began to produce more weapons, and this was repeated until the arsenals were filled to the roof with necessary and often unnecessary weapons, and we became stuck in the quicksand of the arms race.

Does this mean that our involvement in the arms race at all post-war stages was always unnecessary? Could it have been avoided from the very beginning? In the post-war period, in my view, there was a time when we had to take part in the arms race in the interests of protecting our security and the survival of Socialism.

There was basically no alternative. The USSR could not but start developing atomic weapons under the circumstances where the US atomic monopoly spelled dangerous and far-reaching military and political consequences. Our policies felt the pressure of this monopoly for several years. When in 1949 the USSR got this weapon of mass destruction, it became the first sobering warning to the United States, which limited the latter's capacity for blackmail. It introduced significant and positive changes in the balance of forces. Later events justified this step and eventually – forty years later – led to the real possibility of closing the nuclear circle and eliminating completely nuclear weapons by the beginning of the next millennium.

It was as necessary and, from the point of view of military and political strategies, inevitable for the Soviet Union to take the decision to develop and deploy modern strategic carriers – heavy bombers and intercontinental ballistic missiles. The TASS statement of 26 August 1957 on the successful testing of a Soviet ICBM signalled the emergence of a new quality in the USSR defence potential. The same role was played by the development in the USSR in the middle of the 1950s of bombers capable of carrying out a nuclear strike against US territory.

The vulnerability of US territory to a Soviet retaliatory strike became the second sobering warning on our part for the hotheads in Washington, DC, who planned to carry out a preventive strike against the Soviet Union, as was revealed by the recently opened US archives of the late 1940s and 50s.

The appearance of new strategic systems in Soviet armed forces did not by itself solve the task of ensuring the security of the USSR, since the question was, 'What level they should be limited to?' How many were considered sufficient? The absolute appreciation of the fact that this level should be that of the United States was remarkably evident in the analysis of the outcome of the Caribbean crisis of 1962, which, as we have already noted, occurred with the US having a considerable superiority in strategic offensive weapons. Hence the goal of the USSR of achieving strategic parity to guarantee against accidents and tragic misunderstandings.

It is logical to conclude that our involvement in the arms race prior to achieving strategic parity with the USA was forced on us and unfortunately inevitable. However, a cardinal question immediately arises: How should we have behaved after that parity was achieved?

It can be suggested that the implications of solving the historic task – achieving a strategic balance with the US in the early 1970s – were not analysed thoroughly enough with respect to a required shift of emphasis to political ways of maintaining state security and easing tensions in the world. Strategic parity made it senseless to continue the nuclear arms race. Furthermore, a continued build-up of nuclear weapons, according to a genuinely creative conclusion which the Soviet leadership has now reached, can undermine the insurance value of parity, and, at some point in the escalation, it may not be able to serve as a guarantor of strategic stability. Therefore, the task of making substantial cuts in strategic arms on a mutual basis is becoming a key area in foreign policy activity, which, while protecting the national security of the USSR, at the same time promises a substantial economy of means and resources for the benefit of the economy under restructuring.

To resist the magic spell of the total numerical parameters of the present-day levels of strategic arms, one should know that the steep turn in the spiral of the strategic arms race started by the USA in the early 1960s was in fact rooted in improvisation and the lack of sufficiently grounded estimates. At the time of the Caribbean crisis, the strategic forces of the two sides, particularly ICBMs and SLBMs, consisted of a few dozen missiles. Then the Kennedy administration – which gave the greatest acceleration to the strategic arms race – took a decision to deploy 1,000 ICBMs, 'Minutemen', and forty-one submarines with Polaris missiles.

Why 1,000 ICBMs? To be honest, this question has long interested me, since I could not find a convincing explanation or calculation from which this figure originated in any published documents, memoirs or monographs. Three or four years ago, in a conversation with a former close aide to John Kennedy, who was in Moscow, I asked what the motives for their decision had been. Now, after so many years, not being tied to considerations of secrecy or 'departmental honour', he recounted that John Kennedy and Mr McNamara, the then Secretary of Defense, took this figure out of the blue without any in-depth preliminary studies by the Pentagon or scholars. 'From the political point of view,' he said, 'since during the election campaign John Kennedy talked much about the USA lagging behind the USSR, the figure of 1,000 ICBMs probably was used to catch people's imagination. It was as simple as that.'

The same figure became our target too in the development of our strategic forces. Life has given us a great lesson. One cannot but recall what Confucius said: 'We learn wisdom in three ways.

Thinking is the noblest way, imitation, the easiest, the third one – that of life experience – is the hardest.' Have we not sometimes been following the easiest way in arms production?

The Chernobyl tragedy, however paradoxical this may be, served as a crushing blow to the magic spell of huge numbers by which the 'required armament levels' are measured. It turned out that the radiation leakage alone (without other destructive consequences of a real nuclear blast), equal to one-third of the smallest nuclear charge, made half of Europe shudder. Now what would happen if one side, even taking advantage of the surprise factor, carried out a nuclear strike against the other side using a thousand nuclear charges? The answer today is crystal clear – this would bring about the death of the aggressor's opponent, and the aggressor, as well as the destruction of the rest of civilization. We must therefore get rid of nuclear weapons, and the sooner the better. No one needs any additional proof of their lethal danger any more.

That is why the leaders of the USSR and the USA have to look now for a cardinal solution to the problem of 'nuclear interdependence'. For the armed forces to continue to be a reliable protector of a country's security, and at the same time to promote the economic stability and prosperity of the country, a thorough and detailed analysis is required or, still better, a revision of the cyclical process 'action – reaction – counter-reaction – action' in our relations in the area of the development of military technology and determination of the structure of the armed forces.

We, as well as Washington, vitally need the decisions in R & D and arms production to be fully economically justified. One of the USA's strategic goals is to exhaust the USSR economically, among other things by imposing military programmes, very often leading to a technological and strategic impasse through bluff, disinformation and demonstration of a costly 'example'. The time of gigantic figures and 'ceilings' of military expenditures seems to be passing, if our perestroika – and there is no alternative – is to put our country on the road of a powerful and rapid development. In his report Mr Gorbachev stressed in this respect that the effectiveness of our defence development 'should be henceforth ensured by predominantly qualitative parameters – both in terms of technology, military science, and the composition of the armed forces.' This should become a positive trend for the rest of the world.

III

Many state and political figures in the West, regarding the development of the new thinking as a major factor of present-day international life, are at the same time inclined to think that it is a purely 'Soviet phenomenon' and therefore there is no question of whether one should or should not share the main elements of this thinking. Briefly stated, the initial response was that, since the USSR remains a 'Communist' society, and, furthermore, a 'closed' one, the West should not introduce any corrective elements into its attitude toward the processes of perestroika in the domestic and foreign policy of the USSR. It is being stressed that the Soviet Union remains a powerful 'military monolith', and therefore the West should further build up its forces 'to maintain the balance'.

This is, one should say, one of the sources of those miscalculations which are quite often committed by those who shape Western policies, where the confrontational-ideological approach continues to prevail. Developments in the USSR are seen solely as a tactical phenomenon. If one is to be completely frank, the West does not want to change either its thinking or its actions. Yet this situation may turn out to be risky. The West may lag behind us in terms of thinking. This may generate future misunderstanding and additional complications at negotiations, difficulties in reaching agreements, particularly on issues of principal importance. The risk of the West becoming an antique-shop of stale thoughts and ideas should worry serious politicians. The last decade of the twentieth century has become critically important for the construction of a new world and new relations. The old approaches would make it impossible.

The West's ability to manifest a new thinking in world affairs has become a vital issue on the international agenda. One should not say that there are no prospects here. Evidence of the new thinking is starting to be found in the statements of Western leaders. In this context one should note an interesting idea in

FOREIGN POLICY — A NEW COURSE

President George Bush's speech at a Texas university. 'The time has come,' he said, 'to move beyond deterrence to the new policy of the nineties, the policy which will recognize the extraordinary changes in the world and in the Soviet Union.' Adherents to the old school of thinking are persistent in opposing attempts to look at the world and at all of us in a new way. They believe that the major thing is not the novelty of thinking, but how it can be used to promote Western interests. This reveals the inclination of many politicians and political scientists, particularly of those who made their careers in the 'cold war' years, towards the tendency to simplified thinking, using the formula: 'the worse for them, the better for us.'

Today it is important to reduce and then completely eliminate the stark asymmetry of thinking in the East and in the West.

Vladimir N. Kudryavtsev

A distinguished Soviet scholar of constitutional law, Vladimir Kudryavtsev has been the Director of the Institute of State and Law for fifteen years. He is the author of many books published both in the USSR and abroad on the Socialist legal system, law and sociology, the theory of criminal law and criminology. His books include: *Reasons for Infringement of the Law* (1976), *Law and Behaviour* (1978), *Social Divergences: An Introduction to General Theory* (1978, Editor-in-Chief), *A Course in Soviet Criminology* (1985), *Law, Action and Responsibility* (1986), and *The Principles of Soviet Criminal Law* (1988). He is a member of the USSR Academy of Sciences, a fellow of a number of foreign Academies of Sciences and Vice-President of the Association of Soviet Lawyers. He also contributes to the work of a number of other Soviet public organizations such as the Association of Legal Sciences, the International Society of Criminology and the International Society for Social Defence. He is a member of the Board of the International Criminal Law Commission as well as other international organizations.

The Congress of People's Deputies became a triumph for many of them. It became a triumph for the orator, Academician Vladimir Kudryavtsev. Speaking many times on a wide range of important issues, he skilfully used his competence, impeccable logic and eloquence to convert even his most ardent opponents to his point of view.

Political Reform in the USSR: the First Stage

VLADIMIR N. KUDRYAVTSEV

The process of perestroika now under way in the Soviet Union has many aspects. It encompasses radical changes in the economy and state management, the development of social and spiritual life, etc. A key component of this process is the reform of the political system which was given a new impetus after the 19th Party Conference in the summer of 1988.

The necessity of reforming the political system of the USSR was not yet realized in 1985, when perestroika started, because all attention was centred on changes in the economic mechanism. It became clear that it would be impossible to implement economic reform without changes in the social sphere. And only gradually was it understood that there was also a need to democratize human relations in our society, and that meant reshaping the political system itself.

The years of perestroika have brought it home to us that the old system of management, which we call the command and administrative system, has completely outlived itself economically, socially and politically, both in domestic and foreign policy. The control of the state over all spheres of life, excessive centralization of management and its bureaucratization have resulted in a number of serious destructive processes. First, the lowering of efficiency and overall management skills, the reproduction and in the long run the domination of incompetence at different levels of management. Second, diminishing responsibility for work. And, third, as an inevitable result of all this, stagnation in the development of society and gross mistakes in major domestic and foreign policy decision-making.

POLITICAL REFORM IN THE USSR: THE FIRST STAGE

The democratic institutions, though in a rudimentary form provided for by our political structure, were reduced to nothing and merely feigned fruitful activity. This is particularly true of our legislative bodies. Suffice it to say that after the adoption of the Soviet Constitution in 1936 and until last year, the Supreme Soviet of the USSR had never really seriously discussed major draft decisions of state importance. In fifty years it unanimously adopted about eighty laws, but at the same time its Presidium approved more than 600 decrees, none of which was submitted for discussion to the Deputies. As to the number of rulings and regulations issued by the USSR Council of Ministers, individual ministries and state agencies, their number cannot be calculated. Even now that many regulations have been abrogated, our estimates show that about one million normative acts issued primarily by ministries are still in force in the Soviet Union.

Science and practice have repeatedly put the question not only of the long overdue democratization of the legislative bodies, but in fact of the complete restructuring of their work. The first stage of political reform in the USSR went along this road by carrying out considerable changes in the structure of the supreme bodies of power, in the way they are formed and their work organized.

First, we should name the changes in the electoral system. I shall point out three major ones. First, in addition to the election of Deputies from territorial and national-territorial districts, it was proposed to nominate candidates and to elect Deputies from public organizations as well. Second, two supreme bodies of power were established: the Congress of People's Deputies of the USSR convened once or twice a year, and the Supreme Soviet of the USSR elected by the Congress. Third, the legislative, executive and judicial functions were separated from each other consistently enough. A new body – the Committee for Constitutional Supervision of the USSR – is being set up.

The election campaign based on the new principles was characterized by a high degree of political activity on the part of the voters which had been denied to them for many years during the personality cult and stagnation. This increased activity was visible at all stages of the electoral process, but it was particularly heightened when candidates were nominated, their platforms were discussed and voting took place.

Increased political activity of the electorate was encouraged by the general course of the CPSU towards perestroika, the democratization of social life in the country and the specific norms of the new electoral law, among them the following:

• granting the right of nomination of candidates for Deputies to voters' meetings at their place of residence (earlier, candidates could be nominated only at their places of work);

• discussion and nomination of an unlimited number of candidates, and as a result of this, the right to include any number of candidates on the ballot. A total of 1,431 candidates ran for election in 750 territorial districts;

• broad coverage of the preparations and the elections themselves and of the returns;

• a new level of canvassing both in favour of candidates and against them. First, each candidate had his own election platform, and second, canvassing for the candidates was mainly done by their campaign managers.

All this made it possible to hold genuine elections for the first time in many years. While in the preceding years we actually had elections without any real choice, since we had merely voting, slogans and applause to show unanimity (which in fact was non-existent), the latest elections of the People's Deputies of the USSR reflected the real will of the people.

A sociological study conducted by the Institute of State and Law and the Institute of Sociology of the USSR Academy of Sciences in major regions of the country (the Russian Federation, the Ukraine, the Baltic region, Central Asia) in January and February 1989 showed that the new electoral procedures were approved of by a considerable part of the electorate. Nomination meetings were attended by more than 60 per cent of all the people polled, with more than 20 per cent of them actively involved. Over 60 per cent of all those polled said the meetings were animated and to the point. In some one-third of the cases, relevance and the spirit of debate were ensured from the grassroots by thwarting the plans of the meeting organizers. It is important to note that the degree of satisfaction with the meetings was to a large extent related to how democratic they were.

The voters were all for such new elements of the electoral

system as the competitiveness of candidates (about 57 per cent of the polled), the opportunity for personal involvement in the nomination process including one's own candidacy (22 per cent), the fact that candidates had their own election platforms. Only 19.4 per cent of all those polled failed to notice the essential advantages in the new electoral procedures.

89.8 per cent of all registered voters took part in the elections on 26 March 1989. In the constituent republics, the percentage of voters who came to the polling stations varied from a maximum of 98.5 per cent (Azerbaijan SSR) to a minimum of 71.9 per cent (Armenian SSR). The figure for the Russian Federation (RSFSR), the largest constituent republic, was 87.0 per cent.

As to the composition of the 'Deputies' corps', it can be said to be sufficiently representative and diverse. Party members and candidates for CPSU membership account for 87 per cent of the Deputies (in 1984 the figures was 71.5 per cent), but the number of workers, collective farmers, women and young Communist League members among the Deputies went down. This needs a thorough analysis. One can only suppose that the major reasons for these changes were the unaccustomed new approach to the formation of the Deputies corps; lack of experience in conducting this new kind of election; the refusal of some ordinary workers, collective farmers and women to run because of growing demands on Deputies.

During the elections, some high-ranking officials were voted down because the voters thought they did not have enough connections with the people, did not care enough about the people's needs and grievances. In the course of the election battle, some officials did everything in their power to get rid of alternative candidates they had no control over.

The election campaign brought to light a number of new factors and processes. It exposed problems which people had either failed to notice or were not aware of before. For example, in the USSR Academy of Sciences, relations became strained between researchers at individual institutes and the Presidium of the Academy, or its administration. Ardour, emotions, nerves – all these qualities were very much a part of the scene, which to my mind is quite natural. People remain people and unbiased elections cannot really be called elections. But of course, the interests of the electorate ought to be formed in a quieter situation, in a balanced form and well in advance.

District voters' meetings were the element in the electoral procedure which made it possible to strike some candidates off the ticket even before the elections could show who was who. Some people think it is undemocratic that public organizations nominate candidates. But I see an advantage in this because the broad strata of the intelligentsia are becoming actively involved in the elections. The Deputies elected on the tickets of public organizations were very much in the limelight at the Congress of People's Deputies of the USSR.

The new elections have created a unique situation for the Deputies themselves. The status of Deputy had to be changed through abandoning the old idea that our Deputies always combine their public work with a regular job. Many Deputies are now becoming professional politicians, which is inevitable. Permanent work in a legislative body requires people who are competent enough and politically mature. That means they have to change their way of life and work.

Some theoretical questions emerge in connection with the elections and the functioning of the new bodies of power. Our philosophy and constitutional jurisprudence incessantly criticized the theory of 'the separation of powers' formulated by the early European men of the enlightenment. Even now we view it with a degree of doubt, though, as a matter of fact, we have been moving in this direction, which is, to my mind, correct. It is already accepted that the officials of the executive bodies, including ministers, may not be elected as Deputies to the Soviets. Judges may not be Deputies. There is no doubt that the executive apparatus should be fully subordinate to a legislative body, while the courts and the Procurator's Office should retain their independence from both. This is a primary basis for the organization of a rule-of-law state.

The restructuring of the supreme bodies of power is only a part of the whole. What is important is to ensure their truly democratic action in the future. A representative body should accumulate and express the real will of the people through its decisions. For a long time this will was regarded as unambiguous and impersonal enough, though in reality there existed a whole range of different interests, among them social, political, national, age, professional and so on. The Congress of People's Deputies already revealed this in full. Now that the Supreme Soviet of the USSR has begun working, we are to institutionalize the practice of continually bringing out all these interests, weighing priorities and values; not supressing but, on the contrary, comprehensively developing the Socialist pluralism of opinion and the elaboration of alternative decisions.

A major scientific and practical question is the further path of development of the *Soviet federation*. In the late 1950s the powers of the constitutuent republics were extended, but later the trend towards excessive centralization and the transformation of our multiethnic country into a *de facto* unitarian state became manifest. As a reaction to these distortions in the nationalities policy, undesirable and even tragic events have happened recently in some regions of the country.

It is obvious that we need a scientifically-based review of the principles of Soviet Socialist federalism which, as the 19th Party Conference's decision says, should 'not be *killing unification*, but a full-blooded and dynamic unity in ethnic diversity'. To develop and strengthen it means democratizing the relations between the republics and the Union of these Soviet Socialist republics, more clearly demarcating their terms of reference, broadening the rights of Union republics and autonomous units, transferring some managerial functions to the republics and territories, encouraging the independence and responsibility of the Union republics and autonomous territories in the field of economic, social and cultural development, establishing mechanisms for resolving emerging conflicts and coordinating different ethnic interests. In the light of the new realities, we have to considerably revise the existing legislation on ethnic relations.

As was already mentioned, the reform of the political system encompasses the following: radically to strengthen the rule of law in the country by eliminating all opportunities for arbitrariness; to ensure the equality of every individual before the law, irrespective of his or her position; to withstand bureaucratism; to rule out any usurpation of power and abuse of power. We must fully restore and apply the humanistic principles which have been formulated over the centuries and are now manifested in the crowning achievements of world culture.

There is no need to say how important all this is for our people, especially in the light of the tragic events of the past, which in their severity can hardly be paralleled by anything in the history of mankind.

The Congress of People's Deputies of the USSR issued a statement which emphasizes the necessity of establishing the supremacy of the law and the equality of all citizens, officials and organizations before it. In a rule-of-law state, all citizens bear responsibility for their actions before the law, but the state, as represented by its bodies and officials, should also, without any exception, bear responsibility for its actions and decisions before each citizen and the entire people. The law is the foundation of a rule-of-law state, the protector of the freedom and equality of its citizens, of order and proper organization of society, the guarantor of the principle of social justice.

In its statement, the Congress indicated that it proceeds from the recognition of inalienable human rights and the rights of nations as being unshakeable and sacred: the right to live, the right to freedom, the inviolability and security of the individual and the home, the right to self-determination. Any derogation of or infringement upon human rights and the rights of nations is impermissible. The Soviet legislative system, the courts and the law-enforcement agencies are required to implement these rights consistently and strictly and to uphold them.

The USSR will promote the formation of a world community of law-governed nations on the basis of international norms and principles, including those stipulated in the Universal Declaration of Human Rights, the Helsinki Accords and the Agreements at the Vienna meeting through changing domestic legislation to accommodate them.

The Congress also mapped out the next, second, stage of political reform. It asked the USSR Supreme Soviet to begin working out legislation which would specifically and consistently apply the principle of full power of the Soviets in the economy, social and political life. The necessary conditions for the return of real mechanisms of power to the Soviets will be as follows: the restructuring of the Soviets of People's Deputies at all levels, democratization of the way in which they act, the maximum extension of their rights and powers, the unconditional subordination of the executive apparatus to them. All local affairs should be managed according to the principle of self-government, with a green light given to the initiatives of citizens and accompanied by the growing role of public organizations and democratic movements.

The provision of legal guarantees for economic reform is another pressing task in the field of legislation. The Congress asked the USSR Supreme Soviet to study the question of preparing the unified Law on the Socialist Enterprise, as well as to prepare the laws on leasing, republican and regional cost-accounting, self-financing, a unified tax system, self-government and local economy.

The Congress drew attention to the poor state of law and order in the country. Democratic development can be undermined by arbitrary administrative actions to limit the freedom of will of the people, and by the substitution of extremist violence and arbitrary rule for such a will. In this connection it was recommended to develop further and strengthen the constitutional guarantees for a peaceful constructive development of the democratic process. The Congress abrogated the article on criminal responsibility for 'the discreditation' of state bodies and instructed the USSR Supreme Soviet to study the question of whether the decrees 'On the Procedure for Holding Rallies and Demonstrations' and 'On the Powers and Rights of the Internal Troops of the USSR Ministry of the Interior' are in conformity with the Constitution of the USSR.

One of the problems discussed by the delegates was how to step up the fight against crime, embezzlement and bribery. A proposal was made to work out an All-Union Programme to Combat Crime. There is no doubt that the state must guarantee the security of its citizens from assaults on their lives, health and property. A most important element of the planned judicial and legal reform is going to be an all-round consolidation of the independence of the courts and the greater efficiency of investigation, which is to be achieved by moving it away from any ministerial or departmental influence. This task can be solved only if we provide for the real protection of the legitimate rights of citizens at all stages of court trial, including admitting the lawyer from the very start of the investigation. Unbiased investigation, strong defence and an independent court – this is the triune formula of Socialist justice. The reform of the law-enforcement agencies is worthy of special mention and includes the courts, the Procurator's Office, the bar and the penitentiaries. The press usually uses the term 'the reform of the court system', but the reform does not cover the courts only; it is necessary to organize the apparatus of investigation into an autonomous and independent entity to free the Procurator's Office from other functions so that it can do what it is supposed to do – supervise the observance of laws and enhance the independence of judges. I would say that each stage in social, political and economic development calls for a need for a well-thought-out, exact and viable legal institutionalization.

In the course of the election campaign and at the Congress of People's Deputies, much was said about the command and administrative methods of management and the resulting constraints on democracy which produced a particularly harmful effect on the exercise of political and personal rights and freedoms of Soviet citizens: freedom of speech, assembly, meetings and demonstrations, formation of public organizations, freedom of creative activity, freedom of conscience, inviolability of the home and the individual, etc. Here there was a major discrepancy between word and deed, between slogan and political practice.

The problem is that there are either no concrete legal mechanisms for the exercise of a number of constitutional rights, or these mechanisms are defective and extremely outdated. The second stage of the reform will be to renew legislation on public organizations – voluntary societies and artistic unions, the media, and on the freedom of conscience. Worthy of study also are the questions of ensuring collective rights – those of nations and nationalities, public organizations and work collectives.

The rule-of-law state should operate according to the principle 'Everything is allowed that is not banned by law.' Of course, that applies to citizens. This should be said because some officials in the apparatus would like this principle to be extended to them, while precisely the opposite is important, and that is that the actions of officials should be clearly stated by the law and they should not be extended to the areas beyond their terms of reference.

The time has come to work out the legislative strategy for the next few years. Not infrequently previous bills were of a random nature, because they were prepared by the organizations concerned. Now, every bill is thoroughly discussed by the Deputies in the Commissions, Committees and the Chambers of the Supreme Soviet of the USSR.

Certainly, old stereotypes still play a role in preparing today's normative acts: there are relapses of 'prohibitiveness', the desire to apply administrative methods to the economy and to cultural life, the desire to substitute instructions for laws. But there are also objective difficulties: most of the problems which are to be covered by the new legislation are new, and we do not have any expertise in their legal regulation. Let us take the Law on State Enterprise. It seems that its authors were unaware of possible difficulties with the state order; they did not realize that the main stumbling-block for individual enterprises' independence was to be the state order.

Everything was very 'easy' under the administrative system: any 'command' was unquestionably implemented. It is true, the results often turned out to be deplorable, but this did not bother the bureaucrats very much. Now, any new law must provide for a complex range of various interests, which one law or another should reflect, ensure, protect or channel in a different direction.

Departmental and general state interests may conflict, probably immediate departmental interests *vs.* long-term general state interests. In our legislative practice we have trouble dealing with the real conflicts which exist in society. In the past we were hampered by the dogma of the monolithic unity of the Soviet people, but even now the natural differences are regarded by many as an anomaly, a distortion. But a monolith never really existed; it does not exist now and will not do so in the future: the interests of the individual may come into conflict with the interests of society; the interests of different social groups may vary, etc. And the law should take into account all these differences. Otherwise the decisions are going to be one-sided and detrimental. It is clear that conflicting interests cannot be overcome; not only will the differences of interests not disappear, they will become ever more diverse, because Socialist society is not a 'barracks', but a diversity of interests and opinions. Our judicial system should be built around the diversity of interests and this diversity should be encouraged in the economy, and in political and spiritual life. Meanwhile the strategy of development should be clearly seen.

So, life has put a number of complex questions before the highest bodies of power. All of them require a thorough scientific analysis, substantiation and specific recommendations. The difficulties are not minor. It is a well-known fact that for many years serious and unbiased philosophical, sociological or political studies were discouraged. Now social scientists have to make up for that. In this connection I shall mention two issues that require fundamental, in-depth study.

First, there is the problem of *general human values*, which constitute the historic achievements of all human culture. For a long time, the recognition of such values was viewed as a deviation from Marxism. Severe criticism was made of such democratic principles as an independent court, competitiveness of the parties, the presumption of innocence, etc. Such notions as justice, mercy, humanism, humaneness and decency began to disappear from the pages of scholarly publications. The renovated political system, with the rule-of-law state as a part of it, should widely use all these notions, institutes and categories, and be based on them. Immoral policies are not acceptable for us in principle.

Second, there is the *forecast* of our future political and social development. The reform of the political system is not going to be effective unless we can utilize our own historical experience and that of other countries. We should get as realistic and as full a picture of the path of development of the Soviet state, the entire civic society and changes in its social structure and spiritual life as possible. Unfortunately, these questions were not dealt with scientifically, though we must know how history affects the present, what we can expect in the future and what should be the general strategy of the development of Socialism.

Basic research in this field requires studies on the nature and structure of power, the correlation of political and social forces in contemporary society, the analysis of the decision-making mechanisms, the ways of instilling the pluralism of interests and opinions.

The reform of the political system necessitates the creation of an efficient mechanism for utilizing the recommendations of social scientists in politics and calls for the scientific study of state projects and decisions. The ways to attain this goal can be different. Among them are consultative councils attached to the highest bodies of power, expert assessments made by academic institutes, etc.

I believe that political and legal reform will be a success only if it is based on science. At the same time, political reform itself creates the conditions for overcoming stagnation in political and legislative thought and necessitates the development of the social sciences.

Georgi Kh. Shakhnazarov

Georgi Shakhnazarov is a Soviet political scientist, Doctor of Sciences in Law, a corresponding member of the USSR Academy of Sciences, a winner of the USSR State Prize, President of the Soviet Association of Political Sciences (since 1974) and Vice-President of the International Association of Political Sciences.

He was born on 4 October 1924 in Baku. He fought in World War II. In 1949 he graduated from the Law Department of the Azerbaijan State University. From 1952 to 1961 he was head of an editorial office in Politizdat, from 1962 to 1963 and from 1970 to 1972 he worked as a consulting editor and Executive Editor of *The Problems of Peace and Socialism* magazine. From 1972 to 1988 he was a consultant and Deputy Head of a Department at the CPSU Central Committee and in March 1988 became an aide to the General Secretary of the CPSU Central Committee.

His research interests are the analysis of political systems and international relations, political theories and prognostics. His main monographs are as follows: *The Bourgeois State in an Age of Imperialism* (Yurizdat, 1954), *Socialist Democracy* (Politizdat, 1972), *The Socialist Destiny of Mankind, The Fiasco of Futurology, The World Order to Come* (Politizdat, 1978–82), *Socialism and the Future* (Nauka, 1983), *Where Mankind is Going* (Mysl, 1984). He has written many articles, among them 'The Logic of Political Thinking in a Nuclear Age', 'The World Community is Controllable'.

He is the author of a number of science fiction works such as the novel *The Most Regrettable Story in the World*, stories and short stories in the book *The Trees are like Horsemen* and the plays *Check and Checkmate* and *The Thirteenth Feat by Geraclis*.

The New Thinking: Principal Ideas and Guidelines

GEORGI KH. SHAKHNAZAROV

New thinking in international affairs is part and parcel of the great reformation of Socialism. In essence, it is a question of world order in an epoch when mankind begins to realize that it is an integrated whole, when vistas are opening for it to create a prosperous planetary civilization while, at the same time, there looms the menace of annihilation by a nuclear conflagration or ecological disasters.

How can one assess the processes in the contemporary world from viewpoints of the new thinking, and what is the essence of its principal ideas and guidelines? This is the subject of this article. It touches upon certain problems under discussion that, in my view, are of interest both to specialists and to the general public concerned with the present and future of the world community.

I

If one attempts to expound the new thinking concept in symbols one would get, roughly, the following sequence: internationalization – interdependence – priority of human interests and values – freedom of choice – integration – globalization – management of world development – formation of the new international order.

To be sure, symbols simplify the matter. Yet I think that the meaning of this formula is clear to anyone who follows the tempestuous developments of our epoch, at least watching TV and reading the press, not to speak of political literature. Here, probably, lies the reason for the broad and favourable response the idea of a new thinking has received in the world: in different countries and social strata, and by various political movements. It reflects the profound and pressing needs of peoples and mankind as a whole on the threshold of the twenty-first century.

Here is a generalized evaluation of the world's present situation: 'In spite of deep contradictions in the contemporary world and radical differences between the states that make it up, it is interconnected, interdependent and represents a certain entity. This follows from internationalized economic ties in the world, the all-embracing nature of the scientific and technological revolution, principally the new roles of the information and communications media, the conditions of the planet's resources, the overall ecological menace and the developing world's crying social problems which are of concern to everyone. But the main thing is the emergence of mankind's survival problem, for its very existence has been in question since the development and threat of use of nuclear weapons.'

The interdependent world whose space has greatly compressed due to the scientific and technological revolution, especially in communications, cannot but be an object of some measure of collective management. Had it been otherwise, no trains would have ever crossed national borders, piracy would have been rampant on the seas, aircraft would have collided in the air all the time, and everyone would have tried to shut down all others on the radio. Most probably, though, there would have been no world at all, as it would long ago have perished in a nuclear world. Manageability is a function of interdependence.

Management require *law and government.* International law based on treaties and agreements between states traces its origins to antiquity; by now it has become so much ramified that practically all spheres of international life are regulated with the help of legal norms. There is no government as yet, but we have every reason to speak of its rudiments, such as numerous UN-headed organizations which carry out diverse administrative and managing functions, limited as their powers are.

Is there a way to assess the attained *level of world manageability,* primarily, is it adequate, does it meet in full mankind's need for it at the present stage of development? This is a key question, and it has no single answer. In some areas, yes, in others, no.

Understandably, international management is most advanced in navigation, air transport, automobile and other kinds of transportation, communications, trade, finance, money circulation, and, in a broader sense, in the international division of labour. In other words, it is the traditional exchange of material and spiritual values, as well as joint maintenance of public order necessary for normal international life. Of course, though long regulated by common norms and rules, this area of activity, too, is in need of constant improvement. But the existing international mechanism makes it possible to raise and solve such problems with reasonable promptness. One may say that all in all the manageability level is not too remote from what is customary with states of a confederation.

It is much worse with international relations in what concerns the so-called universal (that is, common to a degree to all countries but solved by every state within its capacities) and global problems. A considerable gradation is evidenced inside each of these complexes. While one may speak of a measure of manageability, or rather of regulation of action by states on a bilateral, group or collective basis in health, education, emergency aid to victims of famine and natural disasters, and crime control, there is as yet no common concern of humanity for joint protection of the environment, vital as it is for all mankind.

Such an assertion may appear arguable. Indeed, there are hundreds of international agreements to regulate, for instance, the use of many waterways, the discharge of slime into the ocean; various Red Books are published, animal protection societies are active, national parks are set up, and poachers are hunted; ecological seminars, 'round tables' and congresses are convened.

All this is true. Yet one can soberly assess what has been done only if the achievement is compared with the scope of the problem. And this is so great, and bears so many dangers for mankind's future, that we are justified in placing it next to the nuclear war menace. Within such a system of reference there can be no ground for a serious discussion of either the manageability or even the effective regulation of work to save man's environment.

To draw a parallel with physical phenomena described by the second law of thermodynamics, one may assert that entropy here builds up faster than mankind's protective arrangements. Suffice it to say that experts are now reconsidering their assessments of the hole in the ozone layer and the greenhouse effect in the atmosphere, nitrate poisoning, and the spread of AIDS and cancer. These and other ills push on at a higher rate than was estimated, so threats to ecology may conceivably move to the front row of global problems and make us speed up the collective protection of nature and man from degeneration.

As bad, if not worse, is the menace of another global problem, that of the gap between economically advanced nations and the underdeveloped countries. This problem is far from being an object of international cooperation. There are numerous regional and global aid programmes, so-called UN Development Decades are being realized, the world progressive public deems it its duty to sound an alarm and draw the peoples' and governments' attention to the urgency of bridging the gap between the rich North and poor South which troubles our conscience and bodes ill for the world community of nations.

Yet one fact alone would suffice to show that the negligible scope of these efforts is incommensurate with the true needs: the gap between the developed and underdeveloped nations is again on the rise in the 1980s. The indebtness of over one trillion dollars played a fatal part in this. The unbridled avarice of Shylocks who give credit at enormous interest has brought about an asphyxiation of world finance and now resounds in stock-exchange panics at the very centres of the capitalist financial world. This situation is an avid demonstration of the degree of manageability or, rather, unmanageability as applied to development.

But the worst so far has been the issue of war and peace. There, too, good intentions were in abundance. The oldest ever norms known to international law are peace treaties, agreements of exchange of prisoners of war, *et al*. By now an impressive corpus of rules has been amassed for the purpose of restraining militarism, and one would say that this branch of international law is well in advance of any other. However, one will have to recognize as well that manageability in this vital area for mankind is extremely low, literally negligible. For instance, there are very few cases in post-World War II history when the combined efforts of states helped to prevent or quench the fires of war. The world community does a colossal amount of work to settle peacefully any of the dozens of conflict situations that crop up on the map of the world. And, of course, the biggest concern of all is the arms race that has been steadily gaining in tempo. Unless it is stopped, it threatens to undermine all and any hopes of mankind for the future, and to doom it to fatal catastrophe.

Through the joint efforts of the USSR and the USA and with the active aid of their allies and, in fact, of the whole international community, we have the first case of slowing down the arms race, at least in one field. Small as the percentage of the armaments to be destroyed is, it provides grounds for speaking of a sizeable step up in the level of war and peace manageability. First of all because solutions were found to the many specific and highly complex problems that are unavoidable in the disarmament process: permanent control at war factories, inspection on demand, exchange of experience in the destruction of certain types of nuclear-carrying weaponry, etc. But even the agreement on two nuclear missile 'zeros' and the prospects of troop and conventional arms reductions in Europe that glimmer after NATO's Brussels session and the Warsaw Treaty's Bucharest conference provide no reason to assert that the manageabiity of the issue of war and peace has advanced to the required level.

The success of the imminent work for peace depends, to a decisive degree, on whether *the development of cooperation can be made spontaneous, and world manageability can be elevated to a possible and required level in future.*

It has long been noticed that any advances on this road both cost much effort and were made possible by a preceding catastrophe. The Caribbean crisis of 1962 brought the world to the brink of a nuclear war; yet it prompted the establishment of the 'hot line' of communication between Moscow and Washington, and promoted some other important measures of prevention. The Chernobyl tragedy gave a strong impetus to cooperation in the field of nuclear energy development control. The emergence, or awakening, of the AIDS virus, this pestilence of the twentieth century, impelled the medical profession to intensify international cooperation. Even the recent Washington agreement had its dramatic antecedents: first Europe was overlaid with missile barrages, and only then did the sides spend much effort to convince each other that both would be better off if they got rid of them.

The question is, what should be done so that from now on dangerous incidents would not be needed to prove the necessity of cooperation and joint management of the course of developments? For it may so happen that after one such incident there will be nobody to draw lessons and shake hands. And again, is it at all possible for common sense to be ahead of prejudice, and for constructive ideas to have headway and prevent catastrophes?

The answer is affirmative, provided all members of the international community *set human interest above any other, be it of class, nation, group or ideology.*

It is not that common human interest eliminates or depreciates the class, national and any other interests (provided, of course, that they are well grounded). The whole point is that in the nuclear-age list of values, common human interests should be put at the top. If mankind fails to survive, there will be no class to look after its interests. Should any country be fortunate enough to live through a nuclear war, like Australia in Stanley Kramer's film *On the Beach*, it will still die in agony because of the 'nuclear winter'.

That is why it would be of common interest to all mankind to create or strengthen such bodies, whether regional or universal, which could purposefully regulate international relations on the basis of the balance of interests and conciliating procedures. They should have adequate authority to defuse conflicts in time. Progress in this direction will ultimately lead to a 'world government', a concert of all powers without a conductor, which, in other words, will carry out its duty as a democratic assembly, as a kind of world council or senate.

The world government idea was born and gained popularity at the end of the nineteenth and early twentieth centuries. Hopes for a centralized international authority to prevent a world war were fanned by the creation of the League of Nations and those dozens of agreements that helped to turn international law into

THE NEW THINKING: PRINCIPAL IDEAS AND GUIDELINES

an integral system. However, the movement peaked in the 1950s and 1960s. After the nuclear bombardment of Hiroshima and Nagasaki, many scientists came to a firm opinion that a world government alone could save mankind from annihilation. In the famous manifesto of Einstein and Russell there cropped up dozens of projects ranging from expanding UN functions to the creation of an international confederation or even a unitarian world state with a strong central government. Meanwhile there continued the process of the formation of numerous non-governmental organizations that support this aim, such as 'The Crusade for World Government' (USA), 'The World State League' (West Germany), 'The World Parliament Association' (Britain), etc.

Initially, Soviet foreign policy theory and practice were unequivocally opposed to the idea of mondialism. There were serious grounds for this. Partisans of world government in their majority were categorical in rejecting sovereignty, and pronounced this principle, as a matter of fact, to be a focus of evil, cause of wars, of all conflicts and tension in the world. This was all at the time when dozens of former colonies and semi-independent states were shedding their yokes and realizing their right to self-determination and political independence.

Objectively, there exists a contradiction between the ideas of sovereignty and political independence. But now the whole point is that now the new international order as promoted is not to be based on the rejection of sovereignty and the independence of nations (such a demand remains Utopian and reactionary) but on accounting for and harmonizing interests.

Recognition of every people's freedom of choice of its way and at the same time all states' participation in the solution of common, global problems on the basis of balance of interests – such is the essence of the concept of the new political thinking, and the only rational response to the challenges of the nuclear age.

Here there is no disregard, not a hint of it, of the sovereignty of any states – Socialist, capitalist, developed or developing. When a nation voluntarily consents to accept decisions of international bodies, be they UN or International Court of Justice, it does not imply the ceding of sovereignty – it is simply applied in the way that is found to be beneficial and useful. It is a basic truth, one known since antiquity: this understanding held together, in fact, that wonderful commonwealth, the union of Greek polises; this was discussed by Jean Bodin, the founder of the theory of sovereignty.

There may be an objection to the effect that states have been very unwilling so far to recognize the jurisdiction of international bodies; why, then, hopes that things would be livelier? But they will, just for the reason that in the nuclear age mankind has no chance to survive without a collective care for peace, without a joint and concerted management of common affairs, because ever more evident is the exorbitant price that has to be paid for manifestations of international arbitrariness and national egoism.

Going back to the controversy of mondialists and 'sovereigntyists', we can say that our epoch is benevolent for those who profess the political philosophy of integralism or globalism. It does not oppose sovereignty, for this principle has not outlived itself as yet; it is going to be the basis for satisfying national needs until the time the integration processes become more effective in doing so. It will be the creation of such mechanisms that will signal the international community's transition to a new epoch when mankind starts developing as one social organism.

II

It is particularly important that our views of relations between two basic social systems of our time, those of Socialism and capitalism, should be brought in accord with the idea of the integral world. The way the East–West problem is settled will largely decide the destinies of states of both systems as much as mankind's very survival. In the final count, a solution of this problem is out of the question unless we overcome the deep ideological confrontation which is at the bottom of today's split in the world. Not economic, not spiritual or even political, but ideological confrontation. It is not the question of eliminating ideological differences rooted in conditions of life, interests and the positions of the main classes and social groups of contemporary society. Nobody has powers to abolish the eternal dispute between different ideologies of social, national and religious origins. The question is only of whether the dispute shall be brought to an irreconcilable confrontation and crowned with a Night of St Bartholomew on a global scale.

Some may object, and, indeed, such a point of view exists and is even disseminated – that ideological confrontation does not by itself hamper peaceful coexistence and cooperation in efforts to solve global problems of our time, above all to prevent a nuclear massacre. To prove the point, reference is made to the détente experience of the 1970s, and especially to the beneficial changes in the international climate related to the line of the 28th Congress of the CPSU, with the application of the new thinking to world affairs.

The arguments are weighty, yet they fail to take account of one fact: in both cases we are dealing with incomplete processes. Détente was interrupted for the very reason that it embraced the tip of the iceberg alone: the foreign policy relations of the states of two systems. As to today's thaw, it was made possible, in a most resolute way, by our perestroika. This fact is universally recognized. Further progress along this road, again, will be related to processes of social development in the East and West.

Above all it should be established whether confrontation is indeed embedded in the very conditions of social progress and represents one of its basic characteristics. In such a case its effect may be somewhat allayed and adapted to; yet, does man rule the iron heel of history, the fates? This is, in essence, the *idée fixe* that has become a kind of constant in our social being, or a symbol of faith. It was commonly believed that there was no need to prove this evident 'truth', and few dared to question it.

But let us have a look at the foundation of the concept of confrontation. It is founded on the idea that our time is a revolutionary epoch of transition from capitalism to Socialism, and that the transition will be achieved through the hard struggle of the world proletariat against the world bourgeoisie. After October 1917 this concept acquired a clear-cut shape, but with a difference, namely, instead of the world proletariat's combat with the world bourgeoisie, there was revolutionary Russia's war with the counter-revolutionary and imperialistic

Entente Cordiale. Thus from the very beginning the conflict, which abstract theory had seen as a clash of classes, turned into a clash of states. Since that time, almost to the present day, the contradiction between Socialism and capitalism as social systems used to be embodied, in fact and theory, in the Soviet state's, and later all the Socialist states' confrontations with the capitalist world states.

This kind of 'substitution', though seemingly reflecting the logic of developments in the intitial post-revolutionary period, was an extreme simplification of the social development scene. Inside the nation, the sectarians saw only two confronting classes – proletariat and bourgeoisie; just as much in the international area they kept within their field of vision only two opposing systems. From then on all things 'ours' were pronounced Socialist, everything 'not ours' was classed as bourgeois. Any phenomenon, from natural sciences (cybernetics and genetics) to dress fashions were classified in the latter category.

Practically all spheres of activity: architecture, medicine, music, theatre, to say nothing of philosophy and politics, were speculatively split into Socialist and bourgeois. The bourgeois stamp was put on everything orginating in the West, ignoring, as it were, that the West is not homogenous and has, besides the bourgeoisie, the working class, the peasantry, intellectuals and other strata with which the possibility of Socialist transformation is linked. The Socialist states, too, especially in the transition period, retained strata not involved organically in Socialism by the conditions of their being, still less by their views and aspirations.

Of even more importance is the fact that international relations, by their very nature, are mostly interactions of states. Of course, states are governed by certain classes and parties which lay down their political course. But even so, the subjects of international relations are sovereign states. So it is a mistake of principle to identify the relations of states or groups of states with relations between systems. What may be termed 'inter-system' relations is totally a matter of ideological sphere, of theoretical and political principles. On the contrary, inter-state relations are material although they may find expression in documents, statements, foreign policy doctrines and slogans.

THE NEW THINKING: PRINCIPAL IDEAS AND GUIDELINES

While states can conduct negotiations and enter into agreements, systems cannot do so, neither are they able to exchange memoranda or seek compromises. In fact, the notion of 'social systems' is a high degree of abstraction, and to translate it into concrete actions would be tantamount to a violation of reality.

One may object to the effect that ideological principles tremendously influence the material world, while doctrinal contradictions always find an outlet in bloody clashes. This is a fact, although nearly all religious wars are linked with quite earthly schemings of one grabbing the goods of the other. Another regularity can be traced in history: however sharp and significant 'inter-system' contradictions are, as a rule, they never come to the forefront, and least of all have they been insurmountable obstacles to the cooperation of states. The bourgeois revolution and Charles I's execution were no hindrance to Cromwell's establishing good relations with a majority of the monarchs of the then Europe. The Russian empress covertly helped republican America to free itself of British rule, Alexander I was on quite good terms with Napoleon before the latter coveted Russia, and so on.

Some may say that all these things are within relationships of the exploiting classes. Well, then, what about the Second World War? Surely the US, British and French ruling circles did not renounce their anti-communist convictions when they formed the alliance with the USSR in the war against Hitler's Germany. That is the whole point: in the life-or-death situation for their peoples they made their choice when they saw the dangers of Nazism. The contradiction between democracy and reaction was much more acute than that between Socialism and capitalism.

However, they did not draw the right conclusions from that fact. Since the confrontational idea was the cornerstone of Stalin's interpretation of international relations in the revolutionary epoch, everything that did not fit in with it was treated as accidental or a temporary anomaly. Of course, the guidelines of official theory were not all that indifferent to the changes occurring in the world. The rigid formulas of the time when the Soviet Union was the lonely Socialist island in the capitalist ocean were yielding to more moderate ones in periods of relatively favourable development of our relations with the West. Such terms as 'struggle' or 'confrontation' were replaced with the words 'competition' and 'rivalry'. Then came a change in the forecasts of the outcome in the two systems' struggle: instead of the initial belief that capitalism would collapse within one or two decades, more realistic views prevailed as time went on.

However, it is only in the documents of our days that attempts were overcome to predict calendar dates of the onset of the world era of Socialism. Having unshackled our socio-public thought, perestroika gave an impetus to rethinking the relationships of the two social systems under present-day conditions. In this sense, particularly important are the fundamental ideas of the priority of human values and the unity of civilization. Their consistent research started by the CPSU's 27th Congress has logically brought about the conclusions that the peaceful coexistence of states belonging to the two social systems should not be assessed as a 'specific form of class struggle', and that the struggle between these systems is no longer the decisive trend of the present epoch.

In the final count, the two conclusions rest on the common ground of recognition that life on Earth, which used to seem as eternal as nature itself, may at any moment come to an end in consequence of a nuclear or ecological disaster. A scale of priorities has emerged both here and everywhere else in the world, in which the struggle for survival is placed above that for class, national and other interests. It is not yet realized in an adequate degree that these scale values cannot follow each other in the order of urgency ('Let us first survive, and then we'll settle class scores and ensure national interests'). Neither can they be a matter of choice, for they both contradict each other and at the same time are bound together. One is not in a position to say: for the sake of peace we are renouncing social progress and bridging the gap between developed and underdeveloped nations. It would be impossible to do so because the socially oppressed strata and destitute nations would never give up defending their interests, and because no peace could be stable and lasting unless it rested on principles of justice. It follows that problems of social progress and national development should be considered organic components of the survival problem. The contradiction between these two aims, real as it is, can be removed by the exclusion of military methods. All just aims in a world facing global threats must be achieved by political means.

However, to limit oneself to a mere statement of this kind would mean stopping half-way and creating prerequisites for the coexistence and even the cooperation of the different sides which are inherently hostile to each other. This kind of objectivized confrontation is incapable of fully blocking the joint solution of global problems, but is quite able to complicate and delay the process. Mankind, however, is not in possession of a large reserve of time. So delays of this sort may prove fatal.

What is to be done? No social movement or political trend would ever renounce its credo. And there is no need for it. It is sufficient to shed blinkers and look closely at reality to see that the thesis of two opposing social systems is not correct.

Suppose we ask ourselves: is it right to speak of opposing social systems one of which was born inside the other and is a product of the latter's development? Socialism was not imported to us ready-made from some Utopian islands, nor can it be shaped by some genius's brainwave. This society inherits two basic elements of social structure which are present in all earlier socio-economic systems: commodity production in the economy and state organization in politics. The different social content both institutions acquire in the new system does not alter their nature. Socialist society retains the continuity of all the previous development; in the language of ethics, this should be classed as its merit, not a drawback. For the negation of social orientation presupposes at the same time the necessity to preserve civilization's durable heritage, including political, legal and moral cultures.

The two basic socio-economic systems have more in common than differences. Imagine a Martian traversing the Earth. As he moves from one country to another he would distinguish them mostly by technological levels, standards of living, and, probably, the last thing he would learn are the details of social structure.

Another question worth consideration in the context of this

subject under discussion is whether the two systems can converge. This theory of Galbraith, popular for a time, was later considered less important because of the aggravated West-East struggle. It seems to be regaining strength of late. Quite a few theoreticians are seeing signs of convergence in the confidence-building process now under way, joint steps in arms-race limitation, conflict settlement, and expansion of economic cooperation.

In my work *The Fiasco of Futurology* I have already attempted to prove why no convergence of the two systems is possible. Capitalism and Socialism being different social essences, they can converge no more than can the two geographic poles. These exist only in the quality in which they exist. They are abstract characteristics we apply to certain phenomena; in starting to converge they would have lost their original properties and thus stopped being carriers of these properties in our minds. Rephrasing Rudyard Kipling, West is West and East is East, and never shall they meet.

As to the nations of East and West, they can and must get closer to each other and borrow from each other. This is fully in human nature and meets the contents of politics in the contemporary interdependent world. The best way to promote this getting together in the interests of all peoples is to push back ideological speculations of who gets the upper hand in the competition of the systems, and concentrate on specific targets: how to raise living standards, ensure human rights, enhance social justice, protect the environment, use better the fruits of technological progress, etc.

Such an approach, to my mind, would eliminate the problem of the comparable advantage of this or that system which still preoccupies too many minds or, I dare say, distracts them from pressing cares to a propagandistic confrontation that could hardly be productive. An endless ideological dispute automatically urges one to try to win over the opponent. Consequently, the opponent is seen as an enemy, so competition motivation moves to the forefront, and not the interests of progress. This is the ground which always regenerates the split of the world into opposing blocs, notwithstanding their newly acquired ability to control their behaviour for the prevention of a nuclear war.

As it is, the best way to treat your enemy is to turn him into your friend, or at least into a common neighbour. To come to this, all ideas of rivalry of the two systems should be abandoned. In this interdependent world of ours with nuclear, ecological and many other threats looming, this approach becomes more than desirable, it is an imperative condition for survival and development. It is the artists, masters or athletes who can and must be rivals. The comparison and choice of the best organizational forms of social life and political establishments may also be referred to rivalry. But, to repeat, to my mind we must overcome the *idée fixe* of 'competition of the systems'.

Well, and what about the relative advantages of this or that system? It would seem, too, that the 'general system' approach must be abandoned. A sum of factors superimposed on historic conditions – this is what is seen in the achievements of the West and the East, of the groups of nations that are parties to economic and political alliances. To give an example, the Western countries are ahead of Eastern ones in labour productivity mainly because they undertook industrial development at a much earlier stage, and because Britain, France, West Germany, and nowadays the USA and Japan, have amassed a huge scientific and technological potential.

Advocates of the West's superiority who ascribe their nations' achievements to the virtues of capitalism should have remembered that many of their accomplishments must be credited to Socialism. Were it not for the Soviet Union and its pioneering in economic planning and the large-scale implementation of the social rights of individuals, and the October-inspired wave of the workers' movements, Western nations would never have become what they are. Another point: the emancipation of the colonies and dependent nations stimulated a rapid expansion of the world market and consequently new possibilities for turnover of the capital accumulated in the metropolises. And again, the liberation processes were largely due to the impetus created by the October revolution and afterwards to the steadfast support of peoples' struggles for national independence accorded by the Soviet Union and other Socialist nations.

And, lastly, the Socialist road of development with all its advantages and disadvantages has illuminated the nature of social progress in our epoch; primarily, it has revealed for all to see the benefits of Socialism and the need to know its measure, to combine rationally social, collective and individual components. The results of our development could have been incomparably greater had it not been for the Stalinist distortions. Perestroika now gives a chance for the renascence of Scientific Socialist values in their full scope and to enrich them with the experience gained by our country and the world; on this basis a new, more viable and effective model of Socialist society can be fashioned.

What are the most essential features of the present transitional conditions of society in global dimensions?

First, *the process of socialization* is a characteristic of all countries.

Second, this process is very erratic and depends on its motive force (revolution or evolution), cultural and economic levels,[1] historic traditions and many other factors.

Third, the epoch when the question of a progressive and just social order was raised with regard to individual societies (at best to Europe) is replaced by one when the question must be raised and settled on a planetary scale.

Fourth, none of the existing models of social order can serve as an example. It is being recognized by many that we are just at the beginning of a new, socialized civilization.

So, what conclusions can be drawn from these statements as they concern international relations?

First, that the idea of contraposing nations by their belonging to this or that social system must be excluded from social and political consciousness. We are indeed different, but we are not antipodes. I shall repeat that the specifics of a social order have no more significance than that which is consequent from differences in economic levels or political régimes.

This turnabout in thinking is not easy but quite achievable, and it promises tremendous benefits for all mankind. I should say, this is that unique occasion when we may gain countless riches by saying the magic words: 'Open, Sesame!', ridding ourselves forever of the enemy image personified by people just

---

[1] A social order cannot be higher than a people's general, political, moral and technological levels.

like we are but who live by different standards, and to turn them into our co-workers for a better future for all.

Then it will be much simpler, faster and more worth while to find solutions to the global problems of our time, to build confidence, settle conflicts, create a new international order, in short, all that we are spending so much effort to make in this divided world with its split consciousness. There would be an ideological and political atmosphere incomparably more favourable for the objective processes of internationalization and intergration, for limiting the spontaneousness and improving the manageability of world affairs. It does not at all mean that at the drop of a hat the world is going to be brought to the paradise of total unity and accord. There have been and are going to be alliances of states by interests, as well as disputes and competition. It is inevitable. But all this will not be accompanied by the intolerance that for centuries used to divide adepts of different faiths, making them wage crusades and jihads. All this is on condition of understanding and recognizing the priority of human interests above any others.

Evidently, for human interests to be protected they first must be realized as such, which would not be possible without searching, doing so jointly, without overcoming the rift in scientific knowledge. In our country the label of 'bourgeois' that used to be applied to social science meant that it was no science at all, just some sort of magic or quackery; on 'the other side', the same treatment was accorded to Marxism. Both sides were the losers, but the biggest loser of them was science itself which is, by its nature, one and indivisible, existing objectively for learning the truth.

The new political thinking opened the way to overcoming the 'great rifts' in science as well. By no means does it imply the giving up of the originality of the main trends of modern social studies, Marxist and non-Marxist, not to mention the various schools and lines inside each trend or on the borderline. Conflict of ideas and competition of concepts is a natural condition of science, which would otherwise be doomed to infertility. Yet it must be a truly scientific polemic, not a mortal combat of warring parties sworn to destroy each other. There was a time when they talked of physics and geography being capitalist or

Socialist, Western or Eastern. Nobody does so nowadays. In the same manner we must recognize that philosophy, sociology, political sciences, law, history, economics, philology and other social sciences exist as indivisible entities.

We have touched briefly upon only the most essential of the probable results of overcoming 'inter-system political and ideological confrontation', of transferring the controversies from the area of intolerance to that of theoretical and political dialogue and interaction.

Whatever has been said above may be generalized and expressed in this summary: East and West, like North and South, are facing the goals not of bridging the rifts that separate them, but of filling these gaps.

Julian V. Bromlei

Julian Bromlei is an Academician, a historian and ethnologist, honorary director of Ethnographical Institute, chairman of the Inter-Departmental Scientific Council on the Studies of Ethnic Processes of the Presidium of the USSR Academy of Sciences.

He specializes in the methodological problems of ethnology, the theory of ethnos, the history of primitive society, the agrarian history of the Middle Ages, the history of culture of the peoples of the world and ethnic processes in the modern world, primarily in the USSR.

His monographs are as follows: *Ethnos and Ethnography* (1973), *Modern Problems of Ethnography* (1981), *Essays on the Theory of Ethnos* (1982), *Theoretical Ethnography* (in English) (1984), *Main Ethno-Social Trends in the USSR* (in English) (1988), *Ethnic Processes in the USSR: Searching for New Approaches* (1988).

Acad. Bromlei is vice-president of the Society of European Ethnologists and Folkologists, and an honorary member of the Royal Anthropological Institute of Great Britain and Ireland.

He was born in 1921 in the family of the professor of antiquity V. S. Sergeev. He holds the chair at the History Department of Moscow State University (MGU), though he began his scientific career as a physicist – in 1939 he was enrolled as a student of physics at MGU. From 1941 to 1945 he fought at the fronts of World War II. After the war he resumed his studies at the Physics Department of MGU, but soon switched on to the History Department and graduated from MGU, majoring in history. For fifteen years he was Academic Secretary of the History Department of the USSR Academy of Sciences. From 1966 to 1988 Bromlei was director of the Ethnographical Institute, and in 1989 became its honorary director.

Ethnic Relations and Perestroika

JULIAN V. BROMLEI

The process of perestroika in our country is increasingly invading the sphere of ethnic relations. In recent years, the intelligentsia, young people and society as a whole have come to take a noticeably more active part in them. The general atmosphere of ethnic realities is being renewed and they are becoming free from dogma and bureaucratic bonds. In many Soviet republics ethnic movements are gaining momentum, including the form of popular fronts in support of perestroika. At the same time, economic reform, democratization and glasnost have laid bare the deformations and problems, accompanied by acute collisions, which have piled up in the area of ethnic relations. They are, for example, the ethnic-tinted conflict in Alma-Ata in late 1986, the requirements of the Crimean Tatars, pronouncements on the ethnic issue in the Baltic region, the events in and around Nagorny Karabakh, the tragic clashes in Tbilisi in April 1989, and the recent unrest on ethnic grounds in some parts of Uzbekistan. Regrettably, the steps that have been taken to deal with these extreme manifestations of nationalistic ambitions were not always well thought out. Simultaneously, the long-standing over-optimistic coverage of ethnic relations and a frequently lackadaisical and dogmatic approach to them have led to a situation where the collisions on ethnic grounds have proved unexpected to many and have shocked the public.

Nor is the public at large abroad, who show interest in perestroika under way in our country, indifferent to such strife. I had a fresh proof of this during my recent trip to Britain and especially after I gave talks there on ethnic and national processes occurring in the Soviet Union. Here are the most typical questions put to me there: What are the real results of the development of ethnic processes in the Soviet Union? What are the reasons for and the gist of these problems? How do they affect perestroika? What specific steps are being taken to resolve ethnic problems? What are the general direction and further prospects of ethnic processes in your country?

Giving answers to all of them, I had to remind the audience first that the Soviet Union is a multiethnic country, populated by more than 100 ethnic communities, which vary in size. More than twenty of them have over one million members, and in total they come to 96.2 per cent of the entire population. The biggest ethnic communities are the Russians (137 million as of 1979), Ukrainians (42 million), Uzbeks (12 million), and Byelorussians (9.5 million). Another thirty ethnic groups, numbering from 100,000 to 2 million each, constitute 3.4 per cent of the population. The remaining several dozen peoples account for only 0.4 per cent of the population, while some of them have fewer than 1,000 members (for example, the Aleutians and Nigidals – 500 each, Yukagirs – 700, and the Nganasans – 900). The history of some of the Soviet peoples dates back many centuries, while others were formed only following the Great October Socialist revolution in 1917.

On the eve of the October revolution, the peoples of tsarist Russia stood at different levels of development. While most large ethnic groups in European Russia (the Russians, Ukrainians and Byelorussians, the Baltic and Transcaucasian peoples) lived under considerably developed capitalism and had formed nations, peoples in Central Asia still found themselves under feudalism and the Northern peoples (the Evenks, Chuckchee, Nenets and others) under the patriarchal tribal system. They lived in small tribal groups and pursued hunting, fishing and reindeer-breeding.

Nor was their cultural development equal, which was reflected, in particular, in their historical and ethnographical divisions, which had taken shape in the course of their previous historical development. The more or less integral Eastern European region with its predominantly Orthodox Christian population bordered, on the south-east, regions where the Muslim culture was spread, and in the west and north-west on regions of Catholic or Lutheran orientation. Each of these regions had its dominating language systems, written languages, cultural and everyday traditions.

In Siberia, the Eastern Slavonic culture was in contact with the archaic cultures of the peoples with Buddhist and Lamaist traditions. Their cultural levels were tremendously different. While in Georgia, for example, 22 per cent of the population was illiterate immediately before the October revolution, in the Turkmen territory illiteracy was as high as about 98 per cent among the indigenous ethnic groups. On the whole, 75 per cent of adults were illiterate nationwide. More than fifty peoples did not have a written language.

The mixed ethnic composition and multistructural character of its economy added special importance to the nationality question in pre-revolutionary Russia. The tsarist policy of national inequality was a weighty factor, and anti-Semitic propaganda in particular led to pogroms and Black Hundred provocations. Tsarism not only supported but often fanned national and religious strife in the country. Acute as it was, the nationalities question stood out in the activities of the Communist Party led by Lenin.

After making the Great October Socialist revolution and toppling the power of the landlords and capitalists, the Bolsheviks began to build their policy on the principles of the complete uprooting of the former inequality and all-round economic and cultural development of the peoples. One of the first decrees of Soviet power was the 'Declaration of the Rights of the Peoples of Russia', signed by Lenin in November 1917. It proclaimed the equality and sovereignty of the peoples of Russia and the abolition of all national and national-religious privileges and limitations. In 1922, after the Civil War ended, the Union of Soviet Socialist Republics was formed. Now it includes fifty-three national-territorial units, the biggest of which are the fifteen constituent republics.

Thanks to the efforts of many generations of Soviet people, the tremendous socio-economic and cultural differences between the peoples of our country have been eliminated in a flicker of time (as history goes), owing to untiring and strenuous efforts to overcome the age-old traditions of national seclusion, egotism and suspicion towards all things foreign. The economic, cultural and personnel potential of all the Soviet republics has grown many times over. They are now linked by thousands upon thousands of economic and cultural contacts. Over the years of Soviet power, the ethnic groups have come to have specific traits in lifestyle, culture and values. A new ethnic entity with its own social parameters – the Soviet people – has emerged. But, still, this is no reason to picture the development of ethnic relations throughout the entire post-revolutionary period as a bed of roses.

The path which Soviet society travelled since the Great October revolution was stony and sometimes even tragic. No tested patterns existed for resolving national-development problems in conditions of Socialism and new solutions had to be found, often by trial and error. Theoretically, it was only possible to foretell the general direction of development and outline its basic trends. The decisive role was played here by the principles of the nationalities policy of the CPSU, which Lenin formulated in his time. However, they were grossly distorted during the rule of Stalin, when the principles of democracy and internationalism were violated and the basic Leninist nationalities policy was not observed.

An opponent of assimilation in a word, Stalin in fact displayed his obvious striving to 'simplify' the country's ethnic structure and was disinclined to recognize the existence of ethnic groups. Indicative in this respect is his allegation in the report on the draft Constitution of the USSR in 1936 that the country had only sixty ethnic communities. Their actual number was at least twice as many. By that time such forms of national-administrative division as National Districts and National Village Councils had been liquidated. In the year 1933, there were 250 National Districts and 5,300 National Village Councils across the country. They were meant to help create favourable conditions for executing judicial and administrative functions, for education and for cultural and instructive activities in the native tongues.

The tendency to 'simplify' the country's ethnic structure also affected the censuses of the population. For example in 1926, it was preliminarily decided that the country had 194 nationalities (true, not all of them were registered in the summing up). The 1939 census said there were fewer than 100 nationalities. This numerical gap is, to a certain degree, connected with the change in the criteria for singling out national units, as well as with the parallel consolidation processes. Nevertheless, the nearly twofold decrease in the number of nationalities over a mere thirteen years can certainly be explained by the neglect of many of them, especially the smaller ones. Gradually, disregard for them spread to their specific cultural, language and daily needs.

Simultaneously, organizations handling ethnic affairs were gradually eliminated. This tendency surfaced immediately following the formation of the USSR, when the People's Commissariat for Nationalities was eliminated. True, some of its functions went to the Soviet of Nationalities of the All-Union Central Executive Committee. But, after the Supreme Soviet of the USSR was formed in 1936, this organ actually gave up handling specific ethnic problems, although the Soviet of Nationalities was part of it.

A similar picture was observed in science. In the first postrevolution years, the country had a scientifically-based service for national (ethnographic) problems – the Committee of the Peoples of the North, the Central Ethnographic Bureau of the People's Commissariat for Nationalities of the USSR, etc. The Commission for the Study of the Tribal Composition of Russia and Adjacent Countries, which was set up before the revolution, reinvigorated its activities. In the 1930s, all of them were closed down. At the same time, the introduction of passports and numerous official questionnaires in which one's nationality had to be named made possible violations of the principle of ethnic equality and sometimes led to exaggerated importance being attached to the ethnic factor in the life of society.

The appearance of the central bureaucratic system of administration in the late 20s and early 30s had a negative impact on ethnic relations. In those tragic years when collectivization was being enforced, cost-accounting in industry cast aside and the scientifically-based and balanced plans for five-year economic development periods sacrificed to the race for arbitrarily fixed economic indices, red tape distorted the ideas of federalism in organizing the country's ethnic life. Many present-day problems of socio-economic development in different regions arose out of the command-administration methods which began during the pre-war years. Such an administration did not consider the ethnic specificities and often had no elementary regard for the history, traditions and needs of a given nation or nationality. Sometimes it amounted to direct arbitrariness in handling ethnic issues.

The Great Patriotic War illustrated the cohesion displayed by the overwhelming majority of the Soviet people of different nationalities and their loyalty to their Socialist homeland. Still, not all was going smoothly in ethnic relations in those years. On the one hand, there were nationalists who conducted anti-Soviet activities in the Baltic, the Western Ukraine, Northern Caucasus and other regions, and individual members of nationalities whose territory was temporarily occupied collaborated with the Fascists. On the other hand, we can neither forget nor forgive the reprisals against ethnic groups, who were 'punished' by resettlement in the country's eastern parts, where many of them died, and the deportations of Germans, Kalmyks, Karachais, Ingushes, Chechens, Balkars and the Crimean Tatars, as well as other peoples and ethnic groups whose national development was thus badly impaired. It was not until the late 1950s that most of them regained their statehood and they were returned to their native lands, where they received tangible help to return to a normal life. Simultaneously, the unfair accusation of their having collaborated with the Fascist occupiers was retracted (with regard to the Soviet Germans and Crimean Tatars the accusation was withdrawn in the 60s).

Nevertheless, in the first post-war years, the tremendous efforts that were made to rehabilitate the economy in the territory that had been under temporary Fascist occupation were not backed up by due attention to the ethnic groups' requirements. Such campaigns as 'the struggle against cosmopolitanism', the anti-Semitic 'doctors' case' and others further hurt the ethnic sentiment. In the mid-50s and early 60s, highlighted by a measure of democratization in some aspects of Soviet life, negative tendencies born of overcentralized administration came to the fore, together with achievements in the further levelling out of the economic, social and cultural levels of the Soviet republics' development. In some republics which used to rely on subsidies, feelings of dependence and ethnic privileges began to take root.

These and other negative phenomena in ethnic relations developed further during the stagnation period. Its ideology and psychology were accompanied by overpraising the results achieved in resolving the nationalities question, by establishing the idea that ethnic relations in our country were free from all problems. As a result, many acute issues arising in the ethnic process were not resolved in time to prevent social unrest.

It is with good reason that ethnic matters feature prominently among the numerous social problems which the Soviet Communist Party raises in perestroika. These matters were given much attention at the Party's 27th Congress in 1986, the January 1987 Plenum of the Party's Central Committee, and at the 19th All-Union Party Conference in 1988. The nationalities question was not discussed at the Congress of People's Deputies of the USSR in 1989, and the Party's Central Committee will hold a special plenary sitting to discuss the improvement of ethnic relations.

Before perestroika, many destructive factors in the life of our society, which also affected ethnic relations, were not disclosed to the broad public (for example, ethnic unrest in Abkhazia and Northern Ossetia during the years of stagnation). Perestroika, democratization and glasnost have brought earlier hidden instances of ethnic tension to public notice. At the same time, perestroika has highlighted deformations in the life of our society, many of which were reflected in ethnic relations. In many regions a rising ethnic self-awareness may partially be explained by the desire to avenge the years of overcentralization and distortion of the principles of social justice with regard to certain peoples.

The command-administration, overcentralized, economic system, which was begun to enforce accelerated industrialization and farming collectivization, has with time become a hindrance to the economic development of the constituent republics and the entire country. Guardianship and assistance, which were indispensable at the earlier stages of development in the republics, have lost their value, because they 'froze' the internal mechanisms of growth in these republics. It is obviously impossible to foresee the importance of the peoples' cultural originality, natural specificities etc. for economic development. Bureaucratic elements in the central and local administration merged under the twisted ideological cover of Socialist internationalism understood as the centre's overpowering priority. All disagreement with the central directives, which often disregarded local specificities, possibilities and interests, was condemned as nationalistic.

The centrally commanded economic management led to an imbalance in the country's development on the regional and especially the republican levels. This is above all reflected in the sizeable differences in the growth-rate of labour productivity in industry between the republics. For example, in the past fifteen years, it has been 1.5 times higher in Azerbaijan and Byelorussia than in Tajikistan. In Turkemenia, social labour productivity has shown no rise at all over those years.

The country's complex demographic situation is also reflected in ethnic relations. In recent decades the satisfactory growth in population in our country has been due to the indigenous people of Central Asia, the Kazakhs and Azerbaijanis, whose rate of population increase is three times the average. The share of the peoples in the Slavonic language group fell from 77.1 per cent in 1959 to 72.8 per cent in 1979, and that of the Turkic language group correspondingly grew from 11.1 per cent to 15.2 per cent. This requires an active demographic policy which would rely on federal norms, but would be simultaneously aimed at stimulating population growth in regions with a low birthrate and not encouraging families to have many children in overpopulated regions. It is proposed, for example, to increase allowances and other benefits (longer childbirth and child-care leaves, shorter workday, etc.) for the births of the second and third child and comparatively insignificant benefits for the fourth and each subsequent child. There are other viewpoints on this question. For example, some people say each constituent republic should conduct a demographic policy of its own. It seems, however, that federal and republican demographic programmes are not mutually exclusive.

The regional and ethnic specificities of demographic processes affect labour resources: labour shortages in some regions (mostly northern) and excessive labour in others (mostly southern). In recent times, the unevenness of the ethnic and demographic processes in combination with different growths in labour productivity have been accompanied by the republics' differentiation in the development of certain individual components of the social infrastructure, including housing, the services, medical institutions, etc. The situation has been made even worse because not every republic put to use the means earmarked for health care (for example, Kazakhstan has used only 68 per cent of such means over the last ten years).

Mass migration, which noticeably reduces the percentage of the indigenous population (for example, in Estonia and Latvia), also has an impact on ethnic relations in the republics. In this connection, the limiting of migration is sometimes linked with the introduction of republican citizenship and residential qualifications. However, the opinion that migration regulation should be indirect and above all through the use of economic channels appears more acceptable. These channels are: the development of highly efficient and, most importantly, high-technology production, which does not require much unskilled labour and, hence, an inflow of new migrants.

Among the many measures which helped the once backwards constituent republics to develop at an accelerated rate, the preferential budgetary and taxing policies played a special role. The general picture in the 1930s was as follows: the subsidies from centralized sources covered more than 60 per cent of the budgetary expenditure in most of these republics. In this way, the state redistributed the national income in the interest of individual peoples. Thanks to this policy, as early as the late 1940s, the Soviet Union attained factual equality of nations in many respects. This goal met, there was no more need to grant many benefits and privileges, but, for various reasons, they are still mostly preserved.

This situation, which was not disclosed until recently, on the one hand engendered dependence among local administrators and, on the other, was combined with the widespread conviction among local populations that their republic was making too great a contribution to the federal budget. The leadership of certain constituent republics encouraged such sentiments and, in line with the leaders' feelings, part of the intelligentsia spread allegations about the 'special role' of their republic through the mass media. The shadow economy also has an adverse impact. Therefore, special attention is being paid to combating these phenomena.

Perestroika, which aims to boost the efficiency of the Soviet economy, develop the principles of democratization, glasnost and strengthening of equality, is called upon to ensure social justice in relations between the peoples and different ethnic groups. In this context, radical economic reform, which opens up broad opportunities for the optimal combination of the interests of the country as a whole and each constituent republic in particular, acquires decisive importance. Guidelines have been developed for reshaping the economic management and guidance of social programmes in the constituent republics on a self-management and self-financing basis. They are directed towards the democratization of the entire system of management of the Soviet economy and the substantial expansion of economic independence and responsibility in the republics. The goal has been set of establishing close dependence between the republic's economic development and a rise in living standards, between its resources and the results of its economic activity, its contribution to the integrated economic complex of our country.

A lot has to be done for fuller realization of the advantages offered by diversion and cooperation of labour in the country, for better utilization of the republics' economic potential. Deepening the direct economic contacts between them, by the removal of various barriers which exist between republics, is crucial. It is a must to preserve the principal link in self-management – the cost-accounting enterprise – from the administrative zeal of the republican administrative bodies. In present-day conditions many such enterprises maintain stable economic contacts which extend far beyond the republic's boundaries. Thus there is a danger that differences may emerge between the interests of republics and those of the cost-accounting enterprises. Any attempts at replacing the existing departmental-administration system by a republican-administration system cannot be permitted. Regional nationalism, which has clearly surfaced, is to a certain degree linked with the command-administration bodies' desire to preserve their positions on the republican scale. In this connection, this proposition is very important; self-management and self-financing cannot be limited to the constituent republics, but must also be carried out in the autonomous and administrative-territorial units. Here, account must be taken of the interests of all ethnic groups.

Special attention is paid to increasing the republics' involvement in environmental protection. Until recently the ecological and economic situation and the population's degree of preparedness for different kinds of work used to be somewhat neglected in planning the distribution of production. If the population is ecologically undereducated and has no special skills, the introduction of, for example, chemical production in such a region leads to irreversible effects for the environment and the people's health. In the process of industrial development in the Northern regions, appreciable damage is often done to the extremely vulnerable Northern environment, above all pastures and hunting and fishing grounds, which has an adverse effect on the smaller ethnic groups' traditional economy. Not infrequently environmental problems have ethnic undertones in our times. So now the issue is that national-territorial entities should be paid by government departments for the use of their resources.

State and legal questions are acquiring primary importance for an optimal development of ethnic and national processes.

The ethnic set-up of the state requires more flexibility. Legislation on union and autonomous republics, autonomous regions and territories will be renewed with due account for new realities to reflect better the rights and duties, principles of self-government and representation of all nationalities in the centre and locally. Will this not weaken the central authority? Actually, a strong centre is possible only with strong provinces. That is why greater scientifically elaborated rights and duties for the republics will consolidate the Soviet multiethnic state. On the one hand, it will boost initiative and activity in republican and local bodies; on the other, it will rid the higher echelons of power of inappropriate tasks and functions which would be better carried out on the republican and local level. Thus it would **improve central leadership in matters of national importance.**

Is it expedient to restore national districts and national rural Soviets? One should bear in mind that most of the republics are multiethnic: alongside the nationality that gave the republic its name, there are other ethnic groups. All in all, ethnic groups which live beyond their national-territorial units or have no such units number 60 million people or 20 per cent of the country's population. (It totals more than the population of France.) So they need a constitutional concept of ethnic group status that could provide for their representation in legislative and executive bodies, their right to study in the native language, further develop their ethnic culture, etc. Cultural centres for the Germans, Jews, Armenians, Tatars and some other dispersed ethnic groups have been established. To cater for the specific needs of ethnic groups and small nationalities is especially important. Currently there are plans to work out several programmes of cultural development for the smaller nationalities of the extreme North, Siberia, Far East, Northern Caucasus, and the Northern European USSR. The programmes should improve the social infrastructure in all these areas – perfect education, expand the press, etc.

A number of Soviet laws on ethnic problems are to be drafted soon including a revised Law on Citizenship. Not only officials but the public in the Baltic republics, Georgia, Armenia, Tatary especially are actively working on amendments to the constitutions of the USSR, the union and the autonomous republics. More often than not there are acute differences between the proposals from the native population and those of 'newcomers'. Regrettably, such contradictions breed armed conflicts. Only just and mutually acceptable solutions can prevent armed clashes. More progressive legislation on ethnic questions should become a vital part of the political set-up in a law-based society.

Perestroika and greater democracy have laid bare the distortions of inter-ethnic relations and could not but infringe on the privileges of people who had capitalized or intended to capitalize on them. Besides, some underprivileged groups became corrupted by the bosses' hand-outs and took advantage of their demagogy, low moral standards and slackened control and discipline. Directly and indirectly it will prevent the elimination of distortions. These people drag their feet, clinging to the privileges they got used to under the cover of nationalist slogans. Red tape, corruption and callousness on the part of some leaders of one nationality or another project social problems on ethnic relations. Anti-social acts are especially dangerous in nationalistic disguise. In a number of cases specific unrealized expectations in a career or mode of life may acquire a nationalistic colouring.

Perestroika opponents, who are afraid of losing their privileges stemming from the ethnic factor, try to use some unofficial nationalist youth groups like the Alma-Ata-based 'Golden Horde' or 'New Islam'. Those discontented with perestroika may set up more unofficial groups or clubs of young people that would cover their nationalist programmes with appeals for greater democracy, which may seem quite appropriate, while in fact seeking organizational advantages for their groups or even a monopoly.

The mushrooming associations and cooperatives represent such forms of public self-management as can be employed for nationalist purposes in the transitional period, in the acute contest between old and new. Among such organizations are 'Krunkh' in Nagorny Karabakh and 'Karabakh' in Armenia, which appeared during the developments in Nagorny Karabakh. 'Pamyat' also ranks among the unofficial nationalist organizations, where some of its leaders try to channel the patriotic sentiments of its members toward chauvinism.

Negative processes could not but tell on some party members, including top executives. Moral degradation, violations of Socialist law and other drawbacks were especially marked in Uzbekistan, Moldavia, Turkmenia, Kazakhstan, some districts in the Ukraine, Krasnodar territory, Rostov district, Moscow and some other areas, as well as in the Foreign Trade Ministry and the Ministry of the Interior, the Party Plenum stated in January 1987. In Kazakhstan, for example, 1,200 workers in the Ministry of the Interior were discharged from their posts for questionable morality in 1987 alone.

We should also be aware of the fact that special care for ethnic intellectuals has lead to tangible disproportions. Since the late

1970s, brain-workers among the Estonians, Georgians, Armenians, Latvians, Lithuanians and Kazakhs constituted from 27.3 to 20.9 per cent of the employed population of their respective nationalities. As for the Kirghiz, Uzbeks, Turkmen and Tajiks, this index ranged from 16.2 to 12.4 per cent. The growth of college enrolment in the union republics went hand in hand with serious changes in ethnic composition. In 1979 the share of natives among college students in Georgia, Kazakhstan, Kirghizia, Azerbaijan, Armenia, Lithuania, Estonia and some other republics exceeded their share in the total population. For instance, in the Kirghiz agricultural institute, Kirghiz youth made up between 80 and 85 per cent and in the university economics departments all students were Kirghiz. Totalling 31 per cent in the population of the Yakut autonomous republic, Yakuts made up 79.5 per cent of full-time students at the Yakut State University. Similar disproportions appeared among the highest echelon of scientists. In the late 1970s in Kazakhstan, natives constituted 16.5 per cent of the urban population, while 39 per cent of Candidates of Science and 43 per cent of Doctors of Science were Kazakhs. This is also typical of some other Central Asian republics. For example, Kirghiz made up a smaller part of city-dwellers – 18.9 per cent – while among researchers, 42.5 per cent had a Candidate's degree and 39.1 per cent a D.Sc. This was a direct violation of internationalist principles in personnel training. The practice of entering college through connections among people of the same nationality or even from the same area became widespread. Thus, many colleges in Kazakhstan admitted an excessive number of applicants from its southern parts formerly inhabited by the Senior Zhus (clan).

The privileges given to boost training of skilled personnel in formerly backward areas started to be taken for granted, thus breeding sponging. According to our press, now that the educational standards in the country have been levelled out it is unfair to grant anybody preferential rights to enter colleges, post-graduate or doctoral degree courses. Such practices lead to ethnic egotism. Besides, accelerated training went on at the expense of quality, which subsequently brought about much abuse in the personnel policy.

ETHNIC RELATIONS AND PERESTROIKA

With the educational level soaring, including among the native population, graduates outnumbered vacant skilled jobs. In 1981–85 in Georgia, 19 per cent of college graduates found themselves outside the job placement scheme. In Uzbekistan in the mid-1980s, about 200,000 graduates of vocational schools and colleges worked in fields other than those they had been trained for.

Inter-ethnic problems are most acute among the young people. It seems strange, because young people are more exposed to internationalized forms of culture, are better educated and socially mobile. In fact, it is only natural, as the youth is sensitive to all social problems, responding to them emotionally rather than rationally. Young people, especially students coming from village schools, are not experienced in positive inter-ethnic labour contacts. Hence, riots in Alma-Ata flared up among the youth in December 1986. Many teenagers participated in the Sumgait pogroms in Azerbaijan in December 1988, in which thirty-two people were killed. Young people also played an inglorious part in the clashes at Erevan airport. So to prevent undesirable developments in inter-ethnic contacts it is vital to regulate the number of graduates and vacancies in specific fields and enhance career guidance, a burning issue at the present stage of societal development. Currently, this question is being given special attention in the Soviet Union. The laws recently endorsed are designated to reform the ten-grade secondary and college education and tailor skilled personnel training to the requirements of regions and the country as a whole.

At the same time there are plans to invigorate inter-republican exchanges of specialists and their training in other republics' colleges. Along cooperation lines, colleges will admit 2,300 students from other republics annually (1,800 per year in the previous five-year plan period). In the past five years, vocational schools in the Russian Federation, Byelorussia and the Ukraine admitted 40,000 students sent from Central Asia and the Caucasus. As fewer applicants vie for entrance to Baltic colleges, more young people come there from other parts, especially from the Transcaucasian republics. A great number of graduates return home due to a poor command of the Russian language, the tradition of keeping close family contacts and an attachment to their habitual social environment. Nevertheless the training of specialists in other republics will help solve personnel problems and promote the internationalist education of the young. This practice will be substantially expanded.

The idea of inter-republican exchanges of experienced Party and economic executives, put forward at the 19th All-Union Party Conference, deserves special attention. It was noted that only with their territorial transfer will the USSR become a close-knit family stronger than the sum of national units inclined to self-seclusion. The Conference also stressed the importance of exchanges of college professors between republics.

The format of governing bodies should reflect the ethnic pattern in the country – this line must be adhered to unswervingly. Yet Party documents have repeatedly stressed that to distribute posts automatically according to people's descent would mean the vulgarization of the principles of internationalism. When appointing to a post, priority should be given to political, business and moral qualities.

The proper representation of small ethnic groups in the republics should also assume a place of importance. Of course, that concerns major national entities, especially non-native ones to the same degree. Actually, Russians, who make up over 19 per cent of population in the fourteen constituent republics (except the Russian Federation) total merely 12.5 per cent (even 11 per cent in the early 1980s) in the local Soviets.

The determination of nationality should be more democratic, duly accounting for people's self-awareness and the environment in which a person was brought up. The notorious paragraph requiring the registration of a person's descent in all kinds of questionnaires is not always so necessary. Obviously, not all the forms which have such an item really do need it.

Changes in the cultural sphere are very important for the inter-ethnic processes in the USSR. Since the first years of Soviet government, cultural progress has speeded up, especially in the provinces. Instruction in native languages helped to eliminate illiteracy, alphabets were devised for peoples which had not had a written language, national arts flourished and the field of applying information generally expanded. From 1921 to 1940, some 60 million illiterates were taught. In Soviet Central Asia, the literacy rate stood at 80 per cent with a national level of 87.4 per cent. In the post-war years, the education of the people in formerly backward regions persisted at an accelerated rate.

Printed matter is a graphic indicator of an ethnic culture's advance. During the years of Soviet government, books and pamphlets were published in 159 languages, including 89 languages of Soviet peoples. There are theatre productions in fifty languages of the peoples of the USSR. Now theatrical art has appeared in such republics as Uzbekistan and Kirghizia, which previously had no professional theatres. TV programmes are broadcast in forty languages of the USSR.

Russian plays an outstanding role in the cultural exchange between Soviet nationalities. Ethnic writers translated into Russian become accessible to a readership throughout the country. Works by ethnic composers and playwrights are on in central theatres and ethnic artists participate in central exhibitions, all of which promotes mutual cultural enrichment. Through the Russian language, many smaller nationalities can gain access to the gems of world culture and scientific knowledge.

According to the 1979 census, 81.9 per cent of the country's population, including two-thirds of non-Russians, had a good command of the Russian language. The centralist bureaucratic system often regarded writers', artists' or teachers' concern about their own languages as manifestations of nationalism.

It is not by chance that language is a real issue for people of many nationalities. Debates frequently focus on the central issue of a state language in the republic. Recognition of the national language must remain within the republican term of reference; moreover, it is hardly expedient or possible to deprive Georgia, Azerbaijan, Armenia and Abkhazia of their state languages as they already had them. Importantly, the proclamation of the state language should not violate the equality of all other tongues of people inhabiting the republic. Much will depend on the specific statutory acts determining the materialization of general principles stipulated by the republican legislation. The recent laws on language in Estonia and Latvia regrettably infringe the interests of, and put severe imitations on, the Russian-speaking people, who make up a substantial part of the population there, e.g.: office work will be switched over to Estonian and Latvian soon. In this context, special priority should be given to the elaboration of all-Union language legislation. Republican or USSR constitutions should provide the rights and the status (possibly state or official) of the Russian language as the chief means of inter-ethnic communication, and guarantee its free usage in all areas of public life. It should ensure the free choice of the medium of instruction, which would also concern Russian.

Religion has long been affecting inter-ethnic ties, frequently impeding contacts between peoples of different beliefs. Nevertheless the church's influence on the national processes in the country cannot be described as utterly negative. Contemporary clergymen of various religions often preach friendship between peoples to their flock, as they well understand the importance of this factor for our society. The appeals by Vazgen I, Catholicos of all Armenians, and Sheikh-ul-Islam A. Pashazade, Chief of the Moslem Board of Transcaucasia, for their believers to preserve the friendship between Armenians and Azerbaijanians in the days of the Nagorny Karabakh crisis are a convincing proof of that. They asked people not to believe vicious rumours and to show restraint.

A knowledge of history is another factor in developing ethnic self-awareness. Hence the heightened interest in the events of the past. Blank spaces in historical science in the Soviet period cannot but tell on the ethnic sense of identity. They mainly cover the not-so-distant developments in the history of ethnic groups which joined the USSR before the Second World War, the Baltic nations in particular.

Now it is extremely important to interpret peoples' history truthfully, especially the things critical for their self-awareness: without self-admiration or denial of positive elements conducive to mutual understanding.

Stereotypes and dogmas oversimplify many aspects of complex ethnic processes; among them, the assertion that there is no nationalities issue to be solved today or the hackneyed idea that Soviet culture is national in form and Socialist in content. Watchful attention is being given to doing away with such clichés.

On the other hand there has emerged a nihilistic attitude

toward notions which stand for nationwide processes, e.g. 'the Soviet people'. This term reflects a reality, a state and territorial entity that has common cultural features, traditions, values and a unified self-awareness. The millenia-long history of humankind has seen many such entities; take the present Indian and Indonesian peoples in the developing world, the people of Switzerland in the West and Yugoslav people in the Socialist countries. Thus the Soviet people is a natural phenomenon which differs from similar societies mainly in its Socialist parameters and corresponding spiritual values.

Clearly, we should bear in mind that the Soviet nation consists of a variety of ethnic groups. This pertains not only to culture and languages, but to all other fields.

New principles of economic management, more democracy and openness have exposed the effect of the human factor both in the economy and politics. Society is facing complex tasks in settling inter-ethnic relations under the new conditions because the pace, depth and forms of economic reform, the advance of democracy and openness are bound to vary in different ethnic environments.

The efforts to eliminate distortions in society's life launched under perestroika have laid bare social contradictions which will inevitably be projected on inter-ethnic relations in a multiethnic state, thus generating disputes and other destructive processes.

A demarcation line must be drawn between distortions and contradictions in inter-ethnic relations. It is universally known that contradictions are inherent in any kind of development, which is true of national processes in the USSR too. Socialism cannot do without asymmetries in ethnic relations: the progress of democracy can only create favourable conditions for their elimination. They stem from miscalculations and economic stagnation, underestimation of social policy, violations of social justice, lack of openness and breaches of internationalist principles. In order to harmonize inter-ethnic relations in the USSR, primary importance should be given to the revolutionary renewal of society now being carried out by the CPSU: to accelerated social and economic advance, to the reform of public activities, to active social policy, greater democracy and openness.

Nikolai N. Chetverikov

Nikolai Chetverikov graduated from the 'Alma Mater' of Soviet diplomats, the Moscow State Institute of International Relations. Although he has held a number of high-ranking diplomatic posts in Soviet embassies abroad, he did not go on to become a career diplomat. He does not regret this, preferring to follow his primary passion for public activities and journalism. For some time after his graduation, he was on the staff of the TASS central office. Later, during the cold war period, he was appointed TASS representative in Belgium and Luxemburg. As he was the only Soviet journalist in those countries, much of Soviet opinion about the situation in Europe was based on his reports. Since that time much water has flowed under the bridge, he travelled and worked abroad for a total of twenty years. He was then recalled to Moscow and appointed to the post of First Deputy Head of the International Information Department of the CPSU Central Committee, replacing Valentin Falin. He later became the Chairman of the Board of the USSR Copyright Agency, the organization in charge of cultural exchanges with foreign countries.

Recently he has been expending much energy as the Secretary of the Board of the USSR Union of Journalists as well as the Chairman of the newly established All-Union Board for Ethics and Law – a kind of professional court of honour for Soviet journalists.

Although he occupies a rather imposing post, Nikolai Chetverikov is a democratic, charming and easy-going person. The stability of his tastes and interests makes him even more attractive to his co-workers.

A Secret no Longer
(Confidence Test)
The mass media at the new stage of perestroika

NIKOLAI N. CHETVERIKOV

Sensation

The public has won the subscription campaign. It seems as though this victory came as a surprise. At any rate, nearly two hundred thousand readers who answered the questionnaire circulated at the end of last year by the USSR Centre for the Study of Public Opinion and the weekly newspaper *Literaturnaya Gazeta* believe that the lifting of all limitations on subscriptions to newspapers and magazines was one of the last year's five major events.

The joy felt by certain sections of the press over this unprecedented turn of events in the subscription campaign did not diminish even after sober voices warned that the public's triumph might prove to be a Pyrrhic victory; that is, no trophies in the form of additional quotas for printing paper have been awarded. Furthermore, it is most probable that readers will not live to see in print books by a number of authors, including those for whose return to the literary world they have been so vigorously campaigning.

However, disregarding this important consideration, the victory itself is significant in that it testifies to a broadening of social and political democracy and glasnost. We have taken one more step towards greater public awareness and the increased activity of large sections of the population. People are pleased by the fact that their opinions have not only been heard but also considered. In short, we have progressed in our efforts to reverse the process of social alienation and apathy that could recently be observed in virtually all areas of our life and work.

Lack of trust

The public demand for the lifting of all limitations on subscriptions was also a reflection of the press's growing prestige which thus received a vote of confidence of sorts. The public has, in this way, expressed an acknowledgment of the sizeable role of the mass media which have done a great deal to both support perestroika and free people's minds from the stereotypes and dogmas of the stagnation period. It was precisely the newspapers, radio and television that undertook the vitally important, albeit unpleasant, task of 'taking an inventory' of all of our past experiences and stockpiled problems.

Judging by the tremendously increased amount of letters readers send to editors, the press on the whole successfully fulfils its main mission – to awaken and spur public thought, to generate and reflect public opinion, and to lead action. The mass media have become a true mouthpiece of democracy and glasnost and a vivid, effective partner in the process of perestroika. This change has become possible only because the press, while promoting these changes, is itself favourably affected by them and proceeds to cleanse itself from the negative burden of the past by abandoning outdated methods. It is appropriate here to turn once again to the above-mentioned questionnaire, although some concessions must be made to *Literaturnaya Gazeta*'s specific readership which is composed primarily of mature people who have higher educational backgrounds and reside in large cities. Of those polled, 84 per cent noted positive changes in the activity of the press and television. In addition, 72 per cent expressed their high appreciation of the newly obtained possibility to 'read, listen to, and watch what one really wants'.

The merits of the last factor can easily be seen, considering the surprising uniformity of views which reigned in our press until very recently. By glancing through one paper, one could know what other papers were writing (the few variations that existed were, as a rule, of no substantive importance). Glasnost has turned the press from a device which taught people the art of reading between the lines and filling in the gaps according to one's imagination, to one which provides direct and straightforward information. It urges people to participate in sensible and lively discussions of events and phenomena, their causes and effects, on the basis of facts rather than rumours, hearsay and guesswork. One *Pravda* reader wrote in his letter: 'Today the press, radio and television are a reliable barometer of the level of our society's openness. It is not accidental that the circulation of our periodicals has soared in the last three years and they are now selling like hot cakes.' The letter came from Yelets, a fairly typical Russian 'provincial' town, and therefore it can serve as a weighty argument against those who claim that perestroika has embraced only the nation's major industrial and cultural centres without spreading to the country's periphery.

Positive changes in the Soviet mass media have been noticed not only by people in our 'provincial' areas but also beyond the USSR. Letters from foreign readers of Soviet newspapers are now much more numerous and varied, both in terms of their content and their geography. Their authors explain their positions openly and raise issues that testify to the unabating interest of the world public in the reforms under way in the Soviet Union.

The Soviet mass media, which are vigorously changing their entire activity, have caught the attention of their foreign colleagues, who see new, rather promising prospects for broader contacts, exchanges and business relations in the information field. A specific example of this is the discussion that was held in Moscow this March on the 'Priority of Common Human Values and the Tasks of the Mass Media: Modern Forms of Cooperation'. Representatives from Italy's *Repubblica*, France's *Le Monde*, Spain's *El País* and Soviet journalists from *Moscow News* and the Novosti Press Agency took part in this discussion. Our colleagues from these three major Western European newspapers said that the level of openness reached in the USSR makes it possible to begin cooperating and offered to issue, jointly with *Moscow News*, a monthly publication. I take this as another testimony of the consistent democratization of the mass media.

A fly in the ointment

However, the critical remarks about the press which were made by a number of delegates to the 19th All-Union Party Conference remain fresh in our memory. Many journalists were accused of having a tendency to be excessively negative. Members of the press were also criticized during the last election campaign. Criticism was also heard at the CPSU Central Committee plenary meeting this April. And, of course, readers' letters contain not only words of praise and gratitude.

The mass media have risen high on the wave of our society's renewal. Sharp exposés, the elimination of yet another 'closed area' or 'forbidden topic' and unusually bold and impartial criticism found a lively response among readers and TV viewers. Having tossed off their agonizing numbness and muteness, people are in a hurry to speak out and express those concerns which have been paining them for so long – and the press has become a mouthpiece for their hopes and criticisms.

But as perestroika proceeded, the sketchiness, lack of competence and knowledge of life and the inability to assess and analyse the dynamics of the quickly swelling wave of events became immediately visible in the work of some journalists.

In many respects the mass media have proved unprepared to work under the new conditions. Journalists have yet to learn how to deal with many issues which had previously been left untouched, such as commodity-money relations, the cooperative movement, individual labour activity, humanitarian and socio-psychological aspects of our life and a host of other current issues. The task is further complicated by the fact that Soviet social sciences have so far failed to come up with anything really new in terms of theory or practical methodology. The press therefore has to rely on the unsatisfactory method of trial and error.

The price of an error

It is said in the Orient that 'a word wounds more painfully than a dagger.' Regrettably, there are still many cases of careless handling by the media of such an extremely sharp weapon as the printed word.

There is, for example, a letter from a reader who works as a medical nurse in a district hospital in the town of Mukachev in Transcarpathia. When someone called the editor of the local newspaper and complained that the nurse was rude to her patients, the paper, without taking the trouble to make appropriate enquiries, published an article which abused an innocent person. Moreover, in response to readers' demands that the paper correct its mistake, it ran yet another caustic article, and this time misspelled the nurse's patronymic!

Another reader, from Armenia, tells a similar story, if not even worse, about the national paper *Selskaya Zhizn* (*Rural Life*). The paper published a garbled story with distorted facts, thereby blackening his reputation nationwide.

If carelessness and haste are impermissible when the good name of one person is at stake, the responsibility of a journalist increases many times over when his writings affect the life of large numbers of people. Last year two articles appeared in the national press in which the authors made accusations against psychiatrists and claimed that healthy people were kept at mental hospitals.

Psychiatric abuse for political purposes is a highly important issue. However, an unbiased approach is essential here as well. The stories became big news, causing much excitement. There were several dozen cases where patients vehemently demanded that they be immediately discharged from hospitals. With newspapers in their hands, they insisted that the 'exposed' psychiatrists immediately certify their good health. However, not a single fact referred to in the articles was later confirmed. All the patients whom the authors described as healthy and who 'had suffered innocently' were found in a second examination by a special board of competent experts to be ill. It is difficult to imagine the consequences that these publications might have had for both the patients and society if the medical personnel had yielded to the pressure of excited public opinion, which was misinformed in this case by sensation-seeking journalists.

The effect of superficial and hastily written outlines of events is hard to predict. A study of all of last year's statements made in the press, on radio and television about the activities of the police showed that a third of them contained factual errors.

Even minor inaccuracies about details in a delicate sphere such as legal information could do great harm. Apart from putting into question the credibility of all information on legal issues, they also undermine people's confidence in law-enforcement bodies as such. Of course, these bodies' activity is not free of shortcomings, but the informational pressure has given rise to a paradoxical and, at the same time, dangerous situation in which the growth of crime is accompanied by a decrease in the number of lawsuits against criminal offenders.

The present possibility of publishing much of what used to be forbidden imposes a new, additional, responsibility upon journalists. This is something like self-censorship, and people's tastes are, as yet, not always impeccable in this respect. For instance, TV viewers reacted differently to a videoclip in which the authors of a popular television programme for young people called 'Vzgliad' ('Viewpoint') attempted to prove that no administrative or economic measures against prostitution can bring any tangible results and, therefore, it should be legalized.

Putting on a show of their boundless humanism, some periodicals demand a radical revision of our laws, making them more lenient towards criminals. I am not against improvements in our criminal law that could bring us closer to the establishment of a law-governed state. I only wish to point out, however, that both society as a whole and each and every law-abiding citizen are equally entitled to humane treatment and protection from crime. The conditions of genuine democracy are such that criminals must be worse off and citizens much better. The true essence of humanism is expressed by precisely this formula.

It would be only fair to note in this context that the media have already done a great deal to call public attention to a number of urgent social problems. It was the media which helped us all to recall vitally important words and notions in our daily life as compassion and mercy which seemed to have been forgotten. Filled with passion and empathy, our journalists' statements and articles are literally breaking the ice of public indifference, awakening their slumbering conscience and drawing society's attention to its very elderly, feeble and lonely members. Vivid and impassioned reports about orphaned children, large families, the less affluent and dependants met with deep sympathy and great appreciation on the part of our readers and TV audiences. One can only hope that when dealing with other, equally urgent, issues concerning our civil relations and mutual responsibility the media will find a proper and convincing tone and be careful to avoid distortion, bias and false notes.

A quotation from a letter sent by a reader from Moscow would be appropriate here: 'I assume that a misprint is possible in a newspaper. It is also possible for an author to have his own interpretation of a particular event. Well, this may be his personal point of view, and he is entitled to have one, just like every one of us. But as far as the choice and authenticity of facts are concerned, these must be as precise as a diamond's facet and even the slightest distortion is impermissible.' This shows the extreme concern felt by readers about questions of journalistic responsibility, professional competence, integrity and adherence to principles. This concern is fully justified, for the negligence and lack of conscientiousness of some journalists deliver heavy blows against glasnost and perestroika. Journalists' credulity, superficial judgments, bias and shameless interference into people's private lives are contrary to the policy of glasnost.

Every violation of professional ethics finds itself the focus of attention of the All-Union Council on Ethics and Law which was established under the Union of Journalists of the USSR in order to promote fidelity to truth and human decency among people involved in the important field of journalism, as well as vigilance, depth and complete objectivity of published materials.

A draft law on the press will soon be issued for public discussion. It is my hope that the law will record the principles of glasnost, elevate the role of the press as an effective means of voicing and influencing public opinion and mobilizing it to resolve urgent social, economic and political problems. Broader rights for journalists entail a much greater responsibility for the trustworthiness of every word that appears in print. The more rights, the more duties – it has always been this way.

Interests and ambitions

No references to pluralism of opinion can hide the following fact. Pluralism of opinion has definitely become a reality in this country and, as never before, is playing a progressive role. When talking of the unity of Socialist society, we do not at all mean a levelling of public life.

Our conception of pluralism is one in which a reflection of clashing interests and of competing views work to the better achievement of one and the same interest. A comparison of many various views and discussion of issues are conducive to searching for and finding truth as well as elaborating the most effective solutions.

As the growth of perestroika has shown, some press organs or possibly their editors interpret Socialist-pluralism of opinion in a slightly different manner. This has recently become especially evident when the discussions on many questions have become heated. A collision of opinion and conflict is quite natural if perestroika is a continuation of the revolution. The struggle in our country is not, however, between opposing sides with irreconcilably different class interests, but rather between the temporary interests of various groups.

This struggle and particularly its forms in the press cause disappointment in many readers. They have come to understand that under the pretext of glasnost, criticism and pluralism in the mass media, attempts are sometimes made at speculation, sensationalism and playing on readers' emotions by some editors in order to raise circulation, implanting clannishness and settling scores.

The practice of pinning labels not only upon persons but also upon publications is widespread – some call others 'yellow press' or 'Black-Hundred press'. The opinion of three men of letters and publicists, who are well known not only in the USSR but also abroad, is worth noting.

'I don't know why we understand glasnost as a flood of criticism,' says Victor Likhonosov. 'Glasnost demands conscience from those who use it ... Hastiness and a thirst for reprisal may crush glasnost.'

Anatoli Aleksin is also indignant over the fact that some people often allegedly try to 'try to "promote goodness" by impudent aggressiveness: groundless accusations, a disgusting desire to hit an opponent as hard, as rudely and as sharply as possible. And all this as though aspiring to the truth. These methods, however, can only distort the truth.'

Ivan Vasiliev takes these thoughts about glasnost and zealous public criers to their logical conclusion. He calls for a cautious sorting out of the people and rostrums from which we hear appeals for renewal. 'Do we frequently hear sound ideas from the press? Many speakers are so zealous in their attempts to prove a point and knee their opponents that one wants to tell them: "Your passions would be better used for a common cause, for inducing people to revolutionary thinking and deeds but not to change one icon for another."'

A unity of opposites

Perestroika has shown many negative facts, deformations and deviations which distorted the appearance of Socialism. It is difficult to overestimate the mass-media's role, which, owing to glasnost, ended the silence that complicated the economic, social and moral problems in our society. Boldly and resolutely it helps to point out the werewolves who stained themselves with profit-seeking and who cast a shadow on all that is sacred to the majority of the Soviet people.

Those who named themselves more radical than Gorbachev seized the opportunity. The ultra-left 'initiators of perestroika' began a campaign to blacken the Communist Party by manipulating the guilt of renegades who discredited the name 'Communist'.

The distorted and non-objective image of the Party functionary as a heartless, total bureaucrat which was depicted by the media was criticized at the April Plenum of the CPSU Central Committee.

Some readers' letters question why, on the one hand, the media give the floor to journalists whose position is incompatible with perestroika and the Socialist way of life and, on the other hand, over-emphasizes the corruption of the Party apparatus, its 'privileged' status, incompetence and their unskilled work. They are creating the psychological stereotype of a Party functionary which declares and imposes the paradoxical notion that the Party whose initiative moved the people to radical changes is an obstacle to perestroika.

The experience of recent years, that is life itself, has shown the failure and impotence of 'ultra-perestroika' phraseology, and the inability of those who abuse it to advance society through hard and persistent work. The danger of the Left demagogy's pushing for 'big leaps' lies in the fact that it feeds the attacks on perestroika by the Right. Because of this we hear accusations of 'undermining the basis' of Socialism, of 'rejecting' Socialist values and ideas, and even of attempts to restore capitalism in our country. They try to accuse perestroika of being destructive, of creating alien phenomena and of destabilizing society. Readers, however, are coming to understand more vividly, with the mass media's help, that conservatism is increasing not only because of dogmatic thinking, of old stereotypes, and fear of changes but also because of mercenary ends. Of course not even one representative of the conservative forces will publicly admit that he is led by the desire to preserve his position.

He attributes his attacks on radical change to a concern for the well-being of the people, for the strengthening and prosperity of Socialism – a Socialism which suits him personally.

Objectively, the attacks from both the Left and Right unite at one point – to torpedo perestroika, to discredit its goals, and to undermine the people's belief in it. By forming an alliance, the 'conservatives' and 'ultra-progressives' are encroaching on our future. They both exploit, from different directions, our recent history, primarily the period of Stalin.

Eventually, as Gorbachev said at the Congress of People's Deputies, conservatism and leftism meet.

Fantasies and facts

A knowledge of history became an urgent need of Soviet society. People look back to history not only out of curiosity and inquisitiveness. There is something more important; understanding Socialism, comprehending how it came about that side by side with the heroic deeds of the people, crimes against them existed.

Quite naturally, under the conditions of glasnost, newspapers and magazines publish material concerning historical subjects. Some make great efforts to analyse the origin of Stalinism and the personality cult honestly and objectively, to return the good name to many victims of the mass repressions. There are, however, some blunt, superficial analyses which are calculated to shock.

As the 'blank spots' disappeared and the vacuum of knowledge of these difficult years in the life of the Soviet people became filled, some reports in the media degenerated, repeated themselves, and fell to the level of street anecdotes.

We see a rush by some authors not to fill historical gaps but to sensationalize, to remind the public of themselves and their importance for the sake of insatiable vanity. Many readers (more than 26 per cent of those responding to the above-mentioned questionnaire) are not satisfied by the manner in which this theme is being portrayed. One reader of *Sovetskaya Cultura* writes: 'The denunciation of Stalinism is an extremely serious issue and we should not allow ourselves to sensationalize it cheaply.'

Readers have the right to demand that the new information from the media be accurate and authentic without distortions and perversions.

Many readers are concerned by the fact that some periodicals publish statements which use excessive licence in dealing with historical facts and material, randomly quoting to suit the author's conception. Some editors in the pursuit of the 'perestroika moment' often forget journalistic integrity – the necessity to check and double check the facts. And readers justly consider this impermissible.

One can find many examples where well-known and competent reporters have made dubious conclusions. Among these was the scholarly article in *Izvestia* concerning the lessons of the New Economic Policy (NEP) which attributed a certain text to Lenin even though it conflicted with his views and conceptions.

Literaturnaya Gazeta recently circulated a distorted 'citation'. *Sovetskaya Cultura* offers a new interpretation of Lenin's description of Trotsky by misquoting, together with the author, Lenin's statements recorded in a verbatim account.

In some cases authors speculate about various political figures and events; sometimes they carelessly pass judgments on the times, the people and the Party which are taken out of historical context; they throw doubts upon the Socialist nature of the society formed in our country. Such an approach to historical knowledge neither benefits the truth nor is advantageous to perestroika. These speculations and rather questionable assumptions, while sheer lies and half-truths are definitely counterproductive.

The revolution continues

Lest there be any doubt, it is necessary to emphasize here that the desire of scholars, writers and journalists to investigate Soviet history's intricate curves seems to be quite a natural, legitimate and laudable idea. However, in these efforts haste, negligence and unscrupulous acts should be avoided. These lead to unintentional and at times deliberate mistakes which can have fatal consequences for the cause of perestroika and can leave the public in bewilderment and confusion. Quite often these fallacies in the analysis and assessment of historical events are widely circulated in various publications and, supported by their prestige, are used by extremists to advocate nationalist views, stir up national hatred and to criticize openly Soviet authorities and the socialist system.

These and similar actions are promptly exploited by the conservatives who accuse perestroika of a disruption of Socialist ideals and the restoration of bourgeois values. In their attempts to impute a destructive and destabilizing character to the revolutionary changes in Soviet society, they almost openly urge the revival of 'iron fist' enforcement of 'law and order', of fear and repression.

Unfortunately, one has to admit that the reports advocating, in a more or less veiled form, the views of the far Right as well as of the ultra-Left elements, also appear in the mass media. This brings confusion to the hearts and minds of the public. Quite often these publications come from well-known authors.

Usually, references to democratization and glasnost turn pluralism of opinion into a fig-leaf covering a lack of principles. It has now become absolutely clear that 'ultra-reformist' attacks as well as the nostalgic demands of the conservatives aim at one common goal, namely, to use the present, diversified processes in society, required by perestroika, gradually to bring about a revision of our historical past and heritage, to question the correctness of the Socialist path chosen by the Soviet people.

However, the idea is not to restructure our past – which is, in any case, irreversible – and even less to reject it. It is not our path starting with the October revolution that is now being reconsidered and restructured but the society which was deformed as a result of deviations from Lenin's concept of Socialism. Therefore we need truth, revealing as it might be, in order to insure perestroika and our socialist society against the bitter mistakes and dramatic crimes of the past. The role of the mass media in this endeavour is as invaluable and crucial as ever.

The second wind

... The period of 'perestroika in words' is passing. The time has come for concrete action and practical measures. With regard to the mass media, this means a new quality of the press, which has been achieved in recent years. Vigorous efforts are needed to address the current problems of perestroika and highlight the existing, progressive methods.

Glasnost, which demands a great deal from journalists, requires not only an elucidation of shortcomings and negative phenomena but also, and above all, a demonstration of the positive changes taking place in our lives and the great creative work being done by millions of Soviet citizens. In the framework of genuine democratization, glasnost and Socialist pluralism of opinion, the gains of perestroika, as well as those who spared no effort to achieve the gains, should also be given access to the mass media.

However, as recent correspondence has shown, readers are clearly concerned by a certain bias in the press. Readers indicate that some authors are thrilled by the search for shortcomings and eagerly denounce them in a rather harsh and cavalier manner. At the same time these authors often resort to banalities, clichés and hackneyed language in describing the many good aspects of our lives, the long-awaited changes, transforming our vast land before the eyes of the entire world. Many readers are not pleased that articles dealing with drug-addiction, prostitution, corruption, criminal abuses and accidents, which are openly extensive and at times too sensational, have noticeably squeezed out other issues, equally crucial and urgent. These issues involve the vital interests and, without exaggerating, even the fate of the most diverse sections of the population.

If these notes, far from being a comprehensive and thorough analysis which would be inconceivable in a single publication, appear to some as having a certain critical bias – this is because the author, along with the majority of readers, sincerely wishes the media to master the art of finding beauty in the simple and prosaic, of portraying the positive changes in a provocative, interesting and attractive manner, which is certainly a more challenging task than the mere denunciation of the shortcomings that inhibit our lives without making any effort to overcome them.

The author has no desire to impose any restrictions on the freedom of the press or to revive some sort of self-censorship. If there are indeed any limits to glasnost and democratization (the two main achievements of perestroika and the guarantors of its irreversibility) these limits are determined only by the interests of the people and of Socialism, which are boundless. Thus, the call for a broader vision of reality implies that the mass media should present a complete picture of on-going processes, reflect the dialectics of life, vigorously promote innovative ideas and experience, naturally not avoiding principles and, more importantly, constructive criticism. This requires that the press should be closer to the people, to their aspirations and concerns, especially since readers observe that their vital needs are often ignored in many publications.

The press is called upon to increase its potential as a champion of perestroika. The main task of the media at this time is the promotion of democratization in the public, spiritual and social spheres, to enhance economic reform, while restructuring itself together with all society. It is essential to generalize the best experience of perestroika, to describe the innovators working at its frontiers, and with this aim to offer the press's rostrum to working people. The economic and political reforms, resolute rejection of any encroachments upon Socialist values, attempts to stir up national hatred, technological progress, social justice, problems of housing and food supply, the service sphere – these are the main contemporary issues.

The times call for a genuine battle against bad management, slovenliness and red tape, factors which jeopardize perestroika and harm our society, both economically and morally. Urgent efforts are also needed to promote state policies aimed at stabilizing the market, invigorating the economy and improving the ecological situation. Therefore the media, and primarily the newspapers, should be more active in publishing theoretical articles on issues which are being broadly debated. While analysing changes in the development of the economy using intensive methods, it is most important to show how the psychology of people and their attitudes are being transformed in a vigorous nd inventive manner, how a new type of worker is being formed. In other words, there is a need to publicize widely the new approaches required by perestroika and innovative forms of economic management, including cost-accounting, leasing relations and the cooperative movement.

The press must acquire a second wind. In order to solve the monumental tasks set before our country and our people, priority should be given to the consolidation of all sections of Soviet society and the effective guidance of them towards constructive processes and activities.

I am convinced that the mass media will prove themselves worthy of this crucial and noble aim – to bring about the democratization of public thinking, to consolidate, even in polemical dialogue, all patriotic forces standing for the reviving of Socialism, for preserving and augmenting Socialist values, for the spiritual liberation of man.

A steady advance towards this aim represents, in fact, the highest duty of the press, which should serve the people using its creative talents and faith in the power of a vivid and truthful word.

The Economy

Abel G. Aganbegyan

Abel Aganbegyan is Academic Secretary of the Department of Economics of the USSR Academy of Sciences. A distinguished figure in the memorable group of 'young Academicians' which was formed in Novosibirsk (the centre of the Siberian Branch of the USSR Academy of Sciences) at the time of the region's scientific upsurge, he became head of the Siberian Institute of Economics and Industrial Production Organization. If perestroika is a 'revolution from above', it is also to some extent a 'revolution from Siberia' – since many fresh economic ideas connected with scientific and technological acceleration, self-financing, profit-making and cost accounting, etc., were developed and discussed in the Novosibirsk academic community on the initiative of Abel Aganbegyan who, like many other champions of perestroika, worked his way up from opposition to general recognition by all social strata and by the country's leadership.

Spearheading the Soviet science of economics, Abel Aganbegyan quickly managed to channel scientific effort towards work on the most urgent problems of perestroika. He was recently appointed Rector of the Academy of the National Economy under the USSR Council of Ministers, and holds the title of minister. Much credit for the tremendous interest displayed by Western companies in collaboration with the USSR must be given to him. He has toured many European, American and Asian countries delivering lectures and speeches on the problems of perestroika.

Ivan D. Ivanov

Ivan D. Ivanov is one of the 'wizards' involved in restructuring USSR foreign economic relations. Since the beginning of perestroika, he has been promoted from the scientific ranks to the post of Deputy Chairman of the Soviet State Foreign Economic Commission – the section of the USSR Council of Ministers in charge of foreign trade. As his background includes research, business and United Nations experience, he has been able to play a major part in designing Soviet legislation on foreign investment. He has been a frequent visitor at international conferences, and is chief Soviet negotiator with the EEC. Ivanov's preferred research topics are the transfer of technology, trade policy and export promotion. For many years he served as a UN expert on transnational corporations, and he is on speaking terms with the top international business circles. He has written several books and booklets on R and D management and transnational and international competition, and has over a hundred scientific studies to his name.

Ivanov's clear and constructive position drastically differs from that of the authors of many directive documents coming from the depths of the State Foreign Economic Commission of the USSR Council of Ministers. This difference became particularly evident when compared with the major failure experienced by his boss, Kamentsev, who failed to gain the confirmation of the Supreme Soviet for his post as Chairman of the Commission.

Profitable for Us and for Our Partner
Perestroika, Foreign Economic Ties and International Economic Relations

ABEL G. AGANBEGYAN and IVAN D. IVANOV

The USSR accounts for 4 per cent of world trade. Its trade turnover is less than that of Italy, which ranks sixth among the industrialized capitalist countries. In practical terms, the USSR exchanges fuel and raw materials for finished products. In 1988 the share of foreign trade earnings in the national income dropped to 8 per cent, down from 10.7 per cent in 1985. All hard currency earnings received from exports are now used to pay for the balance of payments deficit, and new imports are paid for by new credits.

Such are some not very optimistic facts about Soviet foreign trade. It is not accidental that the only Soviet deputy premier who was voted down by the Supreme Soviet was Vladimir Kamentsev, chairman of the State Foreign Economic Commission, the man in charge of this sector in the government.

It is clear that we may not steer the ship of foreign trade in the way we did earlier. We need a radical reform of the Soviet foreign economic complex. Besides the goal of making foreign economic relations add their contribution to the nation's economic and social development, the reforms also aim to form an open-type economy in the USSR which would progress jointly and in competition with the world economy. The contemporary world being interdependent, foreign economic ties promise the added advantage of promoting confidence-building and the realization of new political thinking.

These goals were reaffirmed by the new Soviet parliament; pursuing them, foreign economic reform has made noticeable headway in the last three years, particularly in its conceptual, organizational and legal aspects. However, it is coming up against a multitude of problems which are holding back its progress. All in all, the nation's foreign economic relations are in a complicated and contradictory situation.

The reasons and content of restructuring

It was a peculiarity of the USSR's foreign economic ties of the stagnation period that their accumulated critical phenomena were camouflaged for a time by temporary gains, especially by oil euphoria. So stagnation made itself felt all the more heavily when raw materials and oil prices plunged in the early 1980s.

The outdated export structure brought to a halt the growth of the nation's foreign trade turnover. Changes in price proportions caused a partial loss of national income in transactions abroad. The USSR balance of payments grew worse as foreign indebtedness increased. These manifestations had deep roots in the mechanism of managing the nation's foreign economic exchanges at the time.

Official rhetoric notwithstanding, planning in the stagnation period was subject to the inertia of the introverted nature of the Soviet economy and its separation from the world economy. Domestic prices had no relation to those of the Soviet foreign trade, the ruble rate was padded artificially and could not serve in business transactions. Goods were allocated for export on the 'residual principle', while imports were used mostly to fill current shortages. Common trade was the predominating form of foreign economic relations. On the operations level, with state monopoly on foreign trade interpreted as the departmental domain of the Ministry of Foreign Trade, industries were divorced from export trade and felt neither an inclination nor a liking for it. At the same time, ministries and departments lived under the illusion that imports were free as they were financed from the national budget.

To be sure, even under such conditions the USSR economy was being irreversibly drawn into the international division of labour. But the process was painful and costly. Foreign economic relations were further removed from cost-accounting than any other sphere of the Soviet economy. The nation was on the margin of the world markets and, to all intents and purposes, outside the international system of commerce, a fact which was out of proportion to its potential or its weight in world politics.

As matters stood, perestroika called for political, not managerial decisions, a new foreign economic thinking being a component of the new economic and political thinking outlined by the 27th Congress of the CPSU. It was embodied in a number of Party and government documents adopted in this field within the last three years which in their totality have reshaped and restructured the concept of the part foreign economic ties are to play in the USSR's national economy, and of the ways of developing these ties.

It is presumed by the new foreign economic thinking that the contemporary world is interdependent and that the Soviet economy is a component of the world economy and cannot progress if separated from the latter. Therefore, any technical and economic targets for our development should be set correspondingly at the world level, while Soviet industries should operate in competition with those of other nations. This also assumes that outside factors should considerably influence the rates, proportions and nature of our country's economic growth, internal pricing and regional development. Foreign economic ties, as it were, if managed skilfully, should turn into a supplementary source of growth of national income adding to that of home production, and into a constant factor (or option) present in discussing the means of attaining targets by the national economy.

Such an approach would substantially expand the functions of the export, import and other foreign economic operations in the nation's reproduction processes. Thus, exports, while providing a means for import needs, would cease to be 'residual' and act as a yardstick of the engineering level and quality of the national output, a source of savings due to greater production, as well as an additional tool of regional development.

In their turn, imports, in addition to supplementing current shortages, would be called upon to contribute to a large-scale modernization of the Soviet economy, the replacement of costly national products, to regional development and a better supply for the USSR consumer goods market.

In this way, not barter deals, but comparative costs of national and foreign production would become the system-forming factors; sporadic contacts with outside markets would be replaced with a stable international specialization of the nation. This kind of specialization is to be of an industrial type based on the national machine-building and chemical-forestry industries, with finished goods to reach the 50 per cent level in overall Soviet exports by the year 2000 and the share of energy to drop to one-fourth of the present proportion. The imports, too, are to be basically of the high technology kind, with the added advantage that its raw material component would ease pressure on national natural resources and ecological balance.

The new foreign economic thinking would change the over-the-border relations between the two systems of property. While remaining antipodes socially, they will, nevertheless, develop at their points of contact specific dual or hybrid forms, such as joint venture property within the USSR territory and investment assets of the USSR organizations operating abroad.

The joint ventureship allowed within the USSR territory is intended to attract to the country advanced foreign technology and managerial skills, to help to saturate the domestic market (including through replacement of imports) and build export potential, as well as to expand the financial ground for the modernization of the national economy. Soviet investments in other countries are, in their turn, to set up an infrastructure for the promotion of Soviet exports, especially of engineering goods (stores and depots, repair shops, sales and servicing facilities) and manufacturing facilities for the stable delivery of goods the nation needs. Both of these forms would bring the Soviet Union to higher levels of the international division of labour, namely, to give the status of an international investor in addition to just being an international trader.

These processes are to be launched with a headstart within the CMEA and renew the dynamism of the Socialist economic integration which would be linked to the economic grassroots in addition to the intergovernment level. In future this would serve as the base for the formation of a united market for the Socialist nations concerned as a conjuncture of their national wholesale markets open to each other.

The USSR foreign economic ties are to develop on a balanced footing, with the balance of payments kept stable and foreign indebtedness limited so as to retain the nation's standing of a reliable and solvent borrower.

Of principal importance also is the fact that the USSR's policy toward setting up an open economy is being realized not only via centralized strategic planning. Its backbone is the direct opening of Soviet factories, associations and the cooperatives concerned to foreign markets, foreign economic operations becoming an integral component of their general activities.

The nation's course calls also for a substantial improvement of the very mechanism of the foreign economic complex: and as the pricing reform develops, domestic-to-world price relations should be getting closer, and an extensive system of export incentives and foreign operations insurance should be set up to protect Soviet enterprises against commercial risks.

For the open-type economy to be built at home and for the nation to be integrated into the world trade system, we need purposeful work to make the national currency, the ruble, convertible.

A convertible ruble would make it possible for the Soviet market to be drawn into the orbit of international competition and would simplify all account operations in the USSR's foreign economic relations. Convertibility would be of most service in running joint ventures on the territory of the USSR as it eliminates the well-known rule of 'currency self-repayment'.[1] It would also considerably promote Soviet investments abroad: with a convertible ruble such investments will be made in the Soviet national currency.

These conditions will bring new dimensions to the foreign economic performance of Soviet enterprises, associations and cooperatives. On the one hand, they will have to stand up

---

[1] The law currently stipulates that joint ventures should cover all of their currency expenditures, including transfer of profits, with currency earnings. Some foreign investors find this rule burdensome, although, with the prevailing rates of profit and taxation in the USSR, a joint venture with a charter capital split 50-50 need not export more than 5 to 7 per cent of its overall output.

against foreign competition and be quick to adapt to changing needs of foreign markets. Both manufacturers and exporters will be subject to 'natural selection' by the market. At the same time, convertibility will make it possible for them to practise cost-accounting throughout their foreign and domestic operations, as well as to have an option of foreign or domestic markets in selling and supply procurement. Equally, it will spell the end of those artificial rates of conversion for the ruble in foreign currencies that are in use today and are, in fact, producing a diversity of rates for the ruble.

At the same time, when we speak of the applicability of convertibility to the Soviet Union, one must define its possible forms and limits. In modern practice, convertibility is understood to be the possibility to exchange a national currency for that of other countries without any limitation, including sales and purchase in currency markets. However, very few nations, such as the USA and West Germany, allow this full and universal form of convertibility. Others confine themselves to narrow forms of convertibility which are limited either to certain kinds of deals or the people authorized to conduct currency transactions.

Specifically, sixty-three nations adopted paras 2, 3 and 4 of Article V11 of the International Monetary Fund Charter as a basis for the convertibility of their national currencies. These provisions demand that they introduce no limitations on current account payments and transfers, practise no multiplicity of exchange rates and, finally, buy off their national currencies on demand by foreign holders. In other words, such convertibility is applicable, in fact, to current operations only, with the state having the right and the possibility to regulate them by 'currency interventions'.

The USSR's foreign economic strategy has the aim of turning the Soviet currency into one for world-wide transactions. However, the realization of this aim is a matter of the more or less distant future. As to the foreseeable future, there will rather be a partial convertibility of the ruble along the lines described above, primarily in 'current operations'.

Notably, in the case of the USSR, experts make a distinction between 'foreign' and 'internal' convertibility. The former is applied to national currency operations by foreign physical and juridical persons (non-resident), while the latter is the domain of domestic economic operators. The market economy nations started with foreign aspects of convertibility, and their experience has but limited value for the Soviet Union. On the contrary, the prerequisites of convertibility here are found mostly inside the national economy, being rooted, as we shall show further, in the progress of the general economic reforms.

Therefore there are as yet no prerequisites for convertibility in the USSR. It can be based solely on developed market exchanges and the stable financial and credit systems of the state. Otherwise its introduction would result only in disarranged foreign payments, dislocated money circulation at home, inflation and growing foreign indebtedness.

It follows that the attainment of the goal should be phased and follow transformations of the internal and external economic mechanisms.

Internal prerequisites for developing international economic cooperation

It has been stated above that the process of incorporating the Soviet economy into the world system is inseparable from and very much dependent on radical transformation of the domestic economic system. A radical transition from the administrative command system of management to a new mechanism which will be based on a developed market, material incentives and stimulation is taking place here. The lower elements of the economy are becoming in many respects autonomous and independent of the state, taking on self-financing and self-management. Pluralism is expanding in property relationships: state property assumes new forms, such as leasing and shareholding. The cooperative sector is especially dynamic: over 100,000 cooperatives sprang up in just two years. Family businesses are also on the upswing, including agriculture. Now about one million people are engaged in private, individual production. As of the first of July 1989, 680 joint ventures are registered in which foreign companies participate. So the nation is moving on to a mixed, pluralistic economic structure.

This finds expression in the process of decentralization, and the gradual elimination of the antiquated system of detailed command planning. Shortly, self-accounting autonomy is to be introduced in the Union's republics and regions. As the market shapes up and competition evolves, enterprises and organizations will gain ever greater independence. Citizens' economic rights and freedoms are on the increase.

Measures to pass to new conditions of economic management were undertaken only in 1988–9, that is, quite recently. It took about three years to work out the new concept of a comprehensive management system and to develop legal instruments for the transition to the new system. Furthermore, the nation faces a number of pressing problems which have been given priority by the newly elected Soviet parliament.

The major problems are the financial health of the national economy and the saturation of the consumer market with goods and services. The redistribution of resources is now in progress with the aim of expanding the production of consumer goods, both foodstuffs and manufactured ones, and the total range of paid services. In 1989 consumer goods production grew twice as rapidly as output from heavy industries. The 1990 blueprints stipulate a 20 per cent increase of consumer goods production (non-foodstuffs). More consumer goods are to be bought abroad, with some reduction in imports of other classes. The agribusiness, light and foodstuffs industries are being renovated; for this purpose foreign credits totalling 2.2 billion rubles have been involved; some military factories are being converted to consumer goods production.

This conversion will be stimulated by the cuts in military budgeting. These are to drop 50 per cent before 1995; military hardware procurements will be reduced by 19.5 per cent during the coming two years. As a consequence, the share of civilian goods in military industry output will increase from 40 per cent in 1989 to 46 per cent in 1990 and 60 per cent in 1995.

A major economic target for both foreign and domestic trade is the formation of a wholesale market for industrial goods and resources which are so far being distributed centrally through the state supply system. A switch-over to wholesale trade requires, above all, that the entire funds in the hands of enterprises, organizations and the state be brought into harmony with the actual turnover of goods. At the moment payment resources are very excessive because of the national budget deficit, amounting to about 13 per cent of the GNP, as well as swollen credit facilities.

The budget deficit will be noticeably reduced through cuts in centralized capital investments, military expenditure, grants to money-losing factories and administration overheads. Meanwhile a banking reform was undertaken, with the setting up of six specialized state banks in place of two, and about a hundred new, specialized banks have been launched (commercial, cooperative, innovation, etc.). All these banks will be self-financed and cost-accounting, so that credit retirement and efficiency will be incentives for them. A new banking law is being drafted which is to regulate credit policies and other banking operations.

Another major condition for the transfer to a market is a reform in pricing policies, with changes in pricing procedures. New prices will be oriented to socially-determined costs; their proportions will be brought close to world levels. The list of centrally controlled prices will be drastically reduced; the proportions of contracted prices and producer prices set by the market will increase. The reform of agricultural and industrial prices is to start on 1 January 1991, while retail price reform is to be postponed for about three years because of the strong inflationary currents in the non-saturated market.

A money market (capital market) will appear and grow to complement the goods and services market as the banking and credit system reforms develop. It will be inseparable from the securities market now under formation, and with the issue of bonds and shares. Work is already in progress to draft corresponding legislation. It will regularize the issuing of securities already started by enterprises, while the system of shareholding in itself may prove most important for the progress of many state and cooperative enterprises, for capital transfusions between sectors of industry, and for making the work collectives interested in profits and management.

At the same time, to ensure the harmony of interests of industries with those of the state, the state will be, as before, active in the development and realization of economic policies, although by other, economic means. To cite an instance, The Law on State Enterprise (Association) stipulates a system of orders by the state for products of national importance. In 1989 state orders covered about 45 per cent of industrial output; it was higher in commodity production, while it was 20 to 30 per cent in manufactures. At a later date, as the market forms, the share of the state orders will drop to 30 per cent or less. By way of comparison it should be mentioned that in the USA, state procurements amount to 22 per cent of the GNP. In the USSR, state orders must ensure a higher profitability and guaranteed sales, and so will be placed in many cases through the competitive system.

Other tools of the state economic policy will be taxes, credit, local budgets. Planning will also be a tool, but, unlike the past usage, it will centre on long-term, strategic targets instead of on the smallest items; it will be realized through the distribution of state budget funding and by economic measures and incentives, not through a system of administrative levers.

Matured internally, all these processes, naturally, are reflected in the foreign economic sphere. The monopoly of the Foreign Trade Ministry has been abolished, the right to operate in markets abroad either independently or through intermediaries has been granted to all Soviet enterprises concerned, associations and cooperatives. A new investment policy is being put into effect which aims at a renovation and retooling of the export basis and export industrialization. This work started with machine-building and electronics, where capital investments are to double in 1988–90, with renovation investment to treble. In 1985 3.1 per cent of outdated machine tools, equipment and instruments were taken off the production lists; in 1988 this renovation ratio increased to 9.8 per cent. In 1990 it is planned to be raised to 13 per cent, and to 15 per cent within the next five-year period, thus reaching the index of technologically advanced nations.

The new mechanism of foreign economic relations

In order to bring together the Soviet foreign and domestic economic mechanisms with the world one, the instruments of their interaction are being gradually altered and modified. Since 1990 the so-called 'differentiated currency coefficients' which are, in fact, the reimbursement to exporters of the difference between domestic and world market prices, will be abolished; they will be replaced with 100 per cent premiums against the ruble rate. A further step will be the calculation of a new currency rate for the ruble, which will be suitable for business accounts and based on the comparative purchasing powers of Soviet and foreign currencies. Currency percentages to be left with exporters will be increased and extended to all exported goods.

The state mechanism to regulate foreign economic activities will be along the same lines as the one for the domestic economy; it, too, will have the purpose of marrying higher business independence to overall economic interests.

The basis of this new mechanism will be the new USSR Customs Tariff that will play the part of a flexible 'gear' between world and domestic prices, replenish the state budget and have a direct influence on the competitiveness of imported goods on the domestic market. For this purpose the tariff will be twin-columned, with rates varying by 2 to 2.5 times; the preference column of low rates will be extended to nations that offer the most favourable treatment to the USSR, while the higher rates will apply to nations who refuse us such treatment. The tariff will contain also preferences and examptions for new forms of cooperation, including industrial cooperation, joint ventures and their internal goods movements, as well as 'free economic zones'. The tariff is expected to be in force in 1991.

On the current regulation level, a system of non-tariff measures was introduced in the USSR last March, which includes licences and quotas and can be put into effect for reasons of maintaining the balance of payments or adjusting competition. It was for the first reason, for instance, that since last 1 June specific import licensing was imposed on Yugoslav and Finnish goods.

It should be noted particularly that all these steps are worked out in accordance with international standards, GATT rules included. More than that, the USSR is introducing the Harmonized System of Description and Coding of Foreign Trade

Goods, which has been adopted by the majority of nations. This system is to be the basis for both the tariff and the new foreign trade statistics of the USSR. The new customs declaration form of the USSR duplicates the similar document of the European Community.

All these measures have been undertaken with the aim of technically facilitating international trade talks with the participation of the USSR, so that the course and outcome of such talks may be comparable. Official talks already started last July between the USSR and the European Community on entering into an agreement on trade and cooperation.[1] By about 1991 preparations are to be complete on the USSR application for membership of GATT. This country will claim full membership with all the rights and obligations it implies.

The creation of a developed market in the USSR, the new foreign economic mechanism and the tools that are being developed for this country's trade policies will remove the stigma of 'the nation with state-controlled trade', invented by the West. These will allow us to become integrated into the world trade system. At the same time, they provide the nation with the means of retaliation against discriminatory acts.

The creation of 'free economic zones' has been decided in principle in this country. Preparations are in progress in this respect in the Vyborg area (near Leningrad), in Nakhodka in the Far East, and the Novgorod region. Such zones are the logical outcome of the progress of economic reform; this step will expand the experiment in the selection of market economy forms. However, the Soviet model of such zones will be specific and differ from the known world experience. In particular, while these zones are enclaves in the developing nations and People's China and have few ties to national economies, being export oriented, in the USSR, although oriented to export in a degree, they are to become an integral part of our economy, a source of

[1] This agreement is on a large scale and has no precedent in the earlier trade policy practice of the USSR and the EC. Besides trade, it will be extended as well to industrial cooperation, investments, science and technology, trade promotion; it will also cover sectoral cooperation in energy, agriculture, fishing, nuclear energy, transport, ecology, standardization, tourism, statistics, atomic energy, etc. The agreement will also include currencies and finance and, particularly, will extend the use of the ECU in mutual accounts.

modern goods, technology and management for our domestic market. That is why the zones will be established in inner areas as well as in frontier regions, and possess extensive territories. There is, for instance, a proposal to turn the Armenian Republic into such a zone.

Functionally, such zones may have a customs/transit, industrial, agrarian, comprehensive economic nature, or even 'technopolises' like, for example, Novosibirsk Academic Township.

The USSR's incorporation in the international finance system is equally important. In practical terms, there is no question of this country's joining the International Monetary Fund. However, the USSR is willing to participate in the solution of the world problem of indebtedness. In this area the USSR is both a borrower (mostly from the West with a net debt of 34 billion rubles) and a creditor (primarily to the developing nations, with a net indebtedness to the USSR exceeding 60 billion rubles). Concerning the former, this country has a definite index of allowable indebtedness which it tries not to exceed. At the same time, it diversifies borrowing channels, resorting to operations in money and securities markets in addition to drawing loans from banks and governments.

As regards its creditor status, Soviet financial cooperation concentrates mostly on financing specific projects with repayment in kind. In this way industrial and export potentials are created in the debtor countries, the Soviet market becomes open to their goods, and payments are facilitated. Yet, an irregular situation with world indebtedness is felt in this field as well. There occur delays with payments, and bad debts pile up.

The solution of the debt problem is a matter of principle for the world's destinies. Therefore, as President Mikhail Gorbachev stressed in his UN address last December, approaches to this problem must be international. The Soviet leader proposed that in some instances the debts be written off altogether, or an extended (up to 100 years) moratorium be established on debt repayments for the poorest nations. As to the other developing countries, the proposal is to limit payments on official debts depending on their economic indices. Mikhail Gorbachev backed UNCTAD's appeal for a reduction of debts to commercial banks, including steps to assure governments' support of the market mechanisms for debt settlement, going as far as to setting up an international body which would buy off the debts at a discount.

At a meeting with the UN Secretary General when the debt problem was discussed, an author of this article (Abel Aganbegyan) made a proposal to convene a world conference which would adopt a strategic decision under UN auspices on the solution of the debt problem, including issues pertaining to international credit security.

Convertibility of the ruble: the phased course

So far there has been no precedent for a Socialist nation to introduce the convertibility of its currency. This does not, of course, mean that it is impossible or unfeasible. To be sure, in the case of the USSR it will take time in direct relationship to the progress of the general economic reform in the country. However, based on the above described transformations and mechanisms, experts are already outlining the main prerequisites and phases of convertibility with sufficient clarity.

One group of such experts was specifically engaged in the spring of 1989 to assess the convertibility of the ruble. In their opinion, it requires:

a. that the ruble fulfil entirely its monetary function inside the country;
b. that the base be determined for a new, economically sound rate of conversion of the ruble into foreign currencies;
c. that the stability of the Soviet currency rate be ensured in the world money markets.

It is evident that in the first case the USSR's internal system of finances is to be put in order, as well as backing the ruble with proper amounts of goods and setting up diversified money and wholesale markets. These aims are to be reached around 1990–2.

In the second case, there needs to be a sensible realization of pricing reform and ensuring comparability, through accurate instruments, of domestic and world prices. These aims are planned to be substantially reached by 1991.

Lastly, to ensure the ruble's stability, a competible manufacturing base should be created for export purposes, the balance of payments stabilized and foreign indebtedness reduced. Basic investments in the development of such a base have been planned for the 13th Five-Year Plan (1991–5).

Considering the above factors, the ruble's convertibility for current operations seems quite feasible by the end of 1990. Meanwhile, since the build-up of convertibility prerequisites is spaced in time, it can be developed in specific forms well in advance of this date, with an applicability to certain areas of foreign economic ties. At this point, for example, the regular conversion of the ruble to free currencies at the ruble's official rate is common for business and private trips abroad. Some member countries of the Council for Mutual Economic Assistance (Comecon) commenced parallel (as options) use of Soviet and national currencies in operations of their joint enterprises. Lastly, since 1989, currency auctions are in practice where foreign currencies are sold for rubles at demand and supply rates. This is going to speed up foreign currency turnover inside the country and provide a certain experience in money market management.

Also, as a special case, mention should be made of introducing the ruble's convertibility into currencies of the other CMEA member states. It evidently cannot be achieved by turning the transferable ruble into a convertible one. Being a unit of accounts which serves certain exchanges, the transferable ruble cannot become a collective currency for Community members. This would require the reciprocal convertibility of CMEA currencies, and a realistic common market within this organization that would be a sum total of members' markets.

Choosing their roads of development, countries lean either to evolution or to revolution. The second road has been chosen for the transformation of the Soviet economy. This is more complicated, and it has a price to pay. Yet, it is the only one which can effect perestroika, restructuring, including the sphere of foreign economic relations.

Gavriil Kh. Popov

Gavriil Popov was born in 1936, and graduated from the Economics Department of Moscow State University in 1959. He holds the degree of Doctor of Sciences in Economics, and is a full professor. He has been working at the Economics Department of the Moscow State University since 1963; in 1971 he became chairman of the Department of Organization and Methods of Control over Social Production at the MGU. In April 1989 he was appointed editor-in-chief of *Voprosy Ekonomiki* (*Problems of Economics*) magazine.

He is a People's Deputy of the USSR. At the Congress of People's Deputies he, on behalf of the Moscow group of Deputies, came up with a concept of the USSR Supreme Soviet on the political structure of the USSR.

Perestroika and the Managers

GAVRIIL KH. POPOV

The progress and effectiveness of perestroika are closely connected to the activities of our principal social groups: workers, collective farmers, creative intellectuals, the military, and others. A specific part in it is played by leaders who make up a social stratum, as it is: party leaders, heads of state apparatus, managers of the economy, et al. Among the latter, key positions belong to those who lead producing entities such as factories, plants, building projects, collective and state farms and mines. The name 'managers' may be used to describe them as a category.

What positions do the managers take in perestroika? What are their aspirations, what have they achieved and are they achieving, what will be their goals in the future?

This article is an attempt to study these questions. To do so, I shall start with a description of the managers' role in the past system, the administrative one, and then proceed to their role in preparing perestroika. Yet, what is most important is their stand at the onset of perestroika and the subsequent course of developments. Unless the dynamic of these developments is analysed it would be hard to explain the firm line towards democratization that is distinctive of Soviet perestroika, or the 'managers' attack' against governmental bodies during the election campaign for People's Deputies. Without such an analysis it would be impossible to find an explanation for the appearance of the gap between what the managers were at all major congresses of perestroika from 1985 to the 19th Party Conference of 1988, and their situation at the first Congress of People's Deputies in 1989. Of yet more importance is the question of what our perestroika can expect of the managers in future.

In this article I shall attempt to demonstrate that we are facing a most complex process in perestroika, not unlike launching a rocket that cannot take off unless all its stages function to capacity, yet when in flight has to cast off the spent motors to proceed to success.

The managers and the administrative system

As perestroika develops, we have all the time to readjust our ideas of the society that was created in the USSR after the revolution of 1917. In a nutshell, our society of the past years may be defined as administrative, state-centred and bureaucratic Socialism, or, in short, the administrative system. As Karl Marx and Friedrich Engels were working out their theory, they foretold in a way that that kind of Socialism might be possible when they analysed 'barracks Socialism' in general and in its early version which was advanced by Mikhail Bakunin and some other members of the Russian liberation movement in the second half of the nineteenth century.

In the USSR the administrative system arose as a logical extension of three fundamental ideas of Lenin.

First: to waste no time in waiting for the productive forces to reach a level which would objectively exclude any forms of economy other than those of Socialism as it was presumed by the original concept of Socialism. On the contrary, the building of a new society could be undertaken in a country devoid as yet of a proper material basis of Socialism.

The second idea followed from the first. If Socialism arises not from a simple replacement of private property with that of the whole society, if Socialism is to be created or built, then an instrument is needed for this building. As Lenin saw it, power – the state – was that instrument.

Finally, the third idea. Originally Lenin himself tended to view Soviet power as organization of the popular masses; yet even in his lifetime there was a need for a bureaucracy, or an apparatus. Since power had to be resorted to in a land whose predominant masses were not striving for Socialism because of their conditions of life, it was inevitable that the social majority (primarily peasantry) had to be governed by the minority (the working class). Further, the working class itself had to be led by its vanguard, the Party. Inside the Party its membership needed to be guided by an apparatus reporting strictly to the centre. So the whole mechanism was to rest on what the centre and its leadership considered to be Socialism and what Socialism should be. The mechanism negated any pluralism of ideas and organizations.

Of course, people with foresight in the Party, state and among the intellectuals, Lenin included, could foretell that such a system bore the menacing seeds of bureaucratism, the cult of personality, the inefficient use of resources and the suppression of democratic freedoms. However, at the time, in the post-revolution years, the upper hand was with the conviction that all those dangers could be overcome, and that there was a prospect of replacing the old society with all its defects and contradictions and of building a new and perfect social order, all within the lifetime of one generation. The prospect outweighed all menaces and justified every kind of sacrifice.

As is evident, within this framework the economy becomes subjugated to politics and develops into a sphere under command. Also it is quite a logical desire to have in the state's hands as much of the economy as possible. Further, it is quite as logical to ensure that, within the state economy, centralization should be at its maximum. And, finally, it would be most convenient for the centre to rid itself of any objective limitations, such as the need to ensure the gold content of the national currency, the cost orientation of prices, the tying-in of wages with costs and efficiency, or the need to balance budget incomes and expenditure, to maintain certain proportions of heavy and light industries, of production and social spheres, etc. The more freedom for the centre, the more conditions exist for what Fyodor Dostoyevsky termed a longing for a society where 'there is no God, and everything is permissible', and so the more chances to accelerate the building of Socialism, that society of the future, by those who had set this noble goal before them.

The administrative system views all production facilities as links or gears of the entire mechanism, not as independent entities. A factory may or may not be profitable: it all depends on the interests of the whole. It must turn out what the centre and its instructions say. It gets raw materials and plant on the centre's instructions at prices set by the centre and from suppliers specified by the centre. In turn, it ships its output to customers determined by the centre at prices set by the centre.

In a mechanism of this sort, the basic wages of the industrial workforce have to be stipulated by the centre. It is the only condition by which the mechanism can function: the centre's instructions can be followed unswervingly only when the centre pays the wages.

It is more than logical for this system that managers are centre-appointed. The centre establishes its representatives alongside indents, prices and wage-scales. The manager is first and foremost a representative of the state who looks after its interests. The manager is the first controller at the factory. The manager's career must fully depend on those who have appointed him. It is the manager who ensures the realization of the centre's instructions that are called upon to build the new order. The centre's orders are an incarnation of what the building of Socialism requires.

The contradiction of the manager's position within the administrative system

Wholeness is what was not to be in such a seemingly whole system.

It was dangerous to make the manager an absolute master.

What if he deviates from his role as executor of the centre's instructions? Could he start practising his own ideas of Socialism? What if managers attempt to unite to become society's main force, pushing the Party out? This is one side of the coin. The other side is that a manager's absolute powers and his likely mistakes may greatly affect the factory personnel's conviction that they must work hard for the sake of their own interests, the main one being the wish to build the new order quickly.

An outcome of such apprehensions, as well as of the simple shortage of even elementarily trained managers, was that a mechanism to control the managers had to be evolved. The first was the Party organization of the factory. Under its statutes, the Party has the right to control all activities of the administration.

Then, special procedures were introduced for appointments to the position of deputy manager; they were employed not so much by the manager as by the superior authority. The head book-keeper was both appointed from above and in a substantial measure was independent of the manager in his current work. Still more independent was the chief of the so-called Section 1, who represented the national security service. A system of laws, instructions and statutes proceeding from above used to bind a manager with thousands of threads, and served, in fact, as a powerful restraint.

Still, it was beyond the limits of the possible to turn a factory into a kind of military detachment. The production process and its conditions objectively demanded that the factory be essentially independent. The centre's directives were unable to take into account all the latent capabilities of a factory, commonly referred to as 'reserves' in the country. Granting the factory and its manager a measure of independence was inevitable if directives were to be carried out efficiently. Independence *per se* remained inefficient until there were material interests involved in putting this independence to use. In the final count, the manager had to be granted more rights and incentives introduced.

Both undermined the rigorous centralism and brought about the danger of centrifugal trends.

The situation of managers putting out consumer goods was especially precarious. To work to the central bodies' instructions made sense only in periods of acute shortage, when whatever was turned out by the factories the centre would seize and put on sale right away. As living standards improved and the consumer was becoming 'choosy', the need of demand orientation (here the managers had too few rights) came into head-on collision with the need to have everything fixed by the centre.

In this area, too, the collision reached proportions which were insurmountable for the centre. To disregard the people's demand would mean to subvert concern for money earnings and, consequently, the interest in work for the state. Attempts to grant the factories rights to take demand into account were undermining another pillar of the administrative system, that of complete centralized control over the factories and managers.

Thus the administrative version of the economy found itself pregnant with unsolvable contradictions. The manager was right in the middle of these contradictions. Counteracting trends converged upon him, his office and his decisions. He would be loyal to the centre, yet he saw that the centre's directives were not the best way to use the factory's resources. He believed he acted in the people's best interests, yet he saw that he was producing not what met the directives but what the customer wanted. The collision built up as attempts were made to extend the factory's rights and give it and its workforce a chance to earn bonuses.

It was no accident that the ideas of drifting away from the accepted version of the administrative system were fermenting primarily among managers of the economy, the directors, collective farm chairmen, Party leaders with managerial experience. Proposals of a negative kind dominated in their reports: what should be removed, repealed, cast off.

These managers' reports met with understanding by those Party and government leaders who were concerned with the decline in growth-rates and the potential for the solution of social problems, and with increasing inadquacy of the nation's technological development. Nikita Khrushchev and Alexei Kosygin based the concepts of many of their reforms on ideas advanced by the managers.

Under Khrushchev in the 1950s and early in the Brezhnev-Kosygin period, attempts were made to expand the independence of the republics, ministries, local authorities and managers. In this respect the most thorough attempt was undertaken by Alexei Kosygin when he became Prime Minister. However, these efforts were blocked, as it seemed at the time, by a large majority of the Party's top leadership. What, in fact, was behind the resistance to reform was an understanding, whether conscious or intuitive, that the changes would affect their image of Socialism, or what they identified with it in those years.

Seeing that reforms were being blocked, one after another, the managers had to look for a way out. Some of them went on to insist that the reforms continue. However, their appeals were emasculated by endless resolutions of the Central Committee and the government on fresh steps to perfect planning, management structures, etc. These resolutions overflowed with right intentions, half-steps and pseudo-steps, while their realization would reveal within one or two years what was initially put into them: to announce changes without any change whatever. The outcome was that the proponents of reform were turning apathetic and indifferent. Other managers resolved to resort to any ways and means for bypassing procedures which they thought outmoded, thus settling the problems of their factories. The outcome here was that the managers slid into complicity in the shadow economy or corruption.

The 1970s witnessed quite a tragedy of a generation of Soviet managers, those who found the heart to break the rules of the bureaucratic economy game and got involved in corrupt games. In a measure the process was symbolized by the case of the mayor of Sochi. This talented administrator was exceptionally successful in developing Sochi into the nation's major resort city, turning it even into a 'smoke-free zone'; yet at the same time he got drawn into shadow economy swindles and outright corruption. Sooner or later many of the managers who were trying to do something about the situation found themselves in an identical or similar position.

Seeking 'protection' for themselves, these managers established contacts with the Party and state apparatus, especially locally. A highly complex machinery thus evolved which fused 'everybody who was anybody' by overall guarantees, up to family relationships.

There was a third category of managers: those who knowingly became involved in corruption and directed corporations of accomplices at every level of management and in all its bodies.

The restructuring of the economy and the managers

When the Party leadership launched perestroika in 1985, they assumed, from the past years' experience, that the managers would be a major driving force in the restructuring.

Proceeding from this basic idea, a conference on scientific and technological progress was convened in 1985 in the Central Committee with managers being the principal invitees. Again in

1987, shortly before the Central Committee Plenary Session which dealt with problems of the new economic mechanism, another conference was held in the Central Committee where, too, managers played a leading part.

This was not simply a matter of having them as advisers. After 1985 there began a process of nominating managers to key positions in the Party and the Government. Preference was given to former managers, beginning with the new head of the Government and the Central Committee Secretary responsible for the economy, to the large number of newly appointed ministers. Boris Yeltsin proposed the general manager of the country's biggest ZIL Automobile Factory for the post of mayor of Moscow; other managers were proposed by him for the positions of First Secretary in several districts of the USSR capital.

This 'managerial line', however, failed to yield the results that were expected, though it was still continued: for example, the Central Committee's Plenary Session on agriculture in March 1989 adopted decisions which were largely influenced by agricultural managers.

And yet it became evident as early as the end of 1987 that there was nobody to carry out the management reform decisions adopted in the summer of the same year: the top echelon bureaucracy found them altogether alien, while managers for some reason were too wary to take them up.

The story of the Managers' Club started by the *ECO* magazine in Siberia could serve as an indicator of the managers' attitudes. Headed by Academician Abel Aganbegyan, the club had contributed to the preparation of decisions regarding restructuring. However, its influence declined as the restructuring took off. Abel Aganbegyan's efforts to prod the managers were of no avail. Neither the Academy of National Economy where top economic leaders are trained, nor other managers' training centres, have become foci of restructuring.

What happened?

One of the reasons is the increase in corruption of which I spoke earlier. Each of the nearly fifteen years of stagnation dealt blows to the managers' hopes of changing the mechanism of economic administration. Being pragmatic by nature, many of them saw a way out through decisions by-passing laws, and rules which were obviously outdated.

A record of achievement is not all that a manager has after many years' work. In the command economy, these years also piled up a record of his malpractices. The 1970s were particularly 'productive' in this sense. Even if a manager was not corrupt, he still would be a party to corruption in some ways. The very fact of long service 'in the Brezhnev time', especially a successful career, was a kind of indictment. Indeed, who would dare visit Leonid Brezhnev on his birthday with only a bunch of flowers, without an expensive present bought with money that was not from one's own wages? There were so many Brezhnevs that a manager had to deal with.

Brezhnev's line of keeping leaders in their posts applied to managers, too. Many of them had plainly grown old by 1985. They were still strong enough to deliver a discourse on perestroika in public, but physically incapable of engaging in daily work, all the more so as the work was to bear fruit only after many long years.

A very delicate operation was called for, so that managers would get the least punishments for insignificant offences; they would then feel free to join ranks in perestroika uninhibitedly.

Regrettably, things turned out differently. While Yuri Andropov aimed his anti-corruption drive primarily against the very system of law enforcement and the heads of the Party bodies, Konstantin Chernenko, his successor as General Secretary, let the emphasis be shifted by law enforcement agencies backed by the Party apparatus. Repression came down only on trade directors and other managers, that is, on those in the middle and lower echelons who were 'taking and giving', not on those higher up who were just 'taking'. Managers who had been pressed by Party bodies, as often as not with reason, to break this or that law suddenly found themselves abandoned to their fate and defenceless.

It was a major miscalculation of the pre-perestroika time. Although with Mikhail Gorbachev's ascent managerial persecutions ceased, by 1985 the managers were in dread.

All things considered, however, the main causes of the failure of the 'managerial' approach to the perestroika procedure are to be found elsewhere.

By 1985 the economic situation had changed in principle. Growth was there, but it was one which was debilitating both the trunk and the branches of the tree of the economy. Every per cent of increased volumes and every month of fulfilled plan ate into the reserves of the future. The available machinery was run to the limit. The concrete used in civil engineering, even in earthquake-prone Armenia, was practically devoid of cement. Savings were a must at the expense of safety even of transport, pipelines or atomic power stations.

A situation developed everywhere when the smallest spark could ignite a chain of grave consequences. The difficulties of economy aggravated social, ecological and national problems.

In 1965 a reform of the economic mechanism as it was could have undoubtedly been effective so that its radical change might wait. In 1985 a reform of the existing economic mechanism could produce but a respite before launching a complete overhaul of administrative Socialism.

Our managers were ready for, and demanded, changes within the existing frameworks, radical as they might be. But the prospect of a clean break with administrative Socialism was as foreign for them as for many categories of the apparatus leadership. For instance, managers very much wanted to have guaranteed supplies of raw materials and plant of the right quality. Here they would welcome changes. But the prospect of facing customers in the market, without state planning and state supply committees, boded no good for them.

One more thing has to be taken into account. In the course of numerous reforms since 1965, many a half-measure was discarded or cast off. Yet every success of pseudo-reform had something working for a manager's gain, like a pay rise, a bonus, etc. By 1985, managers were earning legal incomes much higher than the average in the USSR. It was especially noticeable in collective farms whose chairmen lived far above the poverty line, even those who ran their farms at a loss. The transition to a new system promised every manager a doubled or trebled workload with a very uncertain rise of real income which would be out of proportion to the effort spent.

There were other factors, too. Managers had many complaints about various limitations. However, norms and regulations coming from above are not only fetters, they are props and crutches as well. They serve also as insurance policies and indulgences. They make it possible to refer matters to higher authority, to hide behind others' backs; simplified work saved having to think. Risk was reduced to a minimum. A manager might be outspoken in his disgust of too detailed supervision from above, yet at the same time he may be accustomed to it deep in his heart and, one may say, he may have 'unlearned' to do without such supervision.

During the years of stagnation, many managers accumulated acquaintances and mutual obligations. This infrastructure was sometimes stronger than the official channels, and was substituted for the latter. Perestroika spelled an end to these networks. And again the picture is the same: the bad had to be removed, but what would come in its place was either uncertain or evidently no good for a manager.

Cooperatives, too, became quite a real threat, indirectly as competitors, and directly as attraction for skilled men. There was also the prospect of losing the monopolistic position that many factories still possessed. So it is not too hard to understand why the managers were losing heart and drive so fast.

It was this process that hampered the realization of the 1987 transformation programme, moderate as it was. Having no wish to go further and fearing the next phase, the managers, willingly or not, failed to achieve even the first phase in full.

The managers proposed no programme of economic reform that would have promised an exit from the crisis. Their 'representatives' in the Council of Ministers apparatus, departments and ministries continued to hold on to the version of reform that bore no solution to the cardinal problems, though it was as evident to them as to the general public. In a word, the way the managers took had no prospect, but the other way held no prospect for them either.

But there are two different causes of the absence of prospects. The first one allowed the managers to stay in their positions with hopes for some kind of 'miracle', like a brainwave of research economists elevated to government posts, or foreign loans, or resources freed by disarmament.

The second prospect of radical change meant immediate and perilous changes for a majority of the managers. This kind of absence of prospect, obviously, was the least acceptable for them.

So the biggest outcome of the four years of perestroika is that most of the managers have moved to the camp of conservative, apparatus-dictated economic transformation. It is a fact that was not grasped in time by the nation's leaders, or scientists, or by our Western partners who by custom believe that a manager, their opposite number at talks, is seriously thinking of perestroika and not of how to stop it so as to retain his position.

Political reform and the managers

Thus it became evident by the end of 1987 that the economy personnel, managers being the main component, were not ready, or willing, or to some extent able to create any radically new forms of running the economy. Moreover, even the progressive elements of the Party's Central Committee decisions of 1987 June on the restructuring of the economy were either ignored or remained unimplemented by them. On the contrary, the major steps were interpreted in a purely administrative way: state orders were brought up to 100 per cent of manufacturing capacities, with their independence throttled totally, rates were approved for every factory by its ministry on the basis of the early plans, prices unchanged, etc.

A serious crisis has emerged, though it is not outwardly visible. The intellectuals were outspoken in criticizing the past and the present administrative Socialism, repudiating its ideological foundations and the myths of its successes. People whose situation was getting harder were demanding changes. And the apparatus as a whole, managers included, were not ready for any decisive change.

The tensions had to be eased by the convocation of the 19th Party Conference (the first one after 1940). However, the apparatus managed to retain basically its control of the election of delegates to the conference. Some delegates' attempts to present the problems in a new way were met with acclamation outside the Kremlin yet were blocked with traditional orations by traditional speakers who traditionally sharply criticized the details and as traditionally evaded tackling the fundamental issues.

In this situation the Party leadership took a dramatic decision. The question then was of changing the very concept of perestroika, of the idea of who was to be the main driving force of perestroika. With three years' experience of perestroika behind him, Mikhail Gorbachev announced in his speech the line to resolute political democratization, to glasnost. (This line had been earlier approved by the Central Committee Plenary Session in January 1988.) The aim was to stir the masses to greater activity. The idea was the intellectuals' activity should be translated into that of the masses, and with this backing either to make the apparatus act with more resolution, or to start a clean-up of the apparatus by reducing its numbers, reorganizing its structure and abolishing a number of its privileges.

From then on the destinies of perestroika were to be related not to the managers, or the apparatus, or a revolution from above, but to the people themselves. Figuratively speaking, it was not unlike the management of a joint-stock company that, having encountered insurmountable difficulties, appealed to all its shareholders.

This inability of the managers to find a solution to the crisis, and their passivity, were most likely what prompted the Party leadership to take this not-too-easy decision. The line to democratization was to be realized in two aspects: in production and in the state.

Democratization at the production level, including elections for managers, did not produce the desired effect. Indeed, for factory workers to start looking for a new and energetic manager, the factory itself had to be working in new conditions and to be under pressure. Yet, since its ministry, not the market, was the main lever in deciding the factory's destiny, the workers tended to elect mostly those managers who knew how to deal with the ministry, that is, the old ones as a rule. Of course there was some cleaning-up of the most odious, rude and hard-fisted ones who failed to cooperate with their collectives. A typical manager became one who knew how to work in concert with the workers' collective councils and who was carrying out some social programmes for the workers. But primarily the managers who stayed at the wheel were those most skilful in navigating reef-infested administrative seas.

The democratization of the political life of the state and, particularly, its first step, the elections of the USSR People's Deputies, proved to be a primary objective.

Even at the nomination phase, an all-out boycott was in evidence directed against everybody whom the electorate identified, directly or indirectly, with the apparatus, whether they were managers proper, or apparatus functionaries, or their helpers. Feeling that they would not be able to win the elections on their own, the more far-sighted leaders of the local Party and government bodies gave up their nominations. Those who did not had to pay dearly on election day.

The apparatus line was to replace the nominations of Party secretaries with those of managers. A virtual dictatorship-style attack was launched to capture Deputies' seats. In Moscow alone dozens of managers were nominated.

Especially active were managers of military-industrial complex factories who spent some of their abundant allocations to improve their workers' situation by building housing and kindergartens, to keep decent clinics, etc. This managerial stratum with a 'workers' guardians' image counted on election victory, and on them the apparatus placed bets.

Frankly, this line justified itself in part, especially in the provinces. But this ruse alone was not sufficient in the cities. There managers suffered defeat though not as impressively as that of the Party and Soviet leaders. In the city of Kharkov, for instance, the editor of the Moscow magazine *Ogonyok*, Vitaly Korotich, ran against a Kharkov-based manager, and won.

The course of the elections gave rise to a process whose consequences are likely to be extensive, the process of the destruction of the decades-old image of the manager as an opponent of the apparatus-style arbitrariness of the higher bodies. On the contrary, the manager himself as often as not was identified with the apparatus.

The managers' conduct at the first Congress of People's Deputies contributed to this process. There was practically no speech by an industrial manager that expounded a really radical concept of economic restructuring. The agricultural managers were very explicit in presenting all the ills and misfortunes of agriculture, yet they proposed to continue to retain collective and state farms and to help them from the national budget; in other words, to seek solutions outside the sphere of efficiency.

To my mind, political perestroika is bringing in a final verdict on the concept of the manager as the mainstay of perestroika. Sad as it is to state, the largest percentage of our managerial corps proved too tightly bound to the whole of the administrative system apparatus and thus could not be the mainstay of that aspect of restructuring whose centrepiece should be the dismantling of administrative-bureaucratic Socialism. More than that, a trend is emerging of positioning managers in the last line of defence of the administrative system.

The new managers

There was a theoretical chance, a difficult one to carry out but nevertheless realistic, that most of the administrative system managers would gradually turn into managers of new type. Had it happened, the restructuring progress tempo and its very shape would have been largely influenced by the managers. However, as we noted above, the first four years of perestroika have shown that the managerial majority did not take this road.

It is natural that the formation of economic sectors of non-administrative Socialism would need leaders, or managers. The process of the formation of the new-type managers has already begun, and we shall call them the 'new managers'. The managers we speak of are:

- chairmen and chairwomen of cooperatives
- heads of state enterprises being converted to cooperatives
- heads of leased enterprises (those leased from the state by workers employed by it)
- heads of joint-stock enterprises

- peasants starting family businesses by leasing land from the state or from state or collective farms
- heads of joint ventures with foreign participation
- heads of various other joint ventures.

Different as these enterprises are, what they have in common is their independence of the administrative system. On the contrary, the latter now depends on their tax contributions and other payments.

The new managers' relationship with the control bodies narrows down to well-defined fixed payments and other normative limitations defined equally clearly. Basically, these managers are dependent on their workers' collectives, their shareholders, or members of their cooperative. Accordingly, the economic, social and political orientation of the new managers is guided by these bodies.

Of course, the new managers originate in some part from the administrative system managers. These usually are those who held positions of little importance in the system, or who managed non-prestigious enterprises in non-prestigious fields in non-prestigious regions. Even so, the percentage of such former managers is not high. The majority of managers of cooperatives and, even more, of peasant family businesses were never managers in the old system; more often, they had no previous managerial experience at all. Rather, the fact that they had no realistic chance to become managers in the administrative system was what prompted energetic and innovative people to seek the management of independent enterprises of the new types.

The new managers are quite opposite in every respect to the majority of the present-day managers. It seems very important that the formation of the new managers be speeded up; they must be helped to get organized, to learn to lean on each other, and to come to know each other.

To illustrate possible ways of reaching these goals I would cite two organizations which I had the good fortune to help launch and which are now under my supervision.

The first is the USSR Association of Young Managers set up in 1989. The Association is to help all young managers to turn into managers meeting the requirements of perestroika. Young managers comprise the very stratum of present-day managers who are, potentially, the best suited for growing into the 'new managers'. We also admitted into the Association the 'new managers' to enable them to influence the young managers of state enterprises. The Association's path is thorny, and it is not yet registered with the Supreme Soviet as a nation-wide organization. But there is very much interest in it.

The other organization is a cooperative, non-government Management Consultation and Managers' Training Centre under the Moscow Regional Soviet. We acted on the assumption that the new managers needed training and advice, and that it was important to provide both. It is as important to help the present-day managers (especially the young ones) have a better feel of their possibilities and to move their enterprises from under state enterprise conditions to those of independent entities, and for themselves to become new managers. When the prospects are clear, the managers find it easier to make decisions. Training helps to remove, though in part only, the fear of the new. The main line of our Centre's programme is to study how a state enterprise may be turned into a leased, joint-stock or cooperative one. Organizations similar to mine are mushrooming – unions of cooperativists, leasers' associations, family farmers' unions, all kinds of management schools, etc.

It is too early to draw any far-reaching conclusions about the tempos of the establishment of enterprises that are to be separate from the state and market-oriented and whose owners are their workers. Correspondingly, it is as difficult to forecast who the new managers will be. But the very fact of their emergence and their influence and weight both for their workers and in society is highly indicative. There is enough reason to expect that the new managers will be the decisive factor in radical restructuring, and it will be they who compensate, partly, for the damage perestroika sustained following the mass desertion of the present-day managers from the apparatus-style approach to perestroika.

Science

Roald Z. Sagdeev

In dictatorships and other closed societies, the majority of people become conformists. This phenomenon also appeared in the Soviet Union during Stalin's personality cult and the period of stagnation. Indeed, only a few scientists were courageous enough to refuse to sign the letter that was published in *Literaturnaya Gazeta* and other official periodicals in which the opinions and actions of Andrei Sakharov were denounced. Among the few who refused was Roald Sagdeev, although at that time such a defiant position could have cost him his highly successful scientific career. Later, in 1988, he boldly defended Sakharov in *Moscow News*, demanding the return of Sakharov's honours and decorations, which were illegally taken from him during the period of stagnation.

In 1961, at the age of thirty-one, Sagdeev became a Doctor of Sciences in Physics and Mathematics. A year later he was elected a corresponding member of the USSR Academy of Sciences, and by the age of thirty-six he became a permanent member. In the following years many universities and academies elected him an honorary member, among them the US National Academy of Sciences. In 1973 Sagdeev became head of the Institute of Space Research of the USSR Academy of Sciences. He has headed a number of unique research projects dealing with the Cosmos, Prognoz, Venera, Meteor and Intercosmos space vehicles and orbital complexes. He is also a scientific adviser for the major international projects Vega and Phobos.

As a scientist, Sagdeev has an acute sense of responsibility for the fate of the world. As he was able to foresee, perhaps more clearly than others, the disastrous end of civilization which might result from the nuclear arms race, he founded and headed the Committee of Soviet Scientists Against the Nuclear Threat. He is known for his honest and principled position on many problems pertaining to perestroika, democratization, science and society. He often speaks out, giving an open and impartial evaluation of the state of Soviet science and outlining his position in the world today.

The anticonformism of a genuine scientist and his courageous civic stance were also vividly revealed during the period of perestroika. After a fierce election campaign, he won over his rivals and was elected a People's Deputy. When he learned, however, that the USSR Academy of Sciences had refused to allow Academician Andrei Sakharov to be elected on the Academy ticket, Roald Sagdeev relinquished his seat in favour of Sakharov.

Where Did We Lose Momentum?

ROALD Z. SAGDEEV

Science and society

The history of science is in many ways a model of what the current Soviet leadership intends to achieve under the theme of perestroika – the destruction of obsolete ways of thinking, direct and open competition of new ideas, and a never-ending search for a complete and accurate understanding of reality. Unfortunately, science, like government, seldom operates according to an ideal model.

The scientific community acts not in a vacuum, not in isolation, but immerses itself in the life of society, and political conditions and social constraints play an important role in the development of science. Soviet science inherited from the old pre-revolutionary Russia a fairly thin layer of scientific and technical intelligentsia which was mostly scattered in the revolutionary upheavals and the civil war that followed the October revolution. Some prominent scientists and engineers left the country, and the young Soviet State had to start from scratch. The economy was in an extremely poor condition. But the very first decrees of the Soviet Government helped to establish rudimentary scientific infrastructures in Soviet Russia. Lenin himself played an important role in taking care of scientific institutions.

These first years of revolutionary romanticism and enthusiasm were followed by Stalin's harsh measures to suppress not only his political opponents, but to a large extent the intelligentsia as a social group. Many big names in science, the leaders of important scientific schools, were denied scientific work and even perished in Gulags. But largely because of his own ambitions and his intention to keep the country's defences strong, Stalin favoured the establishment of some scientific institutes. Among them were the institutes led by the then young physicist Peter Kapitsa and the chemist Nikolai Semenov. Most of the effort went into the development of applied sciences and engineering, such as aviation, the automobile industry and other direct military applications. To some extent it helped to keep alive some important scientific figures and engineers, but great damage to science resulted from the so-called class approach in which fresh human resources were brought in to replenish the intelligentsia. The attack on the traditional circles of intelligentsia and government aimed to accelerate the re-creation of a new intelligentsia with much stronger roots in the working class and peasantry. If this had been successful, national culture and science would have lost its continuity and its traditional roots. Fortunately, it did not happen. Bright people – scientists, engineers, artists and writers – kept the flame alive and continuity was preserved. In the years directly preceding the Great Patriotic War and World War II the very existence of robust science and engineering in the country was extremely helpful in providing rapid research and application in the military field, which was the most sensitive, and for applied science.

After the war the scientific community was subjected to new forms of ideological and political suppression. Every scientist in every field of science was required to follow the special criteria of 'partiinost' – allegiance to the Party – the definition of which was rather vague. It could mean that every field of science had to be developed in strict accordance with the Party spirit and line. And because of the vagueness of such a definition, certain people with virtually no scientific interest were able to use these arguments to suppress their professional and scientific rivals. Some branches of science even suffered physical repression.

To a great extent, science is a product of the social conditions in which it develops. During the past half-century, Soviet science has suffered deeply, and is still bleeding, from the wounds of ill-conceived government policies. Today, although the Soviet Union has one of the world's largest scientific communities, it has only a modest record of achievement and is contributing too little to the world's scientific knowledge.

Science and industry

We in the Soviet Union have for years been castigating ourselves for our failure to apply fundamental research findings to improve industrial productivity. We have revised policies to strengthen the connection between science and practice; but although such reforms might be necessary, we have not faced up to the real problem, which is that basic Soviet science is too weak to contribute much to practical application.

During a long period of Soviet history the basic sciences received too little support. And it is ironic that in the years of perestroika, when science and engineering are called upon to contribute greatly to the renovation of industry and agriculture and to accelerate the economic recovery of the nation, only now have we reached an understanding of how important it is in doing basic science to keep in mind the need to move to practical application at the earliest possible stage. To accelerate the transfer of scientific discovery to practical application requires an organizational infrastructure which is both sophisticated and robust; ideally such an infrastructure would provide a strong interaction between the Academy of Sciences, as the headquarters of basic science, and the State Committee for Science and Technology, which would play a crucial role in the application of basic science to different branches of industry. Unfortunately until quite recently such an interaction was very weak and sometimes almost non-existent.

The inability to support basic sciences

Soviet science can be justly proud of its contribution to the discovery of the laser, and Soviet technology exhibited its prowess with the launching of Sputnik, and with subsequent space achievements. But such flashes of brilliance are rare. The shortcomings of Soviet science are visible from the subatomic world of physics to the boundless world of astronomy. Of the dozen fundamental elementary particles discovered by our generation, Soviet physics contributed none. Of the hundreds of other subatomic particles and resonances considered to be derivatives of the main particles, we can claim to have contributed to the discovery of perhaps 1 or 2 per cent. As astronomy has opened up new windows in our understanding of the origin and development of the universe, Soviet scientists have added little real value. In the biological sciences, the enduring influence of Trofim Lysenko's stubborn rejection of mainstream science has severely damaged Soviet life sciences, and the consequences are felt even now.

However, the biological sciences were not an unfortunate exception. There were several other scientific disciplines which suffered political subjectivism or even direct manipulation by 'Lysenko' scientists. As another painful example, I should refer to cybernetics – or information science, in modern terminology. In the late 1940s and early 1950s philosophers reflecting on modern technology condemned cybernetics as a bourgeois science. Today we can attribute the lack of computers and the underdeveloped infrastructure of the computer industry to that period of heavy-handed attack on information science. A similar attack even in such an exact scientific discipline as physics, especially nuclear physics, was to come, but the first explosion of an atomic bomb on Soviet test sites in 1949 liberated Soviet physicists from that particular ideological attack.

For too long, Soviet science has hidden its inadequacies behind official panegyrics to its success. In academic and political forums alike, exaggerated claims have been made for the achievements of Soviet science. Science has its own criteria for success, however, and Soviet achievements have not measured up to them.

Bureaucratic dinosaurs

The decline of Soviet science dates back to the acceleration of scientific and technological progress that began during World War II. The growth of 'big science', with its need for expensive equipment and large teams of researchers, spelled trouble. The resulting bureaucracy within the scientific community succeeded in stifling Soviet science.

The managerial machinery surrounding science grows in the same way as bureaucratic systems in other spheres of society. The danger for science is that the administrators may come to dominate the operation and direction of scientific research. Many Soviet scientists can remember a meeting of the Presidium of the USSR Academy of Sciences held in 1964 at which Academicians Keldysh and Artisimovich debated the future of the institution. Academy president Keldysh argued that there was no danger, that scientists would continue to guide the work of the Academy as it grew. Artisimovich warned that the Academy was shifting from being a centre of fundamental research to becoming merely another bureaucratic ministry with a political rather than a scientific agenda.

Unfortunately, Artisimovich's fears were not unfounded. A bureaucratic style gradually permeated all facets of the scientific community. With departmental barriers separating academic science from higher education, the country's best researchers were prevented from teaching the next generation of scientists; university students received their training from second-tier scientists, most of whom did no research. Thus, the centuries-old tradition whereby students learned science by working in laboratories with the country's leading researchers was abandoned, and the research institutes as well as the universities suffered as a result.

The majority of academic institutes grew too large and lost sight of their original function as a flexible, manageable team of scientists sharing common goals. The original form of the institutes, with 100–200 scientists and technicians, had demonstrated its effectiveness in the 1920s and 1930s. The Institute for Physical Problems under the leadership of Peter Kapitsa has led the world in the study of superfluidity. With Nikolai Semenov at the helm, the Institute of Chemical Physics did groundbreaking research in chain reactions. Bureaucracy was minimal at these institutes. The director had time to engage in research and to train students.

Today's typical research institute has a staff of thousands, including hundreds of scientists. Its director is overwhelmed with managerial responsibilities and has no time for training students or for doing research – even as a hobby. The Soviet Union is not yet fully aware that these giant institutions are out of date, but scientists at the institutes cannot avoid noticing the declining quality of the seminars and overall level of scientific discourse. We should have already begun to break up these bureaucratic dinosaurs into smaller and more manageable departments and laboratories.

Scientists cannot shirk their managerial responsibilities because the placing of control of institute management completely in the hands of professional bureaucrats cannot improve the quality of scientific research. Only a scientist can effectively manage research. The danger, however, is that talented scientists can become so overloaded with organizational work that they lose touch with science. Eventually they become little better than the professional managers, unable to distinguish an original idea from eyewash.

Progress by fiat

One result of the bureaucratization of science has been the erosion of scientific standards. Physicist and Nobel laureate Lev Landau once observed that scientists are divided into classes: Einstein and a few others belong to the first class; and the rest are distributed at lower levels. Landau maintained that all scientists in this 'class society' know which is their level. To pretend that the scientific world is a 'classless society', in which all scientists are of equal value, is to deny the existence of a hierarchy that all serious scientists recognize. As Arthur Conan Doyle once said: 'Mediocrity knows nothing higher than itself, but talent instantly recognizes genius.' This is another reason why scientists who are actively involved in research should be managing research institutes.

The loss of objective scientific criteria for evaluating scientific work has resulted in an overall levelling of quality. Rather than letting scientists judge what is significant, the political bureaucracy in the late 1950s established the practice of 'registration of new discoveries' to certify important scientific achievements. Such a public mechanism is unavoidably influenced by political and other forces, with the result that the so-called new discoveries are not what scientists themselves consider most important. Such progress by fiat inevitably destroys morale and lowers the standards of science.

In the 1960s scientists even had to promise to make a specific amount of progress within a designated period. Physicists from Novosibirsk, recognizing the absurdity of the exercise, pledged to make one discovery of worldwide importance, two discoveries of all-Union importance, and three discoveries of Siberian importance to please political leaders at all levels. While a scientist would immediately see this as nonsense, political leaders can be comically naïve as to the unpredictability of science as well as to its inherently global nature.

Another ill-conceived aspect of Soviet science is the current system of lifetime tenure for institute directors. Chemist Nikolai Semenov won the Nobel prize for his early work at the Institute of Chemical Physics. As the Institute grew, so did his managerial responsibilities, with the result that the standards of the Institute's research declined, and Semenov himself lost his opportunity to make further significant contributions to science.

Perestroika has resulted in only marginal reforms to the tenure system. The age limit for those holding high administrative positions is now set at sixty-five years for 'ordinary mortals' (say, a doctor of science), seventy years for a member of the Academy, and seventy-five years for a member of the Presidium. And even this modest change will not take effect for several years. In the spirit of glasnost I often find myself explaining the new rule to interested citizens. I tell them jokingly that the health of my ageing Academy colleagues is the result of natural selection.

The practical experience gained by the rest of the world makes it clear that the Soviet scheme is not a good model for science. In France, research institute directors can serve for no more than twelve years. In the Federal Republic of Germany, the Max Planck Society, which plays the same role as the USSR Academy of Sciences, had a system of collective leadership in which three or four co-directors rotate in and out of the executive director's responsibilities according to a planned schedule. The United States has no formal tenure rule because none is necessary. US scientists have always moved freely and frequently, and first-rate scientific research is done at their numerous national laboratories, institutes and universities.

The value of movement and change within research organizations is reflected in scientific progress. French, German and American science is vibrant with new ideas, while Soviet science is stultifying.

The mobility of scientists, which is taken for granted in other countries, is almost completely absent in the Soviet Union. The rigidity and compartmentalization of the research bureaucracy is part of the problem, but even if this were changed, our national housing policy would severely restrict the movement of scientists. We joke that a Soviet scientist needs dual citizenship – for the USSR and for Moscow. In fact, a Moscow domicile registration, which is necessary to live in the city, is virtually a title of nobility. Because the research institutes are concentrated in Moscow, many promising scientists are prevented from doing research at the best of them. And those scientists who live in Moscow are reluctant to work anywhere else for fear of losing their Moscow base. Changing this policy will be difficult, but a possible first step would be for the Academy to provide housing where visiting scientists could live for extended periods.

Lack of foresight

The planning of Soviet science resembles the efforts of a hapless weather forecaster who always predicts today's weather for tomorrow. Overcautious bureaucrats apparently find security in basing all their plans on ensuring the maintenance of the *status quo*. Little attempt is made to understand where science is going.

Planning deficiencies are sometimes as simple as a failure to anticipate what equipment will be needed to achieve a research goal. For example, all financial resources might be allotted to an information-gathering satellite, leaving no reserve with which to buy the necessary hardware to interpret the data. The 6-metre optical telescope in the Northern Caucasus is a perfect example. This is the world's biggest telescope of this kind, but it does not incorporate the latest detector technology. Smaller telescopes with better detectors have a superior performance.

WHERE DID WE LOSE MOMENTUM?

Do we have 'new thinking' in science?

This lack of foresight in science planning has repercussions throughout society. Without an understanding of where science and technology are heading, plans for agriculture, industry and all aspects of social activity also suffer. This failure can be particularly devastating in those human activities which profoundly affect the environment. A science-based view of the future is essential to avoid potential problems such as climatic changes, acid rain and ozone-layer depletion. Indeed, there is evidence that humans have already gone too far in disrupting the environment.

Unfortunately we in the Academy of Sciences and in industrial research often avoid the difficult work of long-range planning. As a result, we repeatedly find ourselves scrambling feverishly to change already approved plans under the pressure of unforeseen circumstances. Lack of foresight also affects research funding. Little if any money is allocated for research into the emerging areas of science, yet such research often leads to breakthrough discoveries and unexpected results. Not only are these important to scientific progress, they are what make the practice of science so wonderful.

Since the 1960s, basic science has been considered less important than applied science in the Soviet Union; economists assumed that basic science contributed little to the means of industrial production. But the country's leaders are slowly beginning to appreciate the importance of interaction between all levels of scientific and technological work. Neither basic nor applied research is sufficient in itself, and the creation of an intellectual reserve for future practical applications enhances the most advanced means of production. It should not be surprising that Japan, which made a revolutionary leap in technology and the management of industrial production through effective application of foreign science, technological know-how and efficient labour organization, is now devoting more of its resources to basic science.

The question is whether the Soviet Union is ready to adopt a truly integrated approach to planning large-scale programmes for scientific and technological progress. In the majority of cases, the Academy of Sciences, which manages scientific planning, is a weak partner to the industrial ministries. As a result, the personal interests of a narrow group of engineers, designers and heads of industrial agencies dominate planning. They function much as trade association lobbyists do in the United States. The industrial planners control not only the research budget, but the production of the scientific instrumentation needed for research.

The ability to offer long-range forecasting and planning based on a scientific approach and system analysis is becoming politically essential to ensure the future survival of a world on the brink of ecological catastrophe. With the explosion of ecological movements characterized by strong emotions and passionately held opinions, it is not often recognized that only serious scientific research holds the key to non-nuclear ecological survival. Industry in the age of stagnation was stimulated by windfall revenue, and as a result we have developed an infrastructure for our society that does not lend itself to the concept of long-term scientifically-based planning. Just as humankind would be unable to survive against the nuclear threat without the new thinking on universal values suggested by Gorbachev, so also there would be no survival in the face of environmental catastrophes without adopting new scientific thinking.

Unfinished reforms

In spite of the recent efforts to enhance glasnost and democracy in the Soviet Union, reform in the field of science has been minimal. Far too much scientific research remains classified on the grounds of its alleged military importance, and too much research in other fields is still immune to criticism. In addition to these difficulties, researchers also often lack modern tools, such as computers.

Consider the space programme, with which I am most familiar. We have put too much emphasis on manned flight at the expense of unmanned efforts that produce more scientific information at a lower cost. Open discussion might have contributed to a more balanced programme. However, the United States has demonstrated that open discussion alone does not guarantee scientific wisdom. After years of debate over the advantages of manned versus unmanned space missions, the United States has, in the end, put too much emphasis on the manned space shuttle program. US space scientists must wait for the expensive and much-delayed shuttle to lift their payloads into space. The US aerospace industry, like the Soviet industry bureaucracies, used its influence to subvert the logic of science. Space science suffers, while industry profits, but in the end it is the nation that is disadvantaged. Open discussion helps scientists reach consensus, but scientists also must have more influence in making science-related decisions.

An even more striking example of a voluntaristic approach to the taking of serious technological decisions was the decision to proceed with the development of an extremely expensive reusable space transport 'Buran' ('Snowstorm'). Nobody could deny its technological ingenuity, but it is clear for those who have access to contemporary information on the state of the art in certain areas that although it is a technological wonder, it has no mission and no applications in which it could in any way compete with existing expendable boosters. In addition it is a huge economic burden and a severe drain on the budget of the country. The country has more urgent needs during the first years of perestroika. It needs a rapid boost to its economy, to the material life of its citizens. I would say that in such conditions, in which many more direct threats are faced, disposable syringes are much more important than reusable rockets.

To speed computerization

Computers have become invaluable to scientific research, enabling scientists to tackle problems that would otherwise be insurmountable. But while researchers throughout the world are taking advantage of these magnificent tools, Soviet research workers and engineers resemble soldiers attempting to fight a modern war with crossbows. Soviet industry's inefficiency in developing this technology, and the Government's reluctance to become dependent on Western technology, means that Soviet research institutes must build their own computers, which is incredibly time-consuming and expensive. The Space Research Institute, for example, had to build a 'domestic' computer to process the data from the Vega mission to Halley's comet; without this computer we would not have been able to receive the data from the Giotto spacecraft, which encountered the comet a few days after the Vega. Under more routine conditions, access to even the most elementary personal computer for many scientists would dramatically improve their productivity.

Restoring international cooperation

Today, international cooperation is essential for maintaining a significant place in the world of science. We take special pride in the X-ray astronomy research that led to the discovery of hard radiation from the supernova 1987a; this discovery was made by the international observatory Kvant aboard the Mir space station. But we must share credit with the Japanese observatory aboard the robotic spacecraft Ginga.

The Vega mission to study Halley's comet was another striking example of successful cooperation. Nine nations working together from as early as 1980 formed an island of scientific brotherhood and glasnost. The Phobos mission to study the moon of Mars of that name included twelve countries.

One goal of perestroika is to break out of our recent scientific isolation. I can remember when many years ago my young colleagues and I were admonished by an experienced administrator before going to a big international conference: 'It will be difficult to avoid contacts. Therefore your task is to give them a kopeck's worth of information in exchange for a ruble's worth.' Such short-sighted thinking has impaired Soviet science far more than it has helped. Conditions used to be different: Could Peter Kapitsa have achieved what he did without the many years he spent at Rutherford's laboratory in the 1920s and 1930s? Would Lev Landau have been as successful without his work at Niels Bohr's institute in the 1930s? I doubt it. We have begun to restore openness and relax our restrictions on international cooperation, but we have a long way to go.

Vladislav G. Teryaev

It is commonly believed that a surgeon has somewhat unusual fingers. Some compare them with the sensitive fingers of a musician, others with those of a watchmaker. Professor V. G. Teryaev has quite ordinary hands. His everyday, almost homely, appearance makes us think of a rural general practitioner who is a god in medicine and, at the same time, owner of the neighbouring farmstead.

But a closer look reveals behind his unpretentious appearance a man of strong will and energy, qualities so necessary for the manager of the biggest teaching hospital in Moscow, the Sklifosovsky Research Institute of Emergency Medical Care. As a small boy he entered this Temple of Surgery when his mother worked there as a medical assistant. Later it became his home, first as a student and postgraduate of the Sechenov 1st Moscow Medical Institute, then as a junior member of the teaching staff at the Sechenov Institute's Department of Surgery. He then moved as first junior and then senior researcher to the Sklifosovsky Institute of Emergency Care, heading the Scientific and Clinical Section and, finally, became director of the entire Institute. Before taking up this appointment Vladislav Teryaev was for twelve years entrusted with the highly responsible and prestigious post of Chief Surgeon of Moscow.

Unwilling to stop half-way with any of his undertakings, as well as being the Institute director, he carries on with his research and teaching. He is also Chairman of the Scientific Council on Emergency Medicare at the Presidium of the USSR Academy of Medical Sciences, Chairman of the Issue Research Centre at the Ministry of Health, Russian Federation, and Head of the Department of Emergency Care at the Moscow Institute of Stomatology.

He is married, with two children and two grandchildren in whom he takes great pride.

The Whole World Gave Us a Helping Hand
The phase of isolation

VLADISLAV G. TERYAEV

Approximately a year ago I helped to treat the victims of a terrible rail accident. A high-speed train went off the rails, and as I was helping the burnt people to overcome their physical and moral traumas, I heard the following story from one of my colleagues who had arrived somewhat earlier at the scene of the accident. In one of the carriages there was a husband, his wife and their fifteen-year-old daughter. After the accident the girl was trapped between the seats. While the mother got out through the window, the father tried to set his daughter free. At that instant the carriage caught fire, and, propelled by the flow of air, the flames headed for their victims. At the last instant the wife, with a superhuman effort, pulled her husband through the window, while the flames swallowed up their daughter.

How can a human being continue living after that? How can he or she come to terms with the loss of an only child, future grandchildren, and the future itself? Very often recently I sense a vague feeling of anxiety. I cannot rest in peace while nursing the thought: What if the last yesterday, last month or year were the crucial turning point that deprives us of the future? A slow rate of change, and economic and social reforms only half-way through accomplishment, more and more often cause disappointment and irritation in people. They sound an alarm over the fate of perestroika.

We are scared by the consequences of the economic crisis. We are disappointed that the material provisions of our health care system could easily compete in their wretchedness with those of some developing countries. Equipment in our in- and out-patient establishments is obsolete, and when doctors write a prescription for their patients they think not of the most effective preparation, but of the one that is available at a pharmacy.

At the same time we are scared of lagging behind perestroika, our progress towards democracy and openness. I mean not only the discussion of previously prohibited topics in the press and freedom of speech at meetings. I interpret glasnost as a compulsory condition for a breakthrough in my field, that of disaster medicine.

I

At this instant I catch in myself the desire to put this phrase into inverted commas – it grates upon the ears. Decades of complacency, when disasters of different origins and scale were either hushed up or distorted, or habitual statements that 'no victims were registered', make this phrase sound extremely inappropriate and rather harsh.

What was the purpose of concealing the truth from the people? Least of all, I presume, did they worry about upsetting the nation. Most likely the decisive role was played by purely ideological considerations: in the world's most advanced society, man is not scared even by natural calamities. We never learned the lesson of the 1949 earthquake in Ashkhabad that killed 100,000 people. Their deaths were thus unable to help those who, forty years later on 7 December 1988, happened to be at the epicentre of the earthquake in Armenia. For this we must blame the bureaucrat who filed away all the documents of the tragedy as 'TOP SECRET', hiding them together with the victims.

I learned about disaster medicine, previously unknown to us, far from the USSR when extending international assistance to the victims of earthquakes in Peru and Algeria. First came Peru. Jointly with a team of doctors I was supposed to travel in the first of two jumbo planes loaded with medicines and food. But plans changed, and we had to take the second plane. When we reached the site of the earthquake, we found that the first plane had been lost. Several months later, the site of the aircrash was found. Disaster medicine, I realized, has its own specificity. I tell my young colleagues who themselves decide to try in that domain that a hot spot is not at all safe, even when the worst has happened.

Ten years later in 1980 I had to work hand in hand with French colleagues. At the time I was staggered to learn that, six hours after the earthquake, they had arrived at the site, set up an outpatient clinic and begun to dress the wounded. Whereas we arrived in El-Asnam twelve days later – that much time was needed to get passports and visas. Later, reading the specialist literature, I found out that it was a nineteenth-century French doctor, Larret, chief surgeon of the Napoleonic army, who pioneered the idea of emergency surgical care units, delivered by horses to the combat zone. But that did not reassure me, since in similar conditions even Napoleon's healers would have left us behind . . .

On my return from Algeria I wrote a detailed memo in which I proposed, after analysing what had been seen and done, concrete measures for the radical improvement of medicare in emergency situations. They included a complex of measures in preparation for possible natural calamities and other catastrophes. It was proposed to provide special training for doctors, to hold large-scale medical manoeuvres with the involvement of other auxiliary and rescue services. It described even methods for the examination of victims of catastrophes. This memo was sent to the USSR Ministry of Health. Eight years later, after the tragedy in Armenia, I tried to locate the document. Alas, the search was abortive.

Bureaucracy effectively destroys innovations that challenge obsolete dogmas and concepts. It has failed and cannot protect us from the accidents, explosions and natural calamities which regularly occur despite bureaucratic optimism and self-sufficiency. The victims were not left entirely to the mercy of fate, and doctors did their best to save their lives and health. But each time we had to begin everything anew, hampered by muddle and low qualifications, losing precious time. Whereas each lost minute in these conditions cannot be retrieved: an hour after an accident up to 40 per cent of heavily-injured people die, mounting to 60 per cent in three hours and 95 per cent in six hours.

The Sklifosovsky Research Institute of Emergency Medical Care, in which I have the honour to work, was ordered by the USSR Ministry of Health to render emergency care to the victims of the railway disaster near Bologoye only eight(!) hours after the accident and two hours after the admission of the last injured person to the local hospital. But this is not the end of the story. Forty doctors, summoned through the warning system used only in emergency situations, spent another six hours, that is the whole night at the Institute, completely lost, until 'through my own channels' I managed to obtain truthful information as to the scale of the catastrophe and the possibility of taking part in overcoming its consequences.

At the disaster site the turn of events followed the same course as many times before. The emergency action plans, drawn up by civil defence and kept in the nearby medical establishments, turned out to be absolutely useless in a real catastrophe. They were soon forgotten. All the rescue teams operated independently, without contacting each other, making hasty decisions in the heat of the moment. This could not help reducing the effectiveness of their actions. As a rule, decision-makers of every kind did not have information on the development of events and did not clearly understand their functions in organizing rescue operations. Top ranking officials were sent to the accident site 'to act as they saw fit'. But without experience and special training, they cramped initiative and interfered in everything. There was virtually no overall direction of the rescue work.

Leafing through the experts' reports on those events, for the first time based on international methodological principles and criteria, I see how fine is the line separating stupidity and cruelty, incompetence and crime. It was only a miracle that saved us from further tragic events: owing to the slow response of the Ministry of Railways and Communications, a passenger train heading for Leningrad was allowed into the disaster zone when the carriages of the express train were already on fire. It was only a break in the contact wire that stopped the train.

Slowly but surely we learned our lessons. In October 1988

two goods trucks loaded with explosives blew up at Sverdlovsk-Sortirovochnaya railway station, forming a crater 60 metres in diameter and 10 metres deep. (The power of the explosion was such that the points, weighing 1,560 kg, were hurled 1.5 km away.) The rescue services, and doctors in particular, acted more effectively, and medicare for the victims was provided in good time and adequately. Intensive therapy teams began to operate in the accident zone during the first hour after the explosion. Medics sorted the wounded into categories, the most important element of emergency care that helps to save the maximum number of survivors. Thirty-six ambulances quickly transported the injured to hospitals. No doubt there were communication problems due to a shortage of equipment, and they deprived rescue teams of timely information on mutual actions and prevented effective joint efforts. But still there was some progress.

'Each national catastrophe should become an instructive lesson for the whole of mankind' reads the motto of one international organization that coordinates international assistance during natural calamities and technological catastrophes. We have learned this lesson through our own ignorance and miscalculations.

Leninakan on the day of the earthquake staggered me not by the scale of the destruction – I have been through this experience in my life – but by the huge number of people suffering from shock. It was not depression but profound psychic trauma. Those brought to the hospital remained fully immobilized. A frozen look was replaced by arbitrary floating movements of their eyes. Respiration in many of them was almost invisible. It was only when you looked attentively that you could see them breathe. The state of some young people with minimal physical injuries caused greater anxiety than people with serious injuries and crushed extremities.

Unintentionally I am beginning to use medical terminology, but it is rather difficult to describe what we have seen and encountered without it. These were the unusual conditions in which our field hospital based at the central district hospital of Maralik settlement operated not far from Leninakan on the road to Erevan. (We were unable to set up our field hospital in

Leninakan itself, since most of the medical establishments in the city had been destroyed.)

Half an hour after our team arrived we began to operate in the disaster zone. Experienced doctors, who have often worked in emergency situations and had to deal with many wounded, examined the patients and selected those to be operated on and those who needed infusion therapy. In parallel, conservative treatment was provided, plaster bandages applied, etc. For two days our work was virtually continuous. One emergency team would replace another. Eight hundred and ten victims received urgent medicare over a short period of time. The patients with the most serious injuries received further treatment at our Institute in Moscow.

It was in Armenia for the first time that we used a fully-fledged national variant of disaster medicine. Summing up the results of our work, we prepared a document on 'The System of Medico-Social and Medico-Biological Protection of the Population in the USSR Against Natural Calamities and Technological Catastrophes'. It emphasizes that 'the unification of efforts on an international scale is essential for the successful overcoming of consequences of natural calamities and catastrophes. Such an approach would tally with human interests, and the tendency towards internationalizing the efforts of nations to solve ecological and other global problems. It would create a new image of our country in international public opinion.'

This time our memo did not sink into oblivion and the words on the 'internationalization of efforts' were not just interpreted as a whim. Not only did we have new leaders and ministers, which is also very important, but also what we tried to prove became evident for one and all: we need reliable protection from both natural and growing technological cataclysms, and international cooperation in overcoming their consequences.

II

Medics use the term, the 'phase of isolation'. This is the initial period after the injury when the victim may count only on himself or on other victims, on the assistance of those who do not have special training. It is only a doctor who happens to be in the disaster zone who can help the wounded until emergency care teams take over and start the next 'phase of rescue measures'.

The 'phase of isolation' means the delay in treating the injured caused by objective difficulties. The shorter this phase, the more saved lives, the fewer dramas. How unnatural then are past efforts to prolong this phase, by the policy of non-recognition over many years that disregarded disaster medicine. How unnatural to prolong this phase physically and morally by ignoring international cooperation that for a long time has helped many other countries to overcome more effectively the consequences of accidents.

Foreign colleagues with whom I worked in Armenia and then recently in Ufa told me that no country is capable of rendering emergency care on its own for such a great number of mutilated, wounded and burnt people. If the same situation happened in our country, we would also have appealed to other countries for help, they said.

The pain and wounds of Armenia helped everyone to realize that we all live on one planet. Having accepted a helping hand, which is quite natural, we have demonstrated that we are not only civilized people, but that we want to live in one family, sharing misfortune and joy, kindness and compassion.

When Armenians were freed from under the débris and saw the unfamiliar faces of their rescuers and heard a strange language, they not only understood that their lives were safe but tasted the fruit of new thinking. The life that had been returned to them was quite different from the one they lived two, three or four days before.

Quite indicative was the timing of this assistance. Let us take only one day, 9 December. 16.30: 64 French rescuers arrived with medicines and equipment. 18.17: 37 Swedish rescuers were brought by a charter flight to Erevan. 19.00: 85 more rescuers arrived from France . . . Directly from the airport they were taken to Leninakan and Spitak, where they immediately began their rescue work and to provide medical care.

By 31 January this year, material assistance including medicines, equipment and clothes to the value of 117 million dollars had been sent to Armenia, an unprecedented action in the history of mankind. Sixty-seven countries gave a helping hand. Although a characteristic trauma in earthquakes is compression of the extremities, renal deficiency comes first. In December alone, within the framework of international assistance, four artificial kidney machines were sent to hospitals in Armenia by the USA, two from Great Britain, four from Sweden, and also from the Federal Republic of Germany, the Netherlands . . .

When the oil pipeline exploded in Ufa in summer 1989, setting fire to hundreds of people, adults and children in all the carriages of two passenger trains, both Soviet and foreign doctors worked together, helping each other.

During the first stage we did our best to save lives and to promote the functioning of the most vital organs. Besides vast burns of the skin many victims had burns of the upper respiratory tract. We looked into their mouths and were horrified: gold crowns in live people had melted, although gold melts at 800 degrees Centigrade!

To bring them out of shock we needed modern equipment for infusion therapy, artificial ventilation of the lungs. We had to do this not in specialized big hospitals, but locally in Ufa and Chelyabinsk, since seriously injured patients could not be transported. This and other equipment was brought by surgeons, traumatologists and intensive therapists from the USA, Britain, West Germany, Australia, Austria, France and other countries.

Complex medical teams, including all types of specialists from a surgeon to medical assistants and technicians, worked highly effectively. Among them were three teams of US army doctors who arrived at the request of President Bush. Another group, led by the West German Professor R. Hettich, consisted of eight specialists who brought unique apparatus for artificial kidney transplantation with them.

When you thank somebody, you have to thank people personally. But it is very difficult to do, since I did not meet all our colleagues from other countries who came to help us in the hot days of June. And this help is still coming. New medical teams begin to work in our hospitals as burns take long to heal. Therefore I apologize for such a generalization: I thank all those who did not leave us in our hour of trouble.

We are learning to answer handshakes. But one should not

only be ready to accept help, but also to be ready to give a helping hand. To be able to do it we have to get rid our health services of their many shortcomings.

III

I may seem to be illogical, but among all the other problems I would give priority to that of personnel. True, our medics worked selflessly in Sverdlovsk and Leninakan, Ufa and Ferghana, saving hundreds of lives. Neither do I doubt the sincerity of our foreign colleagues who praised the professionalism of Soviet doctors. Still I cannot ignore the low professionalism and plain absence of responsibility among many rank-and-file medics. What other evidence is needed of the profound moral crisis of our medicine if there were cases of infecting children with AIDS *via* syringes, or when rats ate a newborn baby in a Central Asian maternity home? (This case was described by Evgeni Chazov, the USSR Minister of Health.)

No doubt this crisis did not occur today. I am proud that I was entrusted to manage a talented team of doctors at the Sklifosovsky Research Institute of Emergency Medical Care. But, earlier, I did not even dare to think that I would one day become the director of the hospital in which my father had died many years earlier as a result of the negligence of his doctors and the ensuing complications! It so happened that soon afterwards I listened to a lecture by my father's former doctor. He underscored the low rate of postoperational mortality, and all the students applauded him wholeheartedly – nobody knew that my father's case was also included in that 'low rate'.

An essential role in the devaluation of the medical professions and the gradual lowering of their moral and intellectual level has been played by low salaries. Even today, after an increase of salaries, a beginner receives 140–150 rubles and a doctor with ten years of seniority will still only get 160–170. They can only barely make ends meet with this amount.

The famous eye-surgeon Svyatoslav Fyodorov has proved that a miraculous transformation can take place if there is a differentiated evaluation of the quantity and quality of work: surgeons, therapists and nurses work two to three times more effectively than with a guaranteed 'poverty allowance'. But how can you convince the non-specialist decision-makers that this operation is of a higher quality? That this doctor is worth more, and therefore has the right to 600–800 rubles a month? How can you prove the advantages of such an approach?

Fyodorov, from my point of view, has found a brilliant answer. He rented a small dairy farm from a Moscow region state farm which was in a very bad way and introduced there the same system of payments as in his clinic. Two months later a formerly unprofitable dairy farm became profitable and yields of milk almost doubled. His employees now get up to 1,000 rubles a month and say that there is still room for improvement.

We should not economize with medicine. The state that grudges money for doctors reminds me of a miserly landowner in a Gogol novel who scolds peasants for laziness although he keeps them underfed. In the meantime there are two alternatives to make them stop being lazy: to make them free of their labour dues or at least to feed them properly.

We have to raise salaries of doctors differentially in the nearest future. This will allow us to be more demanding in selecting future students for medical institutes and picking their future professions. Besides, an improvement in training would promote the expansion of ties with scientific and academic institutions in other countries, including training abroad. All this would increase the prestige of the medical professions and the quality of medical care.

Another problem is the provision of health services with modern equipment and medicine. If the shortage of the latest diagnostic instruments causes vexation, the absence of the most primitive disposable systems is simply shameful. Luckily our foreign colleagues who arrived in Armenia and Ufa were quite well informed of our problems and did not ask us where to buy disposable syringes or surgical stockings – they brought equipment with them. But how long will this shame last?

Great hopes are placed on military conversion. One may develop an impression that workers at former military plants will put up a good show since they lost their former jobs. But these fine fellows will not only be manufacturing medical equipment; they have also been made responsible for the mechanization of agriculture and for bridging many other gaps in our economy, therefore they will not have too much time for us. And then they are not so simple-minded: people already complain of the high prices charged for the goods manufactured at former military plants and of the unwillingness to produce what does not give immediate profit.

I presume that the hopes for conversion will be justified only in the distant future. Today we need hard currency to purchase the technologies necessary for the manufacture of high-quality medical equipment, diagnostic and therapeutic instruments, possibly jointly with foreign firms and cooperatives.

Of no less importance is the provision of medicines. Many pharmaceutical enterprises are very out of date and their equipment is physically and morally obsolete. Besides, prices for medicines are extremely low and it is unprofitable to produce them. We can revive the pharmaceutical industry by relating prices to the costs of production. To prevent high prices from telling on the patient, we have to introduce a system of social insurance into the health services, when the bigger part of the price is covered by the State, trade unions and the enterprise at which a patient is employed.

True, sceptics reject the possibility of introducing this system into our country, arguing that the majority of enterprises have miserly profits, lack social funds and will therefore not be able to pay for the treatment of their workers.

So we come back to my primary concern: without a solution of the global problems there will be no solution of our specific needs. Without radical economic reform we shall not raise the level of medical care, of which disaster medicine forms an important element.

And, *vice versa*, the phase of isolation will be the shorter, the faster perestroika involves the economic and moral fundamentals of our life. And the shorter the phase of isolation, the more survivors and people rescued.

Religion

Mikhail P. Kulakov

He was born in Leningrad in 1927 and in 1946 finished at the Arts School in Ivanov. In 1947 he was arrested on false charges and sentenced to five years in prison and a life-long exile. He was rehabilitated in 1954. He received his theological education by correspondence at the Adventist Academy in Washington, USA – he is a Doctor of Theology. Now Mikhail Kulakov is a pastor at the church of the Seventh Day Adventists and Chairman of the Council of Churches of the Seventh Day Adventists in the RSFSR (the Russian Federation). He is married, with three sons and three daughters, who all share the religious convictions of their parents.

An Open Door

MIKHAIL P. KULAKOV

> 'Therefore all things whatsoever ye would that men should do to you, do ye even so to them' (Gospel According to St Matthew, 7:12).

The stride of history leaves an indelible mark on our destinies, and the life of each man goes to confirm this unavoidable rule of human existence. My nearest and dearest, my co-religionists and myself, have experienced many hardships and sufferings, and as I look back it is with ever greater hope that I welcome the democratic changes happening in this country, with ever greater willingness contribute, as far as possible, to their advance and have a greater certainty about the future. As a minister of the Seventh Day Adventist Church (which, incidentally, has members in almost 200 countries of the world), I am, of course, primarily concerned with freedom of conscience and toleration. This is not to say that freedom of conscience is not all that important for the Orthodox or Muslim citizens of our country. It is equally important for everyone, believers and non-believers alike, but our church, which emerged in the middle of last century as a result of an unprejudiced study of the Bible, perhaps places a somewhat greater emphasis on freedom of conscience and the freedom to express various views and beliefs, as it has a special reason for doing so.

From what we know of Him, God respects the freedom of the individual, his choice and his self-expression. This attitude of the Creator is the basis for the development and strengthening of a salutary love. It rejects violence as a matter of principle, even for the sake of a noble cause. It should be stressed in particular that even the omnipotent God, who has absolute powers, having shown us the way to truth and salvation, does not permit Himself to *force* us to follow such a course. Would it not be a tragic delusion for believers or non-believers to use violence to bring mankind to happiness? Violence can breed violence, of which mankind's bitter experience is an indisputable confirmation.

There is a certain link between *a* freedom as understood by Christians and freedoms social and political. As can be seen from the history of freedom, the protection of religious freedom has quite often opened the door to political and social freedom. At the same time, it cannot be overlooked that throughout the centuries Christians often committed brutal violence against other people's consciences themselves, in defiance of their teaching and principles. And yet it is in the protestant tradition that we find the religious roots of modern freedom and a basis for democratic ideals.

True, the freedom we have is directly related to the high risk of making a wrong choice. I will not recall the first few chapters of 'Being', which record the tragic circumstances that occurred as a result of delusion suffered by our great-grand-parents. I will not mention Christ, who called on man for a freedom that is real through learning the truth about God, either. I will permit myself to go back to the historical developments of the not so distant past. A thoughtful and unprejudiced analysis will show that the devaluation of notions such as the dignity and the sacred nature of the individual is associated with the erosion of the concept of the divine creation of man. Renunciation of common values for the sake of class interests put above all else and success of the revolution at any price must lead to unfreedom as an *all-pervading principle* of the new society. The idea was grasped by Vladimir Galaktionovich Korolenko, a splendid writer and a great citizen. In one of his letters to A. V. Lunacharsky, which were left unanswered, he wrote bitterly: 'You offer the first example of Socialism introduced by suppressing freedom. What good will it come to? I would not like to be a prophet, but my heart sinks at the feeling that we may be yet on the brink of calamities which will make our present hardships look trivial.' Anatoli Vasilyevich was trying to convince the people's commissar for education when he saw him in Poltava in June 1920: 'You keep saying that you are "compelled" to do what you do, but you have provoked an outpouring of animosity, are breaking off against a swarm of enemies and are becoming embittered yourselves. You have butchers and people who have joined the army only to cut human flesh just as they would slaughter cattle. If you want to have a classless society, a society of communist commonwealth, you must more than anybody else revere the human being. And you trample it under foot.'

Korolenko is for Socialism, since only Socialism, the writer believes, having carefully preserved the best achievements of capitalism, is able to ensure social justice. But at the same time he categorically *rejects* a Socialism which rises out of a trampled freedom and which is sustained through terror against its people. 'You have killed the free press,' writes Korolenko. 'You have made an insurgent and excited people believe that the so-called bourgeoisie ('the bourgeois') is nothing but a class of spongers and robbers who clip their coupons. You have conquered the capital, and it is lying at your feet, all bruised and battered. Only you have failed to see that the bonds uniting the capital and production are so vital that, having killed the capital, you have killed production. Summary executions,' Korolenko goes on to say, 'are carried out in dozens . . . I do not think the good of the people can be served by any means at all. There is no doubt in my mind that the firing squads which have operated on a regular administrative basis for a second year running are a case in point.'

I am not referring to this letter to draw comparisons among or to pass judgment on various political systems, as it is not my business to do so. The above cited letter, I think, firmly supports the truth that the liberation of man is primarily a matter of morals, and so it is to be accomplished by moral means. The Christianity I profess sees the solution to problems facing the world today to be the reshaping of our thinking. A divine solution must and can be found to the problems of mankind.

Religion and believers in this country have had hard times to go through. This is mainly due to a violation of the socially indispensable democratic principles – so much so that we found ourselves deprived of the freedom of choice. At the same time, Adventists are convinced (and they base themselves on the teaching of the Saviour and His Apostles) that if democracy is to remain democracy, it is one principle it cannot do without. Of course, the freedom to express one's views and beliefs and freedom of speech must go together with respect for other people's views and freedoms. However, no president or clergyman has a discretionary right to silence those whose ideas and voices are not in consonance with generally accepted views. Nothing can be more dangerous for society than a conscious and violent suppression of human rights and freedoms, especially the freedom of conscience and the right to express one's beliefs freely.

My grandfather on the paternal side, Stepan Viktorovich Kulakov, was a very religious and orthodox person. He came from a peasant family, lived on the Don, in the *stanitsa* of Tarasovka, Millerovsky region, and in 1906 the Don *host* elected him deputy to the First State Duma. He had no systematic education, but was keen on literature and art. He was particularly fond of things religious, including biblical prophecies. It was in Petersburg that a poster once caught his eye. It announced lectures which offered interpretations of the prophetic books of the Bible. As he attended the lectures, Grandfather became acquainted with the lecturer and, through him, with other Adventists. In a little while, his family, many of his relatives and himself adopted Adventism.

It is said that the Spirit breathes where It will. And, although Adventism was brought to Russia by the Germans (the first community was set up by Konradi in the Crimea in 1886), it is Ivan Chernyi, Fyodor Kuritsin and Feodosii Kosoy, Russian protestants of the sixteenth and seventeenth centuries, whom we consider as our spiritual forerunners. Their views, particularly those of Feodosii Kosoy, are identical with ours on some of the issues. F. Kosoy saw God and His Word as the ultimate authority. He believed that God and man are related to each other like Father and son, not like master and servant. I am saying all this to underscore once again that the Reformation, which had such a strong and profound influence on the historical destinies of most countries of Europe, did involve Russia, although it did not cause any turbulent cataclysms in the form of religious wars. Therefore it had paved the way for Adventism, which came to Russia from abroad.

Speaking about history, I cannot help mentioning the difficulties the Adventists communities in Russia encountered from the very outset. Not only did the dominant church, which, as is well known, was the Russian Orthodox church before the revolution, fail to recognize religious dissent, it bitterly fought all those who sought to find their own way to God and their way to the Truth. As early as the seventeenth century our history had been marked by a bloody persecution of the Old Believers, which did not cease before 1905. The Adventists had their share of persecution. The cup of suffering they drank may not be comparable to the fate that befell Old Believers, but arrests, prison cells and internal exile did not spare members of our church, either. My grandfather on the paternal side, Demidov by name, who adopted Adventism at the end of the past century (my mother was born in 1902 to an Adventist family), was subjected to harassment and persecution by the Orthodox priests of Taganrog, Rostov-on-the Don and Northern Caucasus who were jealous of his success as a preacher. He was often arrested, put in prison and subjected to administrative exile – probably in the hope that no man can withstand violence indefinitely, however firm his beliefs.

The determination to break the will of an undesired personality who dared to espouse and express 'non-standard' views is what is probably rooted in the sinful nature of man, which often takes a dramatic turn in unhappy families and undemocratic states. At the same time, there is no suppressing man's inherent striving for spiritual freedom by violence. Violence is impotent, like the fig-tree which, according to the Gospel, is to be cut down and cast into the fire. And indeed, for all the persecutions, not only did Adventism survive in tsarist Russia, it grew stronger and also won hundreds and thousands of zealous supporters, who firmly believe that the Holy Scripture is the Law of Freedom. As King David, author of many psalms, said: 'I shall walk free, for I have sought Thy precepts.'

Originally the new socio-political system which emerged as a result of the Great October Socialist revolution and which made equality of believers and non-believers constitutional made it possible for members of Christian communities to practise and disseminate their religion and to participate directly in the making of a new life. For example, the Seventh Day Adventists had two magazines published in Moscow and Kiev, and a third one in German came out in Saratov. Adventists even had a small hospital in the city of Marx in the Saratov *oblast'*. The progress Adventists and other protestants made in agriculture was praised by V. D. Bonch-Bruyevich. He wrote to *Pravda* (no. 108 of 1924) that religious believers are so hard working and industrious that it would be a criminal mistake not to use their labour for the purposes of the national economy. Who could have thought then that in just three years' time the Seventh Day Adventist church would be subjected to a persecution the like of which it had never experienced throughout its existence in Russia.

My uncle, Alexandre Mikhailovich Demidov (who now lives in Kalinin) was at the time the editor of *The Voice of Truth*, an Adventist magazine published in Moscow. In 1928 he felt that publishing the magazine was becoming increasingly difficult. The publishers finally told Alexandre Mikhailovich they would no longer produce *The Voice of Truth*, and the manager referred to a Party conference which had made up its mind that religion should die out before too long. The manager was fond of invoking images in conversation. 'You know,' he said to my uncle, 'sugar will dissolve in a cup of tea, anyway. But if you stir the sugar with a teaspoon, it will do so quicker!'

The state was extensively using the royal 'spoon': the Russian Orthodox church had been broken up, tens of leading clergymen, hundreds of priests and thousands of believers had been liquidated or put into labour camps. Prosecution was inflicted on Old Believers, Catholics and Muslims ... It was now the turn of our church, which had about 16,000 members by the late 1920s. By 1933–34 all its leaders and preachers were in prison.

My father, an Adventist preacher, was arrested in Tula in 1935. I was eight years old at the time, and I remember well how we carried parcels to prison and how Father would come up to the window to greet us with a waving hand (the windows were still 'unmuzzled'). This is how our family's crusade began.

AN OPEN DOOR

As a matter of fact, it was nothing out of the ordinary as far as our national destiny was concerned. A similar road to unhappiness was followed by millions of citizens of our unfortunate Fatherland. I am not telling the story of the trying experiences to which my nearest and dearest were subjected to halo myself in the aura of martyrdom. I simply want our drop of suffering and our destiny to be yet another example of the inhuman nature of the spiritual unfreedom which held us all prisoner, believers and non-believers alike.

We lived in internal exile in a remote settlement of the Krasnoyarsk region until 1939 before we moved to Ivanovo. It was from Ivanovo that Stephan, my elder brother, went to the front – to go as far as Berlin and to come home as an officer honoured with battlefield decorations, only to find himself in prison, which he was not destined to survive. In Ivanovo Father continued to preach. A community had been formed, and people were coming to our place for divine services. They had a burning desire for things spiritual, and Father did what he could to help the people, being well aware of the high risk involved. He was convinced that he must bring the divine Word to the hearts and minds of his compatriots. He considered it his moral duty to bear witness to God. He continued his service until that winter night when they took him away.

The hearings of the *oblast'* court were held in camera, but it was possible to hide behind a cupboard in the dark corridor and see Father escorted to the courtoom. One could tiptoe to the courtroom door and try to hear what they were saying. Father was charged with anti-Soviet propaganda. But the charges were so absurd and unfounded that the trial had to be postponed three times because of the lack of evidence. Before he was able to say a word, Father would be cut short by the counsel for the prosecution, who insisted that he keep to the point instead of just speaking about religion. Father would reply that religion was the main point and essence of his life and that it was religion his conversations with people were about, those conversations they were trying to portray as anti-Soviet propaganda. The court-appointed lady counsel for the defence ended up with a passionate and positive statement about my father's innocence. He was sentenced to ten years in a labour camp.

The community Father had established was now my responsibility. I began to conduct services and to preach, and now that I recall that difficult and wonderful time I feel that I was really happy. It was as though I took over a burning candle from Father's hands and stood up at the doorway, the doors wide open, inviting people to hear the divine Word and to follow His truth and His way.

Quite soon I graduated from a college of arts, not without difficulties, and saw that there was no place for me in Ivanovo, except in prison. We moved to the city of Daugavpils in Latvia, and lived there for eight months. I took up a job as a schoolteacher. I read a lot, as I was fortunate enough to find in Latvia the literature in German I needed to resolve distressing spiritual predicaments. It was there that I met some of my co-religionists . . . Two security officers came to arrest me at school. 'To have such a snake nurtured in the bosom of the nation,' one of them said as they drove me to prison. 'And an educated man at that,' replied the other. I felt no anger or hatred for these people, nor for Mr Kurochkin, the investigating officer who conducted the case in Ivanovo (where they took my brother, who was arrested the same day as me, and myself), nor for the prison governor, who even prided himself on a model inmate, which I was. I had realized already that those people, subservient and miserable in their own way, were not the only reason for all that was happening. These were some general laws, a national blindness and a nationwide and profound delusion.

The questions of who made all this happen and what for are still very relevant. For if we are to have a truly democratic society, we must clearly understand the reasons why religion and believers were subjected to harsh persecutions for several decades. The root causes of these highly anti-democratic processes are to be found, let me repeat, dear reader, in the sinful nature of man, who is liable to suppress and oppress his fellow men. At a certain time in our history, this brought the country to a command-and-adminster system of government and set our society on the course of a barrack-room Socialism, characterized by a dreary uniformity of thinking and the suppression of freedom of conscience. Such an intolerance of dissent has manifested itself under all totalitarian systems and régimes and at all times. In their extreme forms, such secular or spiritual systems of power did not only hinder social development, but also, quite often, provoked intercommunal violence, the attitude to religion and believers invariably playing an important role.

In other words, there is good reason to believe that a disregard for the individual and the rights of the individual, which have a divine origin, and a lack of democracy will most certainly be coupled with a bitter rejection of religion in any form. The command-and-administer system, produced by complacency and power-seeking in all its forms and manifestations, will not tolerate people who are spiritually independent. And a man of religion is spiritually free.

I was sentenced to five years in a labour camp and internal exile. I have experienced a lot of hardships, but let me repeat that the last thing I want is to make myself out to be a martyr. It would be a shame for me to put on a crown of thorns, for there were beside me soldiers and army officers who languished in captivity only because they had happened to be taken prisoner after being wounded or encircled by the enemy. Having gone through the horrors of German captivity, they ended up with a twenty-five-year sentence in a labour camp. I was certainly much better off where I was – at least I knew I was suffering for my convictions. And what about them? What was their crime against the land they defended so courageously? Mindful of those people, I do not think I have a moral right to speak about my sufferings.

There is one other thing about our everyday life in the labour camp that I would like to recall. I am referring to the large ID numbers printed in black and white on our prison jackets, underwear, hats and trousers. My number was 2K839, and I shall always remember it until I die. Some of the Orthodox inmates believed their number to be the sign of an apocalyptic beast, and refused to wear it. They tore up their clothes and, of course, landed up in solitary confinement. One young man had reached the point of near exhaustion, and was dying. They were taking him out of the cell again when I came up to him, put my arm round his shoulders and tried to make him see that the God-given life charges him with a much greater responsibility than his agreement or disagreement to wear a number, which was nothing but man-printed characters. I could not make him change his mind, and he died soon.

What a great deal of trouble has been caused by violence! How many lives broken and ruined by a total disregard for freedom of conscience! It is vital to return to that principle if our Fatherland is to regain spiritual sanity. Today, freedom of conscience is still severely restricted by the letter of existing legislation. The title alone ('On Religious Cults') is bad enough. Strictly speaking, the *cult* is primarily about the rites, the prayer and the sacrament, which is what serving the divine being is about. But it is only a part, albeit a central one, of religion, which has a much broader significance. If the prohibitive Article 17 of the Soviet Government Resolution 'On the Religious Associations' of 8 April 1929 is compared to the Gospel precepts, which are moral obligations for any Christian, we shall see that Christians are unable to practise their religion in this country without running the risk of being taken to court for breaking the law. Groups studying the Bible are banned, whereas the Gospel teaches us 'to study the Scripture'; mercy and charity are prohibited, whereas, according to the Gospel, 'Thou shalt love thy neighbour as thyself.' Furthermore, a Christian ought to express this love in words and in active social deeds. All forms of religious education of children and adults are prohibited, and Jesus said: 'This Gospel shall be preached in all the world unto all nations . . .' The list goes on and on.

How on earth did the 'cult' come to replace everything else? That is the question. How was a sensible and creative profession of faith narrowed down to performing religious rites? How did believers in the Soviet Union find themselves, to all intents and purposes, the focus of constant suspicion?

Article 13 of the 1918 RSFSR Constitution said: '. . . every citizen is free to engage in religious or anti-religious propaganda'. That is a truly democratic principle which gives believers an opportunity to defend their philosophy! The principle was confirmed by Article 4 of the 1925 Constitution. However, the critical year 1929 saw the article on the 'freedom' of conscience amended. The amendments, which would be stipulated in Stalin's 1936 Constitution, read: 'Every citizen is free to perform religious rites and engage in anti-religious propaganda.' So, church and prayer for the believers, and printing houses, mass media and powerful government agencies for the atheists. They are still calling the same old tune about the enemies who had to be denied the opportunity to use religious activity against the Soviet State, in order to make us believe that such amendments were necessary. The example of my father and myself is striking evidence of the socially damaging effect of the wrong tenet of Stalin's that the class struggle intensifies as we advance to Socialism. But suppose enemies there were, and the church had to be contained here, there and everywhere. Why did the Constitution under the 'developed Socialism' leave believers with nothing but a freedom to 'perform religious rites'? Was it not a new attack of fear of enemies?

To be sure, this is not really the case. In 1929 and in 1936, genuine guarantees of freedom of conscience in the USSR were the last thing the authors of the Fundamental Law were concerned with. If N. I. Bukharin did not care about religious believers in this country, what can we say about comrades Stalin, Khrushchev and Brezhnev?

The above legislation, which is still in force *de jure*, is no longer complied with *de facto* as it is repudiated by the spirit of the modern life and by the democratic changes now under way. To give one example, members of the Seventh Day Adventist church have built out of their own resources and free of charge a new boarding-school house in the village of Zhelybino in the Tula *oblast'*. The work done was of the highest order, which has always been true of work equated with prayer. The local young people's *Molodoy Komunar* newspaper wrote: 'It is a two-storeyed brick house with a non-rusting roof. Each of the six classrooms has walls of a different colour, and the floors are made of lacquered parquetry. The first floor, which has made an excellent gym, was built by the voluntary workmen of their own free will. In fact, the entire building is a splendid piece of workmanship.'

The same newspaper published a letter from a Muscovite who had a grandmother taken ill in Tula. After a few unsuccessful attempts to find a nurse, she came to our church for help. 'It seemed a miracle that these people should be so marvellous about it, after the ordeal to which we had been subjected. The very same day, they had Grandmother taken home from hospital, arranged a twenty-four-hour vigil beside her sickbed and gave her badly needed medicines . . . They were doing all this for no payment at all. On 21 August Grandmother gave up the ghost. They stayed with her until her last breath and shared with us the grief of the funeral. I would like to express my gratitude to these people, the Seventh Day Adventists, from the bottom of my heart. Thanks to them, we were able to grasp the true meaning of the word "Mercy". Signed, G. Rybakova.' (I would like to point out in this context that serving people's needs promotes the spiritual growth of the individual. The experience of serving fills one's life with a special joy and meaning and is a step that brings one closer to God.)

The Adventists are taking care of patients in one of the Moscow hospitals. In a joint venture with a baby-food corporation owned by the Adventist World Union, and with the Soviet children's fund named after Lenin, they propose to set up production of the much needed baby-food and to run a printing house to publish secular and religious literature. Our church has helped doctors from Leningrad to visit Loma Lynda, an Adventist international medical centre in California, which is world famous for its heart transplant operations. All these are wonderful examples of the practical mercy so badly needed by our society. And is it not an irony that the same examples testify to a violation of existing legislation?

This is why the existing legislation must be changed, starting from a review of Article 52 of the USSR Constitution. The Constitution, in the spirit of the present reform of the Soviet political system, should stipulate the right to freedom of religious and anti-religious propaganda. Freedom of conscience must be ensured for everybody! We, the Adventists, think we must campaign for freedom of conscience for atheists as well. We are convinced that one man cannot be truly free if another man is unfree. One man cannot enjoy himself if another man suffers. A society cannot have spiritual sanity if at least one of its members is insulted, as his pain ought to be felt by everybody else.

* * *

AN OPEN DOOR

I was taken in an escorted truck to a settlement named Murzukul' in the Semiozyorsk region in Northern Kustanaisk *oblast'*. The settlement, surrounded by boundless steppes and populated by Kazaks and a few ethnic German families, was the place where I was to spend the rest of my life. After all, it was a lifetime exile! The terrifying meaning of the word came through to me as I looked around, hoping to see at least one tree, in vain. It was all steppe as far as the eye could see, and in the distance, a lake glittered under the burning sun.

It is a long story how little by little my life changed as the life of the country changed. Those who had sentenced me to lifetime exile had miscalculated, having counted on the stability of the existing régime. In 1955 I was already in Alma-Ata. Members of our church, who had been dispersed in the years of terror, were coming together again. Things seemed to be straightening out, and we were hoping we would be included in the thaw of the 1960s. But, unfortunately, religion and believers were in for a lot of trouble. The bureaucratic stranglehold stifled the church, and our nationwide organization was closed down by decree in December 1960.

There are two conversations from that time that I remember particularly well. 'Give us the complete list of believers!' demanded an official of the Council for Religious Affairs in Alma-Ata, when I went to see him about the registration of our Adventist community. I would reply that his demand was illegal and, to support my argument, would hand him a booklet on freedom of conscience issued by the 'Znanie' foundation, which ran a popular series. 'Those are written laws,' he would grin, 'we have unwritten laws of our own.'

I had a job as a travelling photographer in a consumer service establishment in a town of Soviet Central Asia. When they were dismissing me, the chief of personnel exclaimed: 'What a terrible mistake I have made about you! What a failure of intuition! And whoever could have told . . . You look such a decent man. Don't you see that religion is going to wither away within the next two years?'

Those conversations reflected pretty well the spirit of the time and a social attitude to religion as something of a hangover which is doomed to disappear. Well, this is only natural, as to harp on the church as the carrier of hostile ideology for the past seventy years, year after year, to regard the priest and the preacher as aliens and the believer as a 'third class' citizen is to develop a social stereotype, particularly in the minds of the Party and government officials. It is that stereotype, incidentally, which frees one's hands to use violence and makes it possible to disregard moral and legal standards.

At the same time, any violence to life, any attempt to squeeze it into a rigid system or dogma and any violation of common standards of human behaviour will entail huge economic and spiritual losses. V. I. Vernadsky, a major scholar of our century, said that democracy is freedom of thought and freedom of faith. (No Adventist would hesitate to subscribe to these words.) We have spent a long time violating these two principles, which are a *sine qua non* of normal existence of a democratic society, and are now trying hard to make them part of our life's flesh and blood.

What shall we do about it?

Education is a top priority. An education which will foster respect for freedom of conscience and tolerance of other people's views and of any kind of dissent. We, the Adventists, consider it our duty to help society to grasp the importance of dialogue and realize that it will not do to impose a uniform and mandatory philosophy, much less by brutal violence. The right to have one's own opinion is an inalienable right of any individual in a democratic society.

Society must be ruled by law. I have mentioned the necessity to amend the relevant Article of the USSR Constitution. Furthermore, a state which implements consistently democratic principles must be neutral to both religion and atheism. Let the separation of church and state be a two-way street. In that case the propaganda of atheist philosophy will probably be carried out by the Communist Party, Komsomol and independent self-financed atheist agencies. But not the State, which now uses budget resources derived from the labour of all citizens, including tens of millions of believers.

As far as the Law on the Freedom of Conscience is concerned, which we hope will soon be the subject of nationwide discussion, it must definitely grant the church the right of a legal person to enable it to protect its own interests. Besides, it must, according to the final document of the Vienna Conference, give our citizens the right to produce, purchase and use religious literature, making it equally possible for the State educational establishments to teach both atheism and religion. Our country's history has shown that entire generations were not given a basic knowledge of religion or were taught by ignorant teachers of atheism. Thereby they were deprived of access to a huge layer of world culture. This could not but affect the moral and spiritual cast of mind of the nation. It is our firm conviction that the Law on the Freedom of Conscience must open the doors of hospitals, orphanages, prisons and labour camps for the charitable activity of religious organizations. The field of mercy is unlimited!

There is a very apt observation that 'the world's fate hangs on the string of recognition of moral values.' The God-inspired longing for these values in man is great. And I am grateful to Him for the many people, believers and non-believers, who in word and in deed instil love, mercy and tolerance in human relationships. This makes me want to continue to pray that those who work for good and all those who begin to see that this work may well be the point of their lives, come united in the recognition of spiritual and moral values as those of paramount importance.

All this has tremendous significance not only for the church and believers but also for our entire society, which is striving for a democratic setting, for the State to work out a legal basis and for the people which is starved for a respectful attitude to its physical needs and to the requirements of its heart and soul. To impede this process is to attempt to split our society. We have been over that before, and, in fact, the split is so deep that it will take a great deal of moral effort to achieve the necessary understanding. We were split by Stalinism, a terror against our own people, by a spectre of a class struggle which intensifies with the building of Socialism and by fear. The years of stagnation split us by social indifference, lies and the glaring gaps between words and deeds. And now that a difficult and painstaking process is under way on the basis of democratization of the State and society, to drive a wedge between believers and non-believers will be tantamount to an outright damage to perestroika.

We consider ourselves to be staunch supporters of perestroika. We support and are committed to the new thinking. We understand it as an invitation to a reasonable and patient dialogue in international relations as well as inside the country. We see a force in perestroika which is able to break the chains of spiritual unfreedom. Now we have built an administrative and training centre in the village of Zaoksky, in the Tula *oblast'*. We also have a theological college with external instruction, hopefully with internal instruction in the near future.

We do believe, according to our religion, that a second advent of Christ is imminent. And it is our duty, as Fyodor P. Gaaz, a great Christian, put it, *to do good, wasting no time.*

For the good, the door must be wide open.

Culture

Mark A. Zakharov

Mark Zakharov was born in Moscow on 13 October 1933. He is a graduate of the Lunacharsky State Institute of Theatrical Art.

From 1955 to 1959 he was an actor at the Drama Theatre in Perm; from 1959 to 1960 he worked as an actor at the Gogol Theatre in Moscow; from 1960 to 1964 he was an actor and the director at the Moscow Theatre of Miniatures. From 1964 to 1965 Mark Zakharov was a director at the Students' Theatre of Moscow State University; from 1965 to 1973 a director at the Satire Theatre in Moscow. Since 1973 he has been with the Leninski Komsomol Theatre in Moscow, first as its main director, then as its artistic director, and now he is the manager of this theatre.

He is a People's Deputy of the USSR and a Merited Actor of the RSFSR (the Russian Federation). He was awarded the Order of People's Friendship and won the USSR State Prize for his direction of two plays, *Yunona and Avos* and *The Dictatorship of Conscience*.

Nostalgia for Meyerhold

MARK A. ZAKHAROV

It was in the summer of 1989 that astrologists made their first appearance on Soviet TV. Oddly enough, they were not insulted, as they had been in the old days, and not even laughed at. They were politely referred to as scientists. That fact alone might soon be regarded as controversial, as has often been the case in our history and art. Furthermore, our direct dependence on the configuration of celestial bodies may even soon be found totally erroneous and contradicting Engels's idea of the space system as a whole. Engels, we are convinced, knew everything we need to know, especially after joining up with Marx, and people who spent many years exposing astrology, parapsychology, telekinesis, clairvoyance and at the same time cybernetics were never in short supply.

Nevertheless, hearing new space concepts set forth on the official TV channel is a remarkable development to me. In the past two or three years, we all without exception (my optimism making itself felt) suddenly wanted to expand the borders of the universe and look into the spheres of being and spirit we did not bother about before. First, we did not, because we were afraid of too many things unknown, past and present. Second, there was no point. What was possible to learn in our art and history had already been mastered by the above classics of Marxism-Leninism and by an army of new home-grown philosophers, put together by the Central Committee of our poor one and only Party in peculiar sorts of nurseries, reserves and similar establishments, which are as mass as they are gloomy and which are raised to the level of State propaganda agencies with high salaries and secret catering services for the staff. The latter have always encouraged political loyalty and professional inspiration.

Everything beyond that inspiration remained a mystery. There was no incentive whatsoever to unravel the mystery, for, as Tutchev, a Russian poet, put it a long time ago: 'Russia cannot be understood by wit alone. Common measures cannot be applied to her. One must simply believe in Russia.'

No political or economic deadlocks in our historical development could break the habit of believing. This may be due to an unfortunate and permanent deficiency. If it runs in the genes, misbehaviour will not be corrected even by the best upbringing. If you are not going to be a thief, you will probably end up giggling as you walk past a church, anyway, and will go on breaking the traffic rules into the bargain.

It was far from me to consider myself as a completely normal and sane person as I found myself in the Kremlin as a People's Deputy in May–June 1989. But, at the same time, I insist on being one of those people who, although aware of their own limitations and bad moral and intellectual deformities, have set out, with a typical self-irony about any of their intentions, to 'take it down to the nuts and bolts'. To understand and reassess the place of the theatrical art, which I love, in the history of arts in general, with the eschatological bias typical of the Russian man. As I let myself use the phrase I was well aware of the fact that eschatology is my permanent intention to grasp the purpose of the universe, the history of the world and their ultimate destiny.

I have several clear-cut, perhaps highly subjective, views on the past and present of the Russian theatre. And many more vague guesses and dim premonitions, many of them falling short of hypotheses and remaining but a shadow of an obscure intuition. It is that secret mechanism which is often referred to as the arm of Providence, that suggests to me the most appropriate *mises en scène* and at the same time answers questions which defy reasonable answers. Nothing can be more dear to my heart than something which is completely devoid of all logic and scientific substantiation.

To be sure, N. A. Berdiayev, the great Russian orthodox philosopher, has had a far greater influence on me than K. S.

Stanislavsky. He did so both as a founding father of existentialism and as the author of the revelations that follow: 'The Russian people is highly polarized and is a combination of opposites. It can charm and disappoint and will always surprise. It has the ability to arouse extremes of strong love and strong hatred. It is the people that makes the nations of the West worried'.[1] And, finally, a judgment which, I think, has a direct bearing on my beloved Russian theatre: 'The Russian soul is like the Russian plain – immense, unbounded and infinite. Therefore, the Russian people found it difficult to have these vast areas of land managed and put into shape. The Russian people has been strong on spontaneity and relatively weak on shape. The Russians were not predominantly a people of culture, unlike the West Europeans. They were a people of revelations and inspirations. They never knew where to stop and easily leaped to extremes.'

My initial remarks on the modern theatre are based on that incomprehensible desire to leap to extremes as often as possible. N. A. Berdiayev has probably defined better than many of our theatre critics the foundation of the modern Soviet theatre on which our theatre grew, took shape, flashed and fertilized world theatrical art, went through a troubled and turbulent experience and plunged into a spell of gravest crisis, which, incidentally, is not to be seen as the end, for all our traditional affinity to the apocalyptic frame of mind.

Russia was in the prime of its spiritual and intellectual life in the late nineteenth century, according to the assumptions of the above astrologists and as foreordained by the Creator. To quote Lev Gumilev, a seditious philosopher and the son of Anna Akhmatova and Nikolai Gumilev, the outstanding Russian poets: 'The ethnic processes are driven by the same sort of energy as that which stirs up swarms of rasping locusts. It is described by Academician Vernadsky as the energy of living matter, which is biochemical by nature.'

To make a long story short, I surrendered to the idea that unpredictable and turbulent changes occurred in the Russian

---

[1] This and the following quotations are from N. A. Berdiayev's *The Russian Idea* (YMCA Press, Paris, 1971).

mind and in the minds of the peoples around during a period of some special sort of cosmic activity. Those changes went beyond utilitarian and natural processes. I do not rule out a pathology which borders on genius. I have a feeling of a historical anomaly which came down upon us with runaway energy values to form a special ecstatic mass in the Russian ethnos (from, approximately, the turn of the century to 1929).

Leaving aside the revolution in Russian painting with an unmotivated thrust into the Russian vanguard which had an astounding impact, and without referring to the music of Stravinsky, the phenomena of drama, ballet, law or poetry, I just want to single out what is most important to me: to break through to the theatrical enlightenment of Vsevolod Emilievich Meyerhold, a major producer of the twentieth century.

As someone who was for a long time subjected to discipline, sometimes with the help of a stick, I must, above all, mention the Stanislavsky system, which is the origin and genesis of Meyerhold. A producer of my age cannot make too many hints about his profound understanding of the Stanislavsky system, which is a fairly harmless business, for our common teacher wrote and said so many things throughout his life that any speaker on Stanislavsky has a great deal of trouble making himself clear. People usually nod a polite agreement, their faces extremely thoughtful.

The Moscow of the 1920s had become literally a theatrical Mecca. First, though, there is yet another cosmic value that I am about to introduce in my subjective interpretation, superficially as always and with the usual extremes. I should like to pay tribute to Velimir Khlebnikov, a terrific genius of Russian poetry.

At about the same time as Meyerhold, that poet discovered within himself an extraordinary gift that could not fail to affect all his contemporaries. I think it is Khlebnikov who has made a superhuman contribution to overcoming our genetic shapelessness, on which I quote Berdiayev as saying the afore-mentioned rough words. Russian poetry now had the benefit of a man of such remarkable thinking that I believe his psychic energy alone could be enough to produce the effect of levitation; i.e. to rise in the air in defiance of gravitation. Those who do not believe in levitation should take a look at his acts of clairvoyance, presented as mathematical calculations. To those who mistrust clairvoyance or mathematics and who doubt the recurrent appearance of Nostradamuses, big and small, on our planet, I offer some of Khlebnikov's amusing verses which to a certain extent reflect our national destiny, our historical intentions and, possibly, even some of the material hardships experienced by today's perestroika:

> It is nice to see
> A small puffing mermaid,
> Which has crawled in from the woods,
>
> Carefully wipe out
> With a bit of dough
> The law of universal gravitation!
> (V. Khlebnikov, 1922)

Small children who lack vitamins often eat chalk, as they instinctively look for something to substitute for the missing elements needed for their growing organism. Like Khlebnikov and other children of Russia's 'decadent renaissance', Meyerhold declared a painful war on the shapelessness inherent in their genes. It was a state-and-political rather than aesthetic programme. The vigorously growing people needed revolutionary and constructive ideas. Born in the unimportant provincial town of Penza, Meyerhold came out against the inhibiting psyche of plain people whose key instincts had always pushed one to leave one's native land for the sake of an illusory ethnic reflex: it is good to go to other places, and it is good to expand the territory to unreasonable proportions, rather than inhabit one's God-given land.

Meyerhold managed to fulfil his historical destiny in the limited but mysterious world of the stage, where at the turn of the century his stunning *mises en scène* and hitherto unknown scenographic representations began to generate the energy society needed to mould its own shape.

Meyerhold's contribution to Russian and world art is usually explained by the influence of the revolution of October 1917. The reader will recall that I have a different view on the subject.

This is not to deny, of course, that the Bolsheviks' coming to power in 1917 had a bearing on everything, almost, anyway, that is now happening on our small planet. However, I am convinced that the skyrocketing creative potential of the nations that inhabit the territory of what used to be the Russian Empire continued to have a transforming effect not thanks to, but despite, the revolution. The chaos in industry and economy that set in and a crackdown on the outstanding representatives of philosophy and the creators of a new art – all these could not stop the processes of turbulent transformation. To demolish the advanced Russian art, it took Stalin many years of hard work and a new administrative apparatus, which carried out the most massive genocide in the history of our civilization and a monstrous deformation of our genetic fund.

Do I attribute the new forces of global destruction and degradation to cosmic laws of our history or entertain the ideas of blaming it all on one organized criminal? I do fear new unidentified values and am afraid of indulging in hopeless idealism. But, despite myself, I draw a mental analogy with the dynamics of the psychic processes, which is characteristic of man in general. It was explained to me once by an experienced psychiatrist that an emotional upswing which borders on creative euphoria is about as dangerous for a healthy man as sinking to the level of depression.

Any kind of analogy is a lame duck. But let me refer once again to the much-quoted Lev Gumilev: 'Ethnos is a dynamic system also.' After reaching certain heights (history has many examples to that effect), a people may and probably must experience an energy slump. A mobilization of its entire intellectual resources is probably necessary so that the relaxation does not become a downfall from above the clouds. The naturally cyclical slidedown is a temporary retreat to regroup forces before a new recovery. This is something which did not materialize in our experience. The destruction of the forces of production in 1929–30 raised our Fatherland out of the crisis only to drive it into a lasting historical degradation.

The destruction was resisted by all sections of our doomed society; the theatre, perhaps, being the most fervent opponent. It was particularly strong, with a core of producers having an unprecedented concentration of innovators who left an outstanding legacy in world theatrical culture: K. Stanislavsky, V. Nemirovich-Danchenko, V. Meyerhold, E. Vakhtangov, A. Taïrov, K. Mardzhanov, L. Kurbas . . .

I do not want to play down the accomplishments of E. Piskator, B. Brecht and other Western European innovators, including foreign and domestic cinematographers, but it was the Russian theatre of the 20s and, above all, the strikingly heretic theatrical pieces produced by Meyerhold that they often claimed as a source of their inspiration.

The break-up of the Meyerhold theatre in 1938, the arrest of the great producer in 1939 and his execution in 1940 made it impossible for me to be personally involved in his theatrical discoveries (I was born in 1933). And yet, like many of my colleagues, I feel something like nostalgia for Meyerhold as a forerunner of all of today's shape-making acts in the theatre and all stylistic research and feeble impulses. The Master's tragic finale of a martyr was a quite natural outcome of his life and participation in our unfortunate cosmic course.

A record from an unburnt prison manuscript of his final remarks at court martial February 1, 1940, hours before the firing-squad, reads: 'It is strange that a man, aged 66, should give whatever wrong evidence was wanted by the prosecution as he told self-incriminating lies after merely being beaten with a rubber stick. He thought he would rather lie, then, and be executed. He is innocent and has never been a traitor . . .'

It calls for an interval of silence and puts one in mind of some of his great discoveries, such as the final dumb show from Gogol's *Government Inspector*. In 1926, the audience at the Meyerhold Theatre, known as GosTIM, would suddenly see lifesize puppets and plaster casts appear on the stage and stand still in lieu of the actors and actresses. It was the producer's to some extent scenographic stunt, or, to be exact, a creeping finale which reproduced with the mathematical accuracy of Madame Tussaud the faces and postures of what had been the living beings of Gogol's Homeric nightmare.

Did the Master know or could he possibly anticipate how many people in our history would be gone in an apocalyptic string of plaster casts? What is it, this propensity to mass and deadly sculpturalization – a historical forecast or a play of theatrical intuition that science cannot explain?

It will probably be unfair to go into the fabric of Meyerhold, the producer, without defining the origins of his professional development, or his structural methodological foundation, to be more precise. He started out as a like-minded pupil of K. S. Stanislavsky, whom he left in 1902. I am convinced that there can be only one reason why Meyerhold left a prestigious capital city theatre – he dared not resist the mutation that befell him. Nurtured on Stanislavsky's theatre, being the image of his master, as I believe, on the basic, cellular level and remaining his follower, Meyerhold made a breakthrough into another aesthetic quality.

But what is a creative organism which is a product of Stanislavsky's system, anyway? It is something impossible to describe! Stanislavsky is studied inside out. In fact, sometimes I feel he is both studied and stifled. Not being a scientist, I can afford to take some stylistic and even factual liberties. Too much information about Stanislavsky's greatness has piled up throughout the world, so I can use only some very particular and subjective judgments.

I had been giving my diligent teachers the benefit of the doubt about Stanislavsky's genius for so long that I woke up one morning and saw that I believed it. It was an inbred sincere conviction. When a four-volume chronicle of Stanislavsky's life and creative work came out, I read about an offer which was made to him once at a country estate. It was suggested that he act out a scene from A. Chekhov's *Seagull* on a real bench and in a real garden. Stanislavsky liked the idea and started a rehearsal in the new setting, then stopped suddenly and said something like this: 'If it is real, natural foliage beside me, than I should act differently, not like on stage.'

Stanislavsky was probably the only man in the world not a biochemist to link two highly complicated organic systems in an oddly sophisticated cause-and-effect sequence and in such a strikingly aesthetic dimension! And if we go on and on? To be exact, in the opposite direction? Let the leaves die, change their colour, cover them with a thin coat of paint. Than, an actor who has got in touch with them must (!) make some adjustments in his inner and outer world, mustn't he? If the experiment is to be extended by technically transforming the exterior space into interior, the trees in the background cut off from the view by a transparent plastic film, for example, than the mode of the vocal cords and many other things must change at some moment.

Obviously enough, a good (or should I say modern) actor must consciously or better still unconsciously and constantly adjust his mode of existence, checking it against three major objects of the theatre: the material environment, fellow actors and the audience. The actor must promptly respond to whatever changes occur in any or all of the three objects. There must always be some readjustment of energy in the actor's system, otherwise he might fall under a spell of illusory falsehood, artificality and cliché. The latter word was always pronounced by Stanislavsky with disgust, as was his famous angry outcry addressed to the actor: 'I don't believe it!'

The actor's cliché, as I see it, comes down to remembering a piece of a happy interaction between the actor and all of the above three objects, or a fixed recollection of the success. (As a matter of fact, it may well be someone else's success, as actors are liable to imitate one another, but not people who do not belong to the theatre.)

That is basically my idea of Stanislavsky's system, the part of it which, I think, is the least known, which means that we must come up with fresh ideas and efforts. I will not refer to the 'active analysis of the role' (temporarily), but as for my personal meditations about today's sophisticated subtleties in the interactions the actor has with the space (cubic content), his fellows and the audience, I should like to express a cautious hope that the same sorts of feelings (but, surely, in his own terms) were also experienced by Meyerhold. In his notes, I find traces of this quest and a determination to keep this secret and delicate mechanism constantly enriched.

K. S. Stanislavsky was fond of the 'fourth wall' concept, to wit – an interaction the actors had when a direct (frank) message to the audience was apparently not to be found. As for Meyerhold, he set out to develop what I now call 'collective biofield'. What he did was to start filling the auditorium with steady streams of psychic energy and establish intricate energy contacts with the audience by using the clusters of nerve-matter that no instruments are able to pick up. It is also likely that Meyerhold introduced some elements of hypnosis into his productions. On several occasions he put out stimulants into the atmosphere of the hall which could have stirred or torpedoed the audience.

At some performances (*Army Commander-2*) he was known to place several hyperexcitable ladies among the audience, who clicked open their handbags and took out handkerchiefs to fight back the tears as the tragedy culminated. It was the last straw which cast a magic spell on the audience, like the sounds of the funeral march for a close friend or relative.

I think it is a theatrical discovery which is outstanding for its time, as it added a new dimension to the actor's interrelationship with the audience's 'biomass'. Now that many of the theatre's visual effects have been devaluated and the modern producer bends over backwards to come to terms with an audience which is satisfied and oversaturated with artistic information, the number one priority is to create a zone threaded with most subtle and intense emotions. The dynamics of these obscure processes, which cannot be discovered or, therefore, studied in an empty rehearsal space is what, I think, the Master's revolutionary acts are all about. They nourish the modern production, invigorate it and arm it in a rough struggle for the audience's attention at the turn of the twenty-first century.

I shall come back briefly to the practical foundation in Stanislavsky's system which Meyerhold took as a starting point and which later had a considerable influence on the evolution of the theatre both in Russia and abroad. Mikhail Chekhov's pedagogical work in the United States and a pleiad of his famous students who adorned the American theatre and cinema are a case in point.

Stanislavsky's 'active analysis' is the cornerstone of his system. In a nutshell, he urged: rather than illustrating stage feelings, 'basking' in one's own emotions and enjoying the vocal cords' vibrations, to exert a true and specific influence using the actor's individual intrinsic features and inimitable biological nuances.

NOSTALGIA FOR MEYERHOLD

That was my free interpretation of the methodological foundation from which Meyerhold made his fairy-tale start. Stanislavsky had a particular concern for the common truth and the details of the actors' physical condition, based on his personal experience, which was not so much as described by Meyerhold, but rather expanded out of all proportion as he aestheticized the entire stage process in all its component values.

He was the first to 'strip open' the stage box, bringing the architectural working theatre space up to a lofty aesthetic idea, brilliant for its time. Unlike the Taganka Theatre, he did that only once, whch was always a key element in his strategy as a producer. Any further development of his own staging discoveries, he thought, was better left to students and imitators. As far as he was concerned, rather than using a discovered and appraised idea, or being a 'coupon-clipper', as it were, he wasted no time and set out to explore the 'unknown shores'.

Having stripped the stage of its defences and after enjoying the naked communications and technological objects of the theatre, Meyerhold was the first to pour some real naturalistic content into it (A. Dumas Fils's *La Dame aux Camélias*, 1934). The miserable stage set was driven out of the play, leaving the stage glistening with genuine crystal and antiques of great value and high quality.

Meyerhold's contribution to theatrical shape-creation and shape-making ideas of high aesthetic infectiousness was indeed spectacular. A cultivated capital city theatre had certainly been serious about the work of the theatre artist even before Meyerhold's discoveries, but that profession had not seemed to go beyond an adequate and fair (albeit expensive, beautiful and moderately aesthetical) *design*. What Meyerhold made was a real revolution in theatrical aesthetics and theatrical technology. The stage act had been given a new dimension and a new artistic value. (I think he was perfectly aware of what arrogance was all about and probably invented it himself.) But there is no doubt in my mind that Meyerhold made a scenographer out of a theatre artist to get a producer, a designer, an architect and an artist – all rolled into one. In other words, he triggered a turbulent process of blending the producer's mind with the purely visual stage act. The theatre artist was now on the way to transforming the former cameraman into the modern operator. Needless to say that the shape-making endeavour is still going on and has probably not yet reached its philosophical and purely professional completion.

The Master offered the world theatre impulses which have not yet received the modern realization they deserve. Incidentally, Peter Brook's spectacular production of the *Midsummer Night's Dream* probably goes back in terms of its theatrical genesis to the famous *Indulgent Cuckold* by F. Krommelink, produced by Meyerhold and starring M. Babanova and I. Ilyinsky, who later became favourites of Soviet audiences.

The artist L. Popova's scenographic creation in that production had no analogy with the preceding theatrical traditions and achievements. It was a most sophisticated cinematographic sculptural composition which had apparently absorbed some ideas of the Russian vanguard, and K. Malievich's suprematism motives in particular. Incidentally, the magic Tatlin may have been at work there, who created and put together mysterious sculptures with paddles, screws and winged planes which slowly accumulated energy for a possible flight. V. Khlebnikov composed in 1916 some incantatory verses about Tatlin and his 'sun-catchers', as follows:

> Tatlin, a clairvoyant of rolling paddles secrets,
> Who sings stern asanna to a screw-propellor,
> Represents the tribe of sun-catchers.
> He uses an iron horse-shoe
> To have the dale of spider's web of tackle
> Tied up, by deadly hand, and turned
> Into the clairvoyance of tongs' secrets.
> The people, who fail to see the essence of things,
> Gape when they look at what he does –
> So unheard-of and prophetic are
> The things depicted with his iron brush.

Daringly and mysteriously, Meyerhold introduced the farce of the country life into that most fancy mix of rolling paddles, modules and the inexplicably harmonious 'dale of spider's web of tackle'. The queer motion of that scenographic abstract creation coincided closely with psychophysical processes in the actors' souls and bodies clothed in the theatrical 'prose-dress'. The emotional high points of a stage character invariably came into close interaction with movements of paddles and huge rolling drums.

Even very endowed actors, not to mention the audience, were not always able to appraise the Master's innovations, which were often far ahead of the average idea of common sense, aesthetic tolerance and stage logic. Meyerhold's talent took shape under the influence of thrilling discoveries, typical of really cosmic take-offs, when evolution developed into a revolutionary breakthrough and the constellation favoured a bracing renewal of Russia's ethnos.

Meyerhold was supported by the progressive revolutionary intelligentsia and protected by revolutionary leaders from Lenin's entourage. However, with the liquidation of Lenin's party (which would be followed by Stalin's genocide, unprecedented in world history) Meyerhold's confidence was shaken, his strength faltered and he became a lonely man, although he always tended to attract the most progressive forces of the world of arts. Men like D. Shostakovich, S. Prokofiev, V. Mayakovsky, B. Pasternak, N. Erdman, S. Eisenstein, I. Ehrenburg and others were always around during what were his final and most difficult years.

The Meyerhold Theatre was dissolved in 1938 by governmental decree, and the disgraced director was unexpectedly invited by the only person who did not consign him to perdition and was not afraid of working with him. K. S. Stanislavsky, founder of MHAT (Moscow Art Theatre), was running an opera school, so Meyerhold spent a few months before his arrest working under his teacher's guidance. Clothed with honours, the teacher was anticipating his death, and it was probably with a sad amazement that he gazed at the smouldering ruins which used to be Moscow's theatrical Mecca.

The dying Stanislavsky was probably well aware of all the sad and inexorable circumstances which would be the result of forced 'MHATization' of Soviet theatres, enforced by Party decrees. Every Soviet theatre was supposed to proclaim its allegiance to Marxist-Leninist teaching and Stanislavsky's system. Every theatre was to bring its repertoire and internal structure in line with the organizational and artistic structure of what was Stalin's pet theatre. In provincial towns there sprang up half-baked imitation-MHAT-theatres run by petty Stanislavskys, which were moulded on Stanislavsky's position as the producer – or on his artistic value, to be more exact. MHAT's founder was subjected to a forced mass circulation. The imitation practice was found disgusting by the audience. It warped the minds of home-grown Stanislavskys, some of whom were able people, but most just turned to monsters under the circumstances.

The Stalin-led campaign can only be compared in scale and tragedy with the forced collectivization that pushed the country's agriculture into the abyss of harvest failure and increasing degradation. Our homeland with its savagely raped culture had entered one of the most tragic stages in its censored existence. Memories of rebel artists were being carefully erased from the minds of new generations, their names banished from textbooks and reduced to a few scornful references. But the discoveries the Russian innovators made during the period of their exemplary cosmic daring were, somehow or other, preserved in the inmost recesses of the national memory. 'Vestiges of the decimated intelligentsia' told succeeding generations about the high noon of Russian theatre.

Hardly had the 'Khrushchev thaw' begun when a group of enthusiasts, who, among others, included law-enforcement officers, rehabilitated Meyerhold as part of our history and art. They did it in an atmosphere of fear and against bureaucratic hurdles.

The energy which had upset traditional ideas of theatrical rules and had made people believe in the virtually unlimited potential of the most ancient art was now coming down as an avalanche of powerful information clusters, invigorating the minds of the young producers who used to be the Master's students and who started out under the enlightening rays of his heretical stagecraft. They were probably the first to start the difficult recovery of the country's staging power that had been lost. N. Okhlopkov, V. Pluchek, A. Goncharov and B. Ravenskikh made their landmark productions in the late fifties and early sixties; their stage aesthetics were definitely inspired by their teacher's discoveries.

The new staging opportunities were also seized by two young theatres which had appeared on a new wave of the inexorable sobering-up processes in society. Those were 'Sovremennik' and 'Taganka'. The latter made a point of having a portrait of Meyerhold attached to its banner. Led by a fearless fighter, citizen and maverick Youri Lyubimov, the theatre set itself to the task of exploring the unknown shores whose outline had been put on the map of staging discoveries by our common teacher.

Initially, 'Taganka' was somewhat stuck with the shell of the teacher's discoveries, as it were. I do not want to cast a shadow on the theatre company that I love, but just want to make it clear that the Russian repertoire theatre produced at the highest point of its aesthetic evolution an artistic pleiad of its own. Those actors, without imitation, embodied and absorbed the new nature of the stage energy. It was the case with Stanislavsky's creation, with the theatre house of Meyerhold and, finally, the same sort of invigorating process broke its way through to 'Taganka', and a bright company of master actors emerged, which was led by the most cherished actor and poet Vladimir Vysotsky.

Having given due credit to 'Sovremennik' and 'Taganka', my relative modesty notwithstanding, I cannot fail to mention Moscow's 'Lenkom', a theatre which I have been running for over a decade. Oddly enough, Sergei Youtkevich, a well-known cinema director, was one of my teachers at the Student Theatre of the University of Moscow. He made an active contribution to my training as a producer during my student amateur years, and, being one of Meyerhold's students himself, he gave several unforgettable lectures, which were not without some witty practice sessions.

The MGU Student Theatre and 'Our House' theatre school, which shared the same university premises, became the centre and focus of Moscow's culture in 1958–64, when the 'Khrushchev thaw' agitated the minds of younger generations and awakened their genetic memory, in which I still find it difficult to believe but on which I continue to insist. I was involved in that tension field of stagecraft and drama that was rooted in the inmost depths of Meyerhold's stagecraft, as a careful examination would suggest. I have no doubt that my best productions and possibly some of the happier thoughts and ideas which crossed my mind during the practical search for a new artistic aesthetic, hypnotic creations of modern scenography and the establishment of magic contacts with the audience's 'biofield', are to be attributed to the never failing influence of the original source I hail with a humble bow.

Having said that, I have no intention of attacking our theatrical hierarchy, being well aware of the significance of Stanislavsky and his system. But as a human being I am entitled to have my own preferences, particularly if they are not without some methodological reasoning.

I am convinced that Meyerhold was a trail-blazer in the indispensable struggle with the audience's ability to forecast.

We have been studied through and through by an audience responsive to a standard set of gimmicks that we use to conjure up stereotyped stage creations which can make the audience give a polite yawn or even wish they had spent the evenng watching TV instead!

Every other production by Meyerhold was always a mystery and a shocking miracle whose parameters and scent were impossible to anticipate. (Even the cast was considered by Meyerhold as a secret of the theatre which was not to be disclosed.) A new production of Meyerhold could be irritating, but it would invariably be the thing to see for anyone who had at least some interest in theatre.

The erosion of the values inherent in Russian art and culture, the coming of time-serving producers, the fear of physical liquidation, the rigid censorship which reigned for many decades and many other consequences of our unfortunate historical experience have done permanent damage to Soviet theatre. Today's particular difficulties encountered by perestroika, now that a flow of sensational information has come down to the people and the entertainment industry has finally passed an embryonic stage, have added to the hardships and the crisis experienced by many theatre companies as the runaway audience flow is now taking its toll.

* * *

Could our theatre wither away as it is being steadily driven out to the fringes by mass culture, for which I feel no pathological hatred, unlike some of our writers? To be sure, our theatre is indeed going through a tough crisis, and its body is now bleeding. But the most ancient art had similar experiences of bitter failures and persecution! If the universal law of energy conservation is true, and if the Bulgakov discovery that 'manuscripts do not burn' is also true, the Meyerhold inspiration will remain forever in the universe as information and energy clusters of thin matter, in which all oriental philosophers believe. The theatrical faith absorbed man's entire intellectual prowess a long time ago. As N. A. Berdiayev wrote: 'Man craves for rescue in the face of death. But since man is naturally a creator and a moulder of life, his craving for creation will never fade.'

That much is also true as far as the theatre's living body is concerned. In the meantime, it leaves us waiting for another favourable constellation, faced with our thoughtful astrologists on TV.

Ecology

Valentin G. Rasputin

Rasputin was born in 1937 in Siberia, in a village on the Angara river which no longer exists, as it is now at the bottom of the Bratsk reservoir. Neither does the Angara river exist, the beautiful Angara outflowing from Lake Baikal; cut by three dams (a fourth is under construction, and a fifth is on the drawing-board), it has been turned into a cascade of man-made lakes with foul water.

He graduated in 1959 from the Department of Philology of Irkutsk University. Then he worked for seven years on the youth newspapers of Irkutsk and Krasnoyarsk, travelled much over Siberia and saw more than enough of its Communist image under construction: the hydro-electric plants of Bratsk, Krasnoyarsk, Sayano-Shushenskaya, the Abakan-Taishet Railway, the world's largest aluminium plants and forestry complexes which at the time were hailed loudly and promised so much.

On publishing his first collection of short stories he was admitted into the Union of Writers in 1967. His principal books are: *The Money for Maria* (1967), *The Last Term* (1970), *Live and Remember* (1974) and *Farewell to Matyora* (1976), as well as short stories, essays and journalism. The Molodaya Gvardia publishers are preparing a book on Siberia, its past and present in history, ethnography, and ecology. He is secretary of the Boards of the Unions of Writers of Russia and of the USSR, and is also active in the Cultural Foundation and Society for the Protection of Memorials of History and Culture.

Hopes and Despair, and Hopes...

VALENTIN G. RASPUTIN

For over a decade I have been amassing something like ecological archives: newspaper clippings, resolutions, expertise reports, letters, decisions of government bodies and statements by unofficial organizations, devious departmental instructions, records of talks with ministers on one side, and with victims of ministries' actions on the other, etc. I know that similar archives have been collected by many who devote themselves to the protection of nature. My file-filled bookcase reminds me of a 'black box' of the kind they install in aircraft. One day when we crash it will reveal evidence of how it happened. If it helps somebody in the future, my sorrowful spirit, if not myself, will find solace after my failure to help anyone in the present.

To an outsider, ecological information should be collected without problems, in passing: something is mentioned in the press, something happened on our sinful earth, you make a note when you have a moment of leisure, arrange it and file it in a dossier. Yet this is not so. With us, nothing is done just like that. In the early years when I was starting this job, almost nothing occurred with us, and little saw God's light: departmental censors would root out anything that ran counter to our ecological well-being. You could feel with your skin and see with your own eyes how hard it was becoming to breathe and how your surroundings were changed, yet you would be assured that your eyes and nose were failing you, that Socialism with its planned economy could have no harmful effect on nature, that it would be as unnatural as for a man, after a taste of civilization, to return to all fours. For a decade and a half, for example, a myth was kept afloat that the cellulose factories on Lake Baikal were making its waters better; to back the myth a ministry set up a research institution with over a hundred learned minds on the lake shore in the vicinity of one of these factories. No wonder that, under these circumstances, any, even the simplest, document contrary to the picture of well-being had to be chased for months.

For information: The chief guardian of this national 'well-being', Deputy Chairman of the State Committee for Hydrology and Meteorology Comrade Sokolovsky, for many years kept the tightest lid on any word referring to ecology. When two years ago the State Committee for Nature was set up he was promoted without delay to the position of First Deputy Chairman of that long-overdue institution for environmental protection. The Institute of Ecological Toxicology, the one that was successful in proving that black was white, has been recently placed under the State Committee for Nature, with no changes in its nameplate, management or scholarliness. These two instances make one doubt the eternal value of the old dictum: he who pays the piper calls the tune. Here, no doubt, the selections and invitations were prompted by reasons of pipe and tune; he who likes them pays the money.

So, unlike the initial years of my sad collecting when any information on air, water and soil pollution was hard to come by, the situation today is so different (I mean with information, not with nature) that it is hard to select the major and the most important information in the torrent of developments, facts and figures. Like a dam burst under a mighty thrust, whatever was kept firmly within the concrete walls of secrecy, whatever had grown unhampered beneath classified covers erupted into the open with uncontrolled power, announcing its name in confusion and haste, outlining the scope of the disaster and appealing for aid. It is a rare issue of any newspaper nowadays that does not bring out more denunciations and data on the true ecological situation of the nation, wiping out the last cloudless hopes. Each publication detonates an explosion of response from diverse parts: it is as bad with us, or it is worse with us. Control services have at last renounced their cryptography, their solid ranks have cracked, and truth is seeping out. The environmentalists have acquired volunteer assistants in departments most opposed to the environment, and the stamp of confidentiality, a favourite of the departmental guards, has ceased to be a guarantee of silence. It appears that ecological promises were present in the programmes of every People's Deputy elected in spring 1989. Ecology has become the most resounding word, more resounding than war and elements; small children and old women deep in the country are learning to spell it. Such problems as the increase in crime and outbursts of national disputes, remote as they may seem from ecology, are being connected, and rightly, to environmental problems.

To repeat, what has taken place is an eruption of information about what we breathe and drink, what food we eat; forecasts of man's future have been made. The right name has at last been given to the phenomenon that has been present for so long. Yet, with all the adverse publicity and discussions, the phenomenon did not even blink. It goes on living among us as it used to live, and is building up to apocalyptic inevitability. To be more precise, it is we who live inside it, it has become our common womb bearing us to ever more perilous mutations. All attempts to alter the ecological situation of the nation have been of little effect and bring no results. Shooed off by noise and cries in one place, the huge and dreary shadow, like a bird, flies on to another, each time growing bigger and more ominous. The names of Lakes Baikal, Sevan, Aral and Ladoga, the Volga, Chernobyl, today are no more geographical: they are the names of pastures which feed the monster of our making; and they sound like one and the same word in different languages.

Is it not strange that man is not willing to employ his brains, or experience, or instincts which seem to have reached through millenia an adequate perfection, to save himself and his own? Man's actions resemble feints designed to provoke the adversary to false moves. It is akin to a paralysis of mind and will, some senile loss of memory, that he cannot or will not grasp the understanding that the time for sobering up is disastrously running out. Reproaches, complaints, warnings and pleas become ever more lost in a void which echoes the very same words, seeking and not finding those who would heed them and get down to business.

It is, unfortunately, true of a man wherever he lives in the world if he does not care to part with the dubious goods of a

dubious civilization. It is particularly true of Russia. It is
Russia's fate to be late, and then to hasten, with eyes turned up
and seeing nothing of what happens around her. Had the West
not been a victim of its own errors, one might have suspected it
of deliberate manoeuvring to make run headlong a country that
does not know how to distinguish good from bad and to follow
its own way. The world's biggest blast furnaces, mines, hydro-
electric plants, factories and projects of the century, unheard-of
scope for the extraction of minerals, half of them to be wasted,
fantastic expense on 'nature's mistakes' (like the Aral Sea was
called, for one) or discharge of the northern and Siberian rivers
to the cold seas all resulted in the gravest ecological situation,
economic poverty and waywardness today and joyless prospects
for tomorrow.

Over a century ago Fyodor Dostoyevsky came in his ponderings
and observations to a conclusion that seems to lie on the surface,
yet has a primordial, parental importance for economics and
morals. In his *Writer's Diary* he recorded in 1877: 'It is a kind of
law of nature, not in Russia alone, but universal . . . if ownership
of land is serious in a country, everything else is serious in that
country, in all respects, in the most general and in particulars.'
That is the heart of the matter.

In a state where land costs nothing, water costs nothing, the
wastage of both becomes inevitable. If, added to that, the power
belongs in that state not to the government, not to the people's
representatives, but has been seized by departmental corruption,
if that state's economy starts not with the product but with the
ruble spent – that is, all work is planned for the sake of working
and not the sake of producing – all is indeed lost. As long as the
economy rests on such foundations, it will be destroying itself
and the government until it either ruins all or comes to its
senses.

But now we find that to come to one's senses is not so simple.
In the past decades the greatest power has been attained in our
nation by the ministries that have already buried more than one
Atlantis. In its most direct meaning, land is being lost; so much
of it has been wasted, equal to an average-size European nation,
or, possibly, several such nations. It is thought that the Ministry

of Electric Power has sunk a France. Ministries of Electric Power and Water Resources are akin in that they shrank dry land with the help of water, fouling the water as well; yet their destruction techniques were different: one was flooding land and turning it into sea bottom, while the other was pumping water into land, thus creating the same result. It is hard to say which of them had the more success because each has had both the immediate results and subsequent, long-term ones that are to reveal themselves gradually, with time. One example. When the Bratsk Hydel was put on the Ahgara River, its lake licked off 550,000 hectares of topsoil. This happened thirty years ago, but up to this day hundreds and thousands of hectares are lost every year when the lake shores crumble. The loss can be calculated, but what is the use? Elements!

This is the case of only one man-made lake situated in my home country. All in all there are over 3,500 such lakes, though not as large, in the whole nation. Here is a France for you. Not to speak of the land overwatered and spoiled that went to hell — the best and fertile land in river valleys!

The same goes for the work of the water resources and amelioration people. Amelioration (land improvement), however, is a figure of speech, because this is just what they do *not* do. They have no time. It is not profitable. Not worth the trouble. Well, at one go these so-called 'ameliorators' wiped out seven million hectares of ploughland (some estimate the figure at ten million hectares), producing, in fact, no additional harvest yield for the nation. They poured money into the drying up of marshes where they existed, and made fresh swamps where there were none. They made more and more outlays because they were a 'success', and because it was impossible in this country to find out what was good and what was bad in the economy. While the Top Leader was discoursing meaningfully on the 'economy having to be economical', there was so much arbitrariness, plundering, debauchery and swindling as was never seen before. It was in that era, when promises were valued more than achievements, that the Ministry of Water Resources and Amelioration reached the apex of its power.

We can get an idea of the acreage lost only from the lists of officially written-off lands. Of late, however, when such information started to cause trouble for the water resources people, they resorted to diplomacy and found ways to convince the local authorities not to be too hasty with write-offs. Evidently, such agreements are worth no more than money. The leaders of regions are happy to get crumbs from the rich pie of the Water Resources Ministry with which to overcome their multitudinous social ills. There is hardly anyone in the Volgograd region or the Stavropol territory who would ever put trust in the ameliorators' promises of rich future harvests; however, the authorities concerned spare no effort to prove that they need land and water improvement projects of giant dimensions: they have the longstanding habit of placing no value on land while friendship and good service will surely bring something. There can be no doubt that the adminstrative and bureaucratic apparatus helped the departments to become all-powerful monopolies.

By the end of the 1970s the Water Resources Ministry had grown so sure of itself that it decided to launch 'the project of the century', the diversion of northern rivers into the Volga on the pretext of saving the drying-up Caspian Sea, and diverting Siberian rivers to Central Asia to save the Aral Sea. Under the original plans, the northern rivers were to give up 100 cubic kilometres every year, and the Siberian ones 210 cubic kilometres – as much as the great Obi carries to the ocean. The Siberian diversion would have required a 2,400-km-long canal. I will not list what else and how much would have been required for the job: what sounds like pleasant music for vested interests is tiresome or simply awful for outsiders. The important thing is that billions upon billions would have had to be spent. With a project like that under way, one could live without care, without need to think of one's future.

However, an unbelievable thing occurred, or, rather, unbelievable things piled up. As if having realized what kind of people it was to face, the Caspian Sea rushed to raise its level. Leaving no hopes for the diversionists, it went on raising its water level year in year out, so that on its opposite shores, in Dagestan, people began to plead for help.

Another unexpected thing was the reaction of people, who had long been silent and willing to swallow any tomfoolery, and who would not have been struck with awe had the Water Resources Ministry proposed building a canal from Lake Baikal to the Moon. These people rubbed their eyes and looked around to see what was happening. Well, I should say, not all people, it did not go that far, but the so-called public: writers, journalists, some scientists and other brains stirred themselves and went on stirring up the people. What, indeed, was happening? The more impudent and uncontrolled are the departments, more honour to them; the more they waste national wealth, the more open the nation's pockets are to them. Why?

To save itself, the Water Resources Ministry had to review the relation of its European projects to the northern rivers. The Caspian card was covered by the sea itself, so a new one was played: the need to irrigate rice and wheat plantations on both banks of the Volga, to achieve the Food Programme recently introduced, and in the final count to save the nation from starvation.

The wording was strong and, I would say, daring: Whom are you against? Whom are you competing with? They turned to their benefit even the fact that the nation had to import ever greater quantities of wheat through their fault: the nation cannot depend all the time on the uncle overseas, and we shall pull the country out of the agricultural crisis at the count of two. By that time the Water Resources Ministry had a two-million-strong workforce.

But the public did not want to be fooled once again. The grumbling grew in force, again and again the economic and ecological inadequacy of the diversionists was revealed, more and more facts came to light showing that deceit, trickery and bribing did not fit well their pretended role of nation's saviours. There was nothing left for the Water Resources Ministry but to curb its appetites and announce reductions in the amounts of water to be diverted from the northern rivers: down from the original 100 cubic kilometres to 80, to 60, to 40, to 6 and – at last – to 2.2 cubic kilometres. The last figure is laughable, or it seems laughable to us; the Ministry wants this to realize the diversion itself, to save whatever is left of the project, and then to see. Later, the amounts of diverted water could be stepped up just as it was cut; means will be found for the purpose. The means were seen in having the Volga water dispersed by large canals; with the river made shallower, the nature-lovers themselves would clamour for the northern water.

As to the second part of 'the project of the century', the diversion of the Siberian rivers, the Aral Sea, unlike the Caspian, was indeed in dire need of emergency help. The Syr-Darya and Amu-Darya Rivers, its feeders, were of late suffering pitiful drops. The major amounts of water were taken for cotton-field irrigation by the Ministry of Water Resources. The autonomous republic of Karakalpakia next to the Aral Sea was swimming in poisonous lakes seeping up from under the ground; the Aral was drying at a catastrophic rate, yet the irrigating ameliorators continued to flood the fields to excess. The worse for the republic and cotton, the more murderous for the Aral, the better for them. One day in desperation the Karakalpaks and Uzbeks would cry out for help, so one day the Government, facing the calamity and pressed by Central Asia's peoples, would consent to the Siberian variant. Meanwhile, no water was to be spared. Experts free of the Water Resources embrace are warning that Siberian water will never reach its destination by passing 2,000 kilometres in an earth-bottomed canal; instead, it will make swamps of huge areas along its route. For the diversion advocates, this is of no account, provided they get their hearts' desire. Even a burglar on his way to a job thinks more of the consequences than they did, accustomed as they were to arbitrariness and impunity.

Here, too, for tactical reasons presented as good-will gestures, they had to introduce modifications: 210 cubic kilometres went down step by step to 30.

The reader outside who knows little of the mysterious Soviet way of life can hardly understand the intricacies of this strange machine designed to operate on the principle of the reverse. Seemingly a harvester, it crosses the field, reaping and threshing as a harvester should, yet what is reaped and threshed is dumped into a deep ditch behind, national money going into its bunker. To an outside reader this comes as something from horror fiction. To be frank, we, too, do not comprehend many things in our life if we look at them with common sense. But if looked at otherwise, well, then, it becomes curious, indeed.

For information: Had the Water Resources Ministry fully succeeded with its ill-fated diversion, irreversible ecological changes would have occurred on a territory of five million square kilometres – that is, on one-fourth of the national territory. They would not have been contained within national borders, of course, so after a time both Northern and Western Europe would have been affected.

The reality is: the diversion project has not been approved, its expediency report is put together in a haphazard manner, with ecological expertise of the least significance, the public is in turmoil, and yet the diversion machine moves at full speed. Dozens of design and research institutions with their tens of thousands of brains have been put on the diversion job; construction has started from two ends in the European part, expenditure is already in excess of one hundred millions. Indeed: 'there were worse times but not as . . .' (in the poet's original it is 'as base', here 'as foolhardy' would be more proper).

So far we have dealt with the Ministry of Water Resources. Yet it has been not the only one to tear this country to pieces, taking no account of its past, present or future, or with moral principles, or with its being their land of birth; all for the sake of personal enrichment. It was a great enthusiasm for devastation (it is our way to fill the cup to the brim). Ore, woods, waters, wealth under and above the ground – all was being uprooted, removed, scattered, spilled, sold out, like an army in retreat leaving nothing to the enemy. The Water Resources Ministry is but one, the most glaring, example. It may be named the leader of devastation followed by dozens of similar ones.

One riddle remains unsolvable, at least for me. It is people. The way I think: the administrative command system promoted departmental monopolism. It had no obstacles to speak of in a rightless and voiceless state. Large sums snatched from the nation corrupted both the departmental top echelons willing to push through any scheme, and those who were to carry out these schemes. Relatively higher salaries did their work there, too. The unbreakability of this chain I can at least understand up to this point. Unlike the state, a department is better organized, though not to such an extent as to be above the average conditions and escape common ills. Besides, a department cannot deceive the state without deceiving its own departmental people; still, there are advantages.

And still again, the people . . . A few decades ago our country was mostly a peasant one brought up by, and deriving its livelihood and morals from, land and amid nature. The land was seen as a provider and nature as a home; for generations a relationship, a kinship was developed and maintained with both.

So the former peasant ripped from the land by industrialization or a campaign to erase 'villages of no promise' joins the Water Resources people, sits behind the levers of an excavator and now is ready for his pay to destroy all that was the mainstay of his father's and grandfather's world. I suppose reasons and causes for this could be found – I am quite willing to provide them myself, knowing as I do how man's conscience used to be distorted for decades and how his fundamental ideas were undermined. But he is a man! one who must preserve, oppression or seduction notwithstanding, whatever it was that began not with him but before his birth, and is in him since the dawn of mankind: an instinct of self-preservation, instinct of fatherhood, of tribe, that enable him to smell danger unerringly.

But here I see a young fellow on the TV screen, apparently nice and wholesome, well-gifted by nature, the operator of an excavator digging the Volga-Chograi Canal, a canal beneficial for Water Resources but of no benefit – harmful, rather – to the nation. The reporter asks him if he is aware of the controversy about the canal. Yes, he is. So, what is his opinion? The fellow smiles acidly: what's it to me, if the pay's good? His colleagues come up and join the talk. So what? If we're told to dig, we'll dig, if to fill in, we'll turn to fill in. The pay is good.

This is more fearsome than the departmental omnipotence, and a cause of far-reaching apprehension. Ages ago man became man through turning a stone into an implement . . . What is to become of him if he turns work into an instrument of indiscriminate wage? Our end is visible beyond it . . .

The Volga-Chograi took me away from the most important development of the environmentalists' confrontation with the Water Resources Ministry. This development happened in the second year of perestroika. When it took off, we all were very enthusiastic because of the chance to speak out and act frankly. So we pressed on with our protests and denunciations of the diversionists. Mindful of the time factor, the other side, the Ministry of Water Resources, also was pressing on, with some sparks flying in certain places of contact. To keep silence would mean a loss of face for the Government, so in August 1986 it made a decision to suspend all work involved in the diversion of the northern and Siberian rivers.

We rejoiced in the victory, clearly.

And we were deceived.

We were used to the fact that, in the past, the Government's decisions aimed at environmental protection were either ignored or cunningly enveloped in ritualistic manoeuvres with the least financial sacrifice. With the dire lessons of the past we relegated such practices to that past. Just to refresh the memory, the latest, perestroika-time, decision on Lake Baikal in 1987 was preceded by three equally highly promising and fine-sounding documents adopted on the same level, which provoked much echo on the stone shores of Baikal but ended exactly in nothing. The gap between 1984 and 1987 seemed to us to last longer than a decade: it looked not like a gap but a chasm. So we expected that the supreme helplessness of the august documents had been left on the other side of the chasm.

There are decisions and decisions. The 1987 one on Lake Baikal requires billions in outlay. The other that cancelled the river diversion, on the contrary, freed billions; one had only to take money off the Ministry's budget and put it to good works, an action seemingly easy but promising great moral satisfaction. Yet, that is as it would be seen by common sense. But look at it from the reverse side of common sense. In short, the 50 billion allocated to the Water Resources Ministry for the last five-year plan were left untouched.

What to do with the money? The question produced no answers, not even the smallest one to encourage us. Of course, money is to be spent. It is the army sergeant's logic, fusing space and time, when he orders a trench to be dug from the fence till sunset, elevated to a national scale. After a redisposition of its forces, the Ministry launched them to carry out that same diversion, without using the name, from the Volga end. There energetic work was undertaken to cut the Volga-Chograi and Volga-Don no. 2 canals. That no. 2 is already 40 metres deep in the ground (one sunset was obviously not enough). To compare: the Panama Canal for ocean-going ships is 16 metres deep. They started to dig the Volga-Chograi without drawings – faster, faster! – and did so until the local people awoke and the public stirred again. Indeed, while eyes were being rubbed to see what was happening, they dug in 50 million. Again protests, meetings, public expertise, appeals to national interest. The Volga-Chograi was stopped, but 50 million cannot be recovered, cannot be dug out. The sum is a trifle for the Water Resources Ministry with its 10 billion annual budget, but it would have done very well indeed for those millions who suffer poverty in silence and for whom we have to scratch resources wherever possible.

I realize that my story of the Water Resources Ministry is overlong and thus favours other ministries which are in shadow though functioning by the same method of 'grab and rule', or 'grab here, grab there, or tomorrow they'll give you nothing.' My excuse is that the subject is very entertaining; one does not find such a *dolce vita* in every night's dreams. Regrettably, this story of the Water Resources Ministry cannot be beautified with some lively details that are abundantly integral to the story. Like, for example, the one of the Government awarding the Order of Lenin, the nation's highest decoration, to Minister Vasiliev by way of moral compensation for the stopping of the diversion project. Or another one, of the lush prizes the Ministry decided to award for the best stories about canal-diggers by way of fraternizing with the authors after they turned too difficult. The author Sergei Zalygin did not want to fraternize with First Deputy Minister Polad-zade, a person too odious and unscrupulous in a turncoat's zeal. Zalygin classified the Ministry's works as national crimes, and added that he did not mind being taken to court by the Ministry if it thought him wrong. The latter did not dare to take him to court, but started a dossier on him. So many curious and serious things are just asking to be printed to characterize our hero!

But to conclude.

My compatriots are well acquainted with fortune's caprices, yet even they gasped to learn that the saving of the Aral Sea had been entrusted to the same Ministry of Water Resources that killed it. A designated Zone of Ecological Disaster, half-dry, no more feeding several Central Asian nations, a breeding-ground of infections, a vividly tragic illustration of human madness – all caused by the Water Resources Ministry, the Aral Sea is again turned over to it. So many billions had been spent to make a 'quiet Chernobyl' of the sea – but who counts the expense? Now the initial phase of the rescue is to take 30 to 40 billion. The giving hand shall not impoverish. That is the way to work – to create jobs and money for oneself for all time. Just like that bitter verse about the ambulance: 'It runs, it hits, it aids itself.' Experts, though, are convinced that the Aral Sea cannot be salvaged after Water Resources did its job, that billions will again be wasted, and that other, not the Ministry's, ways should be found to heal the terrible scourge of the Earth's body. Still the Ministry says: We'll do it, no problem!

So now the Tobolsk-Kurgan Canal is being planned. It has no relation to the Aral, but it is on the same line that is part of the diversion route.

One way or another. It looks as though the major developments are yet to be.

For information. The Ministry of Water Resources is no more, now being called the Ministry of Water Development. That is the correction. At the first session of the new Supreme Soviet as it was approving the new cabinet, Comrade A. Polad-zade was twice proposed for the position of Water Development Minister, the same one who was no. 2 in the former ministry. The chairman of the Council of Ministers, Nikolai Ryzhkov, pleaded for him. No go. Comrade Polad-zade was not confirmed; his name brings shudders to those millions of hectares that are as yet able to yield harvests.

. . . 240 billion rubles is the sum the former Ministry of Water Resources asked for the coming fifteen years for irrigation projects alone.

. . . The Electric Power Ministry plans to build ninety-three new hydro-electric stations in the same fifteen years.

To follow the old advice to look for the roots: these monstrous growths turned state within the state did not spring up spontaneously. It was not the climate that influenced their positions and development. The 'climate' was there, of course: why not take what is given; why not overdo things, why not misbehave, why not damage hectares and souls if there is no accountability? After all, planning, financing and controlling bodies are there, everything is being done under their eyes. As we mentioned before, land and water cost nothing and belong to nobody, so pour, dig, kill, to your heart's content! The law is too feeble to stop plunder and too imperfect to dare to go out and be humbled; the moral undermined, culture left in the past, economy loose: the best possible conditions for the Water Resources Ministry and its counterparts. For seventy years the State behaved like an heir with no legal claim to the property and therefore putting no value on it, wasting it right and left ingloriously with zeal and haste, as if expecting the true owners to appear at any moment. It is only now that the State has undertaken to lay claim to its inheritance, but doing so timidly, weighed down by its position.

Maybe, with property rights finalized, the obligations will come up, too.

Until then – who is to say what is ours and what is not?

The greatest, and the primary, word of today is ecology; it bears the heavy burden of mankind's defeat on its chosen path. The word is learned and spelled in this country as a big question-mark crying for action. 'The Earth is in Trouble', 'The Earth of Discontent', 'The Ache of the Earth', etc. – such are the headings in the newspapers and magazines we read daily. In local papers: 'The Dnieper in Trouble', 'The Volga in Trouble', 'The Obi in Trouble', 'Let us Save the Angara' (too late), all in one voice from west to east and from north to south. All the inland seas appeal for help: Baikal, Balkhash, Caspian, Azov, Lake Ladoga. The taiga is being cut mercilessly. A picture of rape or negligence is the vast north-eastern area of the wooded tundra and the tundra with which Lomonosov two hundred years ago and Solzhenitsin only two decades back connected Russia's future. Siberia itself was considered a short time back to be a 'reserve land' where, should the need arise, Russia could move to and prosper – not in the Gulag, of course. It has never seen development, it is all overturned, robbed and polluted. The coalfields are moonscapes of waste dumps and open mines; oil and gas fields present extensive lakes of oily wash. The taiga looks as if a giant tornado had passed: half of the timber carried away God knows where, the rest scattered over the cuts; rivers are replaced with ugly thicknesses of reservoirs of poisoned water, interspersed with dams. And so on.

As it was making man millions of years ago, nature had no suspicion of the menace that would loom, and so failed to incorporate an alarm clock that might warn *Homo sapiens* of a critical situation for generations to come, and would not let him eat or drink until the danger was removed. Like mutants, we cannot help undergoing changes in our signalling system. It is weakened and dulled.

About 400 kilograms of harmful matter descends on every head in our country from the air alone. Since it descends not in parts, or even in particles, all year long, we are incapable of distinguishing between, say, 300 and 400 kilos, nor can our senses control our feelings. Both amounts are big, too big, both figures are beyond comprehension. In more than one hundred cities industrial pollution levels greatly (sometimes tens of times) exceed the permissible concentrations. This information is several years old, so possibly these now number two hundred; information we are not keen to have unless it helps to change matters.

I wish I could state hopefully that more than four years of perestroika have improved the nation's ecological situation. Unfortunately, this is not so. Anyway, it could not improve after so long a period of energetic conquests: too big is the accumulated inertia, while attempts to change things are too timid. The Government's decisions (regarding Baikal, Aral, etc.) run into dead-ends when facing expensive reanimation jobs, and, secondly, are hampered by departmental reluctance to step back.

Moreover, perestroika added ecological problems of its own to the old ones. One of them is involved in setting up joint ventures when environmental protection is disregarded in pursuit of foreign currency and high-quality goods. 'Disregarded' is not the word! – they are willing to sell their souls to the devil! The latest example, a case of ill fame not resolved as yet, a kind of swelling still unripe, which one side claims is a cancerous growth, the other asserts its worth for the public, is the decision to build jointly with five foreign concerns huge petro-gas-chemical complexes for the production of plastics in the Tyumen region (Siberia). Not one but several complexes, each to consist of several plants. Its raw material is to be the gas that accompanies oil extraction; for years this gas has been burned, finding no application.

Of course such burning is wasteful and can be afforded by our state, and nobody else. At the same time, the project jointly undertaken with Japanese and US companies will place us on a common footing with underdeveloped nations who have to let in 'dirty industries'. One may, of course, say that qualitatively our economy is indeed on the same footing. Yet the project goes to show that we have no intention of rising above this footing, and are sinking deeper.

The chemical engineers believe that the gas can be transported to plants already operating. The economists assert that the project will drive us deeper into debt, from knee-deep as we are, and make us the West's hostages for ever. The complexes would cost us just under one hundred billion. Or more; nobody can name the exact figure. Credit payoffs and profits are estimated at today's prices for plastics; they are bound to fall, naturally, as more goods come on to the market. To stay a reliable partner, we shall have to step up production of the plastics which, in turn, will lower the prices. The process is likely to repeat itself until we find ourselves in a jolly mess and make a global waste-heap of Siberia.

There are heated arguments about whether it will be so or not. But they started after the Government took the decision to build the complexes, and did so in the best traditions of the past: hiding it from the public, without substantial expediency studies or ecological expertise, and failing to take into account the ecological situation in the north of the Tyumen region. It is the same *modus operandi*: haste, lack of deliberation, mania of grandeur, the nation's total effort as it was with the B.A.M. railway, with every republic allotted its quota as in the time of *métayage*. It all makes one sadly doubtful about our ecological eyes being opened.

Yet consciousness changes, and it would be no exaggeration to affirm that it changes daily. Had there been any method to measure it, rather as they do it in hydrology, we would have recorded a level tending to rise above the tolerable limits. To extend the simile: the rise is caused by melting ice-floes of prohibitions as heating by glasnost and democracy builds up. Today it is not merely a bunch of two or three dozens of enthusiasts rushing madly from Baikal to the northern rivers to the Volga to Russia's black soils to Kara-Bogazgol Bay to the Leningrad Weir to the Altai Mountains to Ussuri Taiga. It is a record of losses: Kara-Bogazgol, dammed off from the Caspian Sea, perished; the Leningrad Weir to cut the Neva off from the Finnish Gulf is under construction; the great Russian river, the Volga, is harmed so it would not recognize itself and breathes with difficulty; black soils are either blown away by the wind or poisoned with chemicals; the Sevan Lake is one-third drained; Baikal hardly manages to deal with cellulose wastes.

The ecological movement is swelling. Still, this fact should not deceive us into complacency, because nature wants results and not the decisions of meetings attended by thousands, though these have started to bear fruit. For the third time running opponents of the Katun Hydel Project (Northern Altai) succeeded in beating off the scheme which would have destroyed this miraculously preserved area of pre-historic nature and rich human history. The Katun Protection groups (they counted hundreds and thousands) were active in Moscow, Leningrad, Kiev, Novosibirsk, Barnaul and in other cities. The Public Committee for Saving the Volga has been set up and is headed by the author Vasili Belov. Similar committees are at work to save the Obi and Dnieper Rivers. The Baikal Movement has become international: its aim is to save the lake and its river system – which includes Lake Hubsugul in Mongolia, as well as the Biva Lake in Japan and the Sevan Lake in Armenia. Separately, the Baikal Foundation has been launched, with the first contribution made by the Russian Society for Nature Protection (500,000 rubles). Last year over a hundred unofficial nature protection organizations joined together to form the Socio-Ecological Union. The Ecology and Peace Association headed by the author Sergei Zalygin is, in my view, the first in importance; it is known not so much by its numbers as by the ability of its membership of outstanding scientists and public figures to influence decision-making and expertise in cases involving the protection of nature.

Numerous are the ecological groupings both temporary or long-term that crop up and wither in connection with some local problems in the republics, territories and regions. They are overabundant in energy and protest but often fail in culture and knowledge to withstand the well-bred eyewash and professional demagogy that know only too well how to play on consumers' psychology and the current interests of the State. Still, the time will come. If there is time . . .

Many hopes are pinned on the Supreme Soviet, the first one to be democratically elected under Socialism, and on its Ecological Committee. They are the highest authorities to dam departmental monopolism and wastefulness, the State's squandering of our natural riches. The cost-accounting being introduced at republic and regional levels is also a hope.

Were it not too late . . .

Meanwhile . . .

. . . as before, the richer we are, the poorer we become . . .

. . . as before, woods are cut excessively, half the timber burned or lost . . .

. . . hydro-electric stations are designed in the plains, with huge areas to be inundated . . .

. . . the Government ignores public appeals to hold a national referendum on atomic energy . . .

. . . chemical fertilizers turn ploughlands into drug-addicts, black soils disappear at a disastrous pace . . .

Sport

Lev Yashin

The goalkeeper is a very noticeable figure on the football pitch, if only by the fact that he wears an eye-catching sweatshirt and he is the only player in the team who is allowed to handle the ball. Goalkeepers often evoke admiration, but when it comes to choosing the football player of the year, a country or a continent, they are forgotten altogether.

Even the magazine *France-Football*, whose evaluations are considered to be official in Europe, maintains this annoying discrimination against goalkeepers, awarding the 'Golden Ball' only to field players. There has been only one exception throughout history.

By 1963, football fans in Europe knew, as they know to this day, that Lev Yashin in the best goalkeeper ever. That year the breathtaking successes of the Soviet goalkeeper made him recognized as the best football player on the continent.

In 1956, as a member of the national team, he became the champion of the Olympic Games in Melbourne, and in 1960 the European champion. In 1963, as a member of Moscow Dynamo, he became the champion of the USSR for the fifth time. That season he established a stunning record, having let through only six goals in the twenty-seven matches of the whole championship. The same year he was invited to England to participate in the centenary celebration of this wonderful game, as a member of the world team. The balls which he parried from Jimmy Greaves were shown on TV across the world, and became the pearls of football aesthetics.

Lev Yashin proved that he was top class at four World Cup championships in Sweden, Chile, England and Mexico. Yashin has been a member of the symbolic team of the Soviet Union for the past fifty years and, according to the results of a poll run by *France-Football* in 1979, he was the goalkeeper of the symbolic European team from the 1950s to the 1970s.

As this annual is being prepared for publication, the footballing world is about to mark the 60th birthday of this extremely popular Soviet sportsman. Football stars from different generations like Pele, Cruyff, Maradona, Gullit and others will be coming to Moscow.

Football Requires Competence

LEV YASHIN

The way I see it

When I first got into football as a boy, I naturally did not think that I was choosing my life profession. I just immediately understood that football is a great thing. Now, coming up to sixty, I still think that football is a great thing, but now I feel I know why.

For football is a surprisingly three-dimensional and multicoloured reflection of real life. In it, as in life, Good is juxtaposed with Evil, cruelty is found alongside magnanimity, Chance breaks down the Laws in order to prove them more convincingly, Good Luck turns into Bad Luck and then back into Good Luck . . . And human relations! You are wrong if you think that everything boils down to the competition between 'us' and 'them'.

Football is psychological and social, through and through. And what is remarkable is that a person completely switches off from his psychological and social strains when playing or watching the game. They are left outside the pitch and the stadium. A person does not seem to suspect that he has become a participant in or a witness of the same psychological and social models, and emotions which are distinct from the everyday run of things are turned on. He experiences excitement.

Yes, football is a particle of life, its reflection and model. Some people may say that I am exaggerating. Well, maybe. But it does not bother me. I am still sure that anyone who is deeply taken up with his profession, whether theatrical art or diplomacy, carpentry or physics, surgery or football, can easily distinguish within it the characteristics, signs and bonds of life in general.

I will allow myself another such 'exaggeration'. Football as a social phenomenon reflects the condition and processes of society as a whole. That is why the changes in our football are directly connected with the process of perestroika in the country, and sometimes the parallels are striking.

And so, let's look at perestroika in football. It goes without saying that I am not referring to tactics and strategy, technical methods and physical conditions. No, the ball is still round and the goals do not change in size. I am referring to the restructuring of football, its economic and legislative basis. And if, when speaking about the ways of perestroika in the country, we mention glasnost and democratization, the rejection of the administrative command methods of management, the transfer to economic methods and the strengthening of legislative norms, then our football also needs these, as it needs air.

In general, nobody argues with such a formulation of the question. But when it comes to discussing the choice of priorities, the speed of the changes and concrete actions, there are bitter clashes. Some people strive to sort out everything at one go. Others try to make improvements while actually changing nothing. In short, there are both desperate radicals and arrant conservatives. And, between them, a whole range of different shades.

Sometimes one may get the impression that it is difficult to come to any agreement within such a variety of views. The Football Union was established over six months ago. To a great extent, the discussion of its draft rules took the form of a debate over what Soviet football should be like. They finally gathered at the conference in order to adopt the final decision, and they adopted ... a decision on the creation of a totally different organization – the Union of Football Leagues.

Without going into details, I will just mention that the orientation towards professional football, free of interference from an incompetent and ambitious bureaucracy, has prevailed. This is very much to my liking.

I do not have any sort of separate programme, but I have my own view of things. My priority is the football player, the central figure of football play – may the spectators, coaches and referees, whose rights and interests are also sacred and indisputable, forgive me. Nevertheless, football starts with the player. Only after we have studied his personality, provided him with rights and taken care of his interests, or, in other words, after we have grasped the main link of the chain, will we be able to pull the whole chain from the stagnating swamp, and draw the spectators back to the stadium, make football a profitable business, strengthen the economic independence of our clubs and create the basis for the development of mass football.

But people interpret concern for a person in different ways. The recently-established practice of transferring Soviet players to foreign professional clubs was vehemently criticized by the writer Valentin Rasputin in his speech at the First Congress of People's Deputies, for he saw it as a trade in people.

But here is another example. Having only just become a professional club, Dynamo Tbilisi introduced a new approach to a very common situation where one football player injures another. My Georgian club-mates recently put forward a demand to compensate the losses incurred through the treatment of team member Grigory Tsaava, who suffered a broken shin-bone and torn ligaments during a match against another professional club, Chernomorets from Odessa. I don't know what the outcome will be, but the very fact that the question has been formulated in this way is important. As far as I know, there is no such practice anywhere else in the world.

Which of these two positions shows more respect for the player? I so much want to argue with the writer, whose point of view I have always respected.

Two fates

I have just returned from Kiev after the farewell match of our country's outstanding football player, Oleg Blokhin. It was a real football festival, an event of national and international importance. 'This is the way to leave football!' I thought during the three days that I spent in the Ukrainian capital, feeling sincerely happy for Oleg, whose invitation was accepted by many stars from world football. It was no joke – one and a half million people expressed their wish to go to the stadium in Kiev on that day. There were even three hundred requests from the United States. Blokhin is the holder of all the possible and impossible records of our football. Nobody has played so many games for his club and for the national team, nobody has scored so many goals, nobody has won so many medals and prizes.

At thirty-seven Oleg has retained his health and capacity for work, and has also accumulated invaluable experience. He was the first to overcome the resistance of the bureaucrats in sport and spent two seasons with a professional Austrian club as a playing coach, earning good money by our standards. His farewell match turned out to be an honourable civic act and was conducted in the name of 'Charity instead of Vandalism'. All the takings from the events within the framework of the farewell match were donated to the Soviet Children's Fund for the benefit of orphaned and abandoned children. In this way, an exceptionally valuable charitable aspect of the development of Soviet professional football has been created.

Somehow, all the injuries, bruises and fatigue were forgotten on those days, though they could hardly have been avoided during such a long life in football! It is a different matter when, finishing his sporting career, a veteran is left face to face with his fatigue and bruises, with nothing ahead but the cruel necessity of starting life afresh. And this is at the age of thirty to thirty-five! Alas, until recently this was the end that nearly always awaited our football stars. But there were truly tragic cases against this general background of misfortune . . .

Igor Chislenko was known as 'the magnificent seven' of my club, Moscow Dynamo, and the national team in the 1960s. Oh, how he played! From my goal I could clearly see how he tackled the defence on the right wing of our attack. Thick-set and swift, he would rush forward and boldly go for the defender, his body slightly swaying, looking not at the ball but at the footwork of his retreating opponent. Right near the corner of the penalty box Igor would make a feint to the right, which was impossible not to believe in, but then retreat sharply to the centre and give a lethal kick with his left.

I remember it nearly word for word: 'At the 39th minute, the Russian star Chislenko "crucified" Albertosi in the goal with a terrifyingly powerful shot.' That's what one of the English newspapers wrote the day after the game between our team and the Italians at the World Cup in London in 1966. That goal of Igor's was the only one that hit the net of my Italian counterpart and it took us to the semi-final; this is still the highest achievement of Soviet football in world tournaments.

We played against the powerful West German team in the semi-finals. Igor Chislenko distinguished himself once again – but this time in a negative way. At the end of the first half of an exceptionally relentless match he lost the ball in a very tough tackle with a defender. This was followed by a long pass to the present-day West German coach, the then very young Franz Beckenbauer. And he put the ball in my net.

At that moment Chislenko lost his cool. We had scarcely started from the centre of the pitch when, going in to tackle the same defender who had 'insulted' him, Igor kicked him on the legs. It was obvious that it wasn't an act of cruelty, but rather of dismay. A minute later, the German player was running round the pitch as if nothing had happened. But Igor was sent off by the referee.

I remember how warmly we were supported by the English fans gathered in the Liverpool stadium that day, when ten of us were trying to save the game and even scored a goal, but were nevertheless forced to give up and were deprived of the right to play in the finals against the English team, who became the world champions that year.

However, in the next year in the Soviet team did play against the English at the famous Wembley Stadium. It was a friendly match, but in its relentlessness it could be compared with a championship one. And again Chislenko's talent sparkled. It was he, with the help of another, who twice settled scores with the hosts, enabling the Soviet team to achieve an honourable draw with the world champions.

Such ups and downs were characteristic of this outstanding player. His brilliant, inspired play was changed by some particularly annoying disruptions when weeks of relentless training (during which Igor mastered in a few weeks a vicious kick called the 'dry leaf', which we had been taught by the Brazilians) were followed by grave violations of the training schedule in the company of some dubious people. But still, love of football and Russian hockey, which he also played very well, kept Igor from the final fall.

The finale of Chislenko's sporting career were the matches played by our national team in 1968 ... in Czechoslovakia. I won't go into details about the political situation at that time, which is well known to the Western reader. I will only say that we should never have played football under those conditions. However, in order to gratify our political authorities, our sports authorities decided to show the whole world that the Soviet tanks in Prague did not embitter anyone in the least. Look, we are playing football. As a result of one such 'friendly' match, some players from our team came back home in plaster casts, some on stretchers and some in both conditions. One of these was Igor Chislenko.

Leaving big-time sport is a hard thing for anyone, even for a very strong-willed person. But when it is combined with physical and moral pain, a feeling of emptiness and bitterness, and there are only dubious friends around who know only way to console you ...

Igor's real friends, and first of all his team-mates, tried to help him. They found him a place as a coach in a provincial team. He went there but soon returned: the salary was low and it was difficult work without any special education. But when could he have studied? He played football in the summer and hockey in the winter. He, who could so well overcome the defence of his opponents on the football pitch, failed to overcome normal everyday difficulties.

Eighteen years ago, in 1971, I was saying goodbye to football just as Blokhin has done recently. Incidentally, there was nothing of that kind in our football in between these two events, and that says a lot about the way in which we treat football personalities. Meanwhile, during this time, such heroes of the ball as Albert Shesternov, Murtaz Khurtsilava, Valery Voronin, Eduard Streltsov and others left football. I could name more.

I invited Igor Chislenko to play at least fifteen minutes in my farewell match. I wanted to give him support, to make him wake up. There was no question of his showing his former top class, but nevertheless he somehow pulled himself together and started training. The spectators greeted him and saw him off warmly, despite the fact that there were such stars as Bobby Charlton and Gert Muller there. The fans loved him, even those who were not supporters of Moscow Dynamo.

It is not very productive to compare football players of different generations, but I can say with conviction that, judging by the calibre of footballing talent, Igor Chislenko was on a par with Oleg Blokhin. Some people may object that their characters and purely human qualities are not comparable. Of course, this is true, but it is not only characters that matter. People are different, and a lot depends on the conditions in which they live and by which they are formed.

Very often, our sportsmen have found themselves on the roadside of life. Are things changing now? I think they are, and it's obvious from Blokhin's example. People have been given the chance to be themselves and not to pretend to be something they are not. It is invaluable that Igor Chislenko told his own story in the country's most popular TV programme 'Vzglyad'. It is a good sign that things are improving both in personal and public life. For it was not for nothing that one old book said: 'the Word came first.' We are adapting this idea to our reality, first and foremost through glasnost.

Hero and antihero

Yes, glasnost has liberated the football player from the burden of the necessity to lie and pretend to be a student or a fitter. This lie came to life somehow unnoticed and by degrees. I came to big-time football from the lathe, as we say, and called myself a worker without batting an eyelid, though I then became a soldier who performed his service in goal. It's not an easy way to earn a living, but why should I conceal the fact that I was earning it on the football pitch?

Those were the years of the football boom. Along with football the country was forgetting the war, but along with football it could not forget it. Like war, football was in its own way the continuation of politics. The triumphal English tour by Moscow Dynamo in 1945 was the second major event of the year after Victory Day. And although the team went to an allied country, the task was quite a militant one – to win and to make them respect us. The players did everything not from fear but from conscience, not for the prizes or benefits but purely out of patriotism. After that came the years of the Cold War. Both here and in the West they were actively drawing and implanting the image of the enemy. I remember that as an integral part of any film about football there would be a match against a Western team where players with ominous faces were scheming against our factory boys both on and off the pitch.

I am also a patriot and will remain one, but I have never believed, and don't believe now, any crude propaganda. Factory boys who play football in their free time do not play against Western teams, and those who do play against foreigners are only registered in factories. But stereotypes are dangerous for the simple reason that they influence the subconscious. The dogmatic leadership liked this image of the Soviet football player, and the Soviet football player, in order not to wreck his own life, accepted the enforced rules of the game, very often not realizing that they might be dangerous.

For society, the football player represented a person who quite professionally fulfilled a very important social function both at home and abroad, and got practically nothing in return in terms of social security and assurances for the future. The little he did receive from society he had to hide in order not to ruin the bright image of the Soviet sportsman. This basic lie and uncertainty distorted many souls, turning some people into cynics and others into fools.

But, as is known, one small lie gives rise to others. In contrast to the image of an ideal goody-goody, a new stereotype of the football player as a condescending favourite of fortune began to affirm itself in public opinion. The belief spread that football players have unheard-of privileges, touring abroad and living a life of leisure and fun . . .

I think that the prevalence of such views can be explained by the closed nature of our society, the permanent emptiness of our shop counters and the lack of reliable information. In these conditions, such details from the lives of football stars could irritate people. For example, our team went to South America several times. The takings from those matches were pretty good, but in each country we only received fifty dollars as pocket money. However, even for this money we could buy several nylon shirts and waterproof raincoats, which were very fashionable twenty years ago. If you add the bonus of five thousand rubles for victory in the national championship to these 'sources of luxury', you will get a more-or-less accurate picture of that material wealth a football player could count on apart from his salary at his registered workplace.

I am absolutely sure that lies and double-thinking would have led our football into degradation sooner or later, and this is despite the fact that I consider football to be our national game and that our multinational country is a well of footballing talent. The most important thing we lack is competence and real professionalism. This concerns players, coaches, referees and organizers. We are still at the prepatory level.

We are starting to study

Once again, people may object. How is it that we are the European Silver champions and Olympic champions, our football players are highly rated on the football market? No, I have not forgotten this. But I still remember the complete failure of our clubs in all European tournaments. I remember that quite recently Alexander Zavorov had to break his contract with Juventus in Italy. And one shouldn't treat it as incidental, because Renat Dasayev, Vagis Khidiyatullin and Vasily Ratz all testify in unison that they have a tragic lack of professionalism. But all these are world-class footballers and there is no denying that they are all talented and industrious. And if you take into account that those of our players who play for less famous foreign clubs encounter similar difficulties, it becomes clear how far we are lagging behind.

There is only one way out – to study. In this sense I am expecting a lot from the return of our professionals who are now playing abroad and are receiving wonderful training. Our referee corps needs an influx of competent men. The administrative command system of football management turned our coach into a very unconvincing, dependent and ingratiating figure. What are we speaking about when even the coach of the national team works without a contract? Since there is no contract, that means the term of work is unknown, and legal relations with the State Sports Committee, the Football Federation and clubs are not fixed. The duties of the coach and the players are not formulated in any document which has juridical force. Only one constant demand is clearly seen: to win every match, even if it is a training one. The present-day coach of our national team, Valery Lobanovsky, has recently written about this bitterly in the press. He said that his cherished dream is to become the last coach without rights in the Soviet Union.

During the quarter of a century that I spent on football pitches, I have been sent off only once from my home stadium, Dynamo, in Petrovsky Park in Moscow. It happened so long ago that I do not have any personal reasons for bearing a particular grudge against referees. However, I am very dissatisfied with them. To my mind, it is the weakest link in our football, but a very important one. I can count the number of our referees who would meet international requirements on the fingers of one hand. There is hardly a match that finishes without any complaints to the referee. And it is generally not just one side, but both, that are displeased with the refereeing.

Public opinion was stirred once again by a recent fuss about a howling error made by the referee in the final USSR cup match, when he disallowed a goal scored in the Dnepr net, and the match ended with the score 0:1 to Moscow Torpedo. It is clear that we have to break away from amateurism and switch to professionalism in this field. For apart from the quite understandable disappointments connected with referees' mistakes, there is also the aspect of injuries. I have no comparative data on football injuries in other countries, but I think that we can outshine anyone on this score. Take, for example, Dynamo Kiev. I do not remember a single game this year when three or four men from the regular team were not absent because of injury, and this is the basic team for our national team! In football, as in real life, everything is interconnected. The incompetence of our referees may result in irreparable losses in our national team at the World Cup in Italy.

I am an easy-going man, but one thing has always irritated me – carelessness and incompetence in serious business. At the moment, qualitatively new structures of management, new forms of economic management and new, so to speak, production relations are taking shape in football. All this is very serious. Football must not only pay for itself, but also be profitable. I would have thought it would be clear to everyone, but here is the simplest example to show that it is clearly not so. Football matches start here at 6.30, i.e. immediately after the working day at most factories and offices. A man who decides to go to a match deprives himself of his home-cooked dinner or postpones it for three or four hours.

This is a potential goldmine for trade. But no such luck! For several months last year, in the popular daily programme 'Football Review', the best Soviet sports commentators regularly put to shame before the whole country trade representatives and the management of stadiums for their inefficiency in organizing the sale of such easy and profitable things as pies, lemonade and hot dogs on match days. Do you think anything has changed? If you do, that means you don't know us. The journalists have given up. And if you come to the Soviet Union, to Moscow, and visit the Dynamo stadium where your old friend Lev Yashin served football some time ago, on a hot day, before the match you are able to buy a portion of Moscow ice cream (which is the best in the world) without a queue, you have to realize that you have become the witness of really revolutionary changes in the commercialization of Soviet sport.

We have the chance

It has always been considered improper to predict sports results. Maybe this stemmed from films about football. An exemplary Soviet coach from such films (or a sports leader or a leading player), besieged by importunate Western journalists, utters something like this with modest dignity: 'The ball is round. The game will show the result. The strongest team will win.' I myself have spoken like that many times and I advise you to bear it in mind. It doesn't matter that you will be considered a bore – you will never be wrong.

But of course, like all normal people, we try to look into the future, to guess and to be more sagacious than everyone else. In our own circle we sometimes argue until we are hoarse about who has the best chances of winning. But it is absolutely different to make public statements . . .

So what are we to do? You cannot avoid talking about the forthcoming World Cup in Italy in the summer of 1990. Let's do it in this way – I will simply share some of my opinions with you.

You can undoubtedly put your bets on Italy. This is clear, even to amateurs. When an objectively strong team plays at home, that doubles its chances. But that is not the only factor. Over the past few days I happened to see a couple of TV clips from games played by Italian teams. Of course they were, so to speak, selected extracts. But I was struck by some sort of special ardour in the Italian players. You could sense that they get pleasure out of the game. True, there are a lot of foreign stars in their clubs, and it's possible that the spark of inspiration comes from them. But, one way or the other, the Italian team is the favourite.

The Dutch team, with its own stars like Ruud Gullit and Marko Van Basten, is on its way up. I hope the Soviet team meets this one as late as possible. I am afraid that a couple of previous losses by our lads have created a kind of 'Dutch complex' which will be very difficult for them to overcome. I don't know about you, but I have not been put at ease by the dull play of the Brazilians in their recent tour round Europe. We must remember that the Brazilians and Argentinians can in a matter of months build up a qualitatively new national team. The sixteen-year-old Pele and eighteen-year-old Maradona first appeared in those teams. England? West Germany? One of these great footballing powers will definitely realize its potential and arrive in Italy with a team capable of fighting for the gold.

I think our team also has a reasonable chance of winning medals.

With all the instability of the status of the coach of the Soviet national team, we must remember that there is a specialist of world calibre standing at the helm. Valery Lobanovsky has already announced that, regardless of the result, he will retire from the national team after the championship. That means it is his last chance. His unquestionable competence and ability to put his ideas into practice speak in his favour. Also, the players see in him their older friend and the protector of their rights and interests. It is Lobanovsky who has been pushing many innovations in favour of the players.

We also have the very powerful and well-tested backbone of the team: Morozov, Baltacha, Bessonov, Demyanenko and Khadiyatullin in defence; Ratz, Yaremchuk, Alenikov, Yakovenko, Mikhailichenko and Litovchenko midfield; and Protasov and Belanov attacking. All of them are matured masters. Let's only hope that they will recover from their injuries and come to the championship in top form.

It seems that I haven't named Zavarov. Alexander's unlucky season in Milan's Juventus may, as they say, arouse the beast in him. I don't think anyone doubts that he can play. So in Italy he will want to show his true worth. There is also a group of young players (but already tried out in different games, including the Olympics) at Lobanovsky's disposal. These are defenders Gorlukovich and Luzhny, the midfield player Dobrovolsky and attacker Savichev. There are also one and a half to two dozen players with good potential, who might at any moment achieve good results.

I myself greatly rely on the very sharp attackers from my old team, Moscow Dynamo, who have only just made themselves known. Make a note of their names: Kiriakov, Kolivanov and Dobrovolsky.

And now a special word about goalkeepers. We have many of them who are quite good. Dasayev's experience is very disarming. But there are a couple of others who can compete with him. For example, in Moscow Dynamo, there are two strong goalkeepers – Kharin and Uvarov – so sometimes it is difficult for the coaches to choose one even within the same club. In general I think that there is a lot of the goalkeeper in our national character. Sometimes we retreat to a critical limit and then start to save the situation. However, all this is very debatable.

When speaking about our team's chances, I always subconsciously weigh up what changes will take place in our football, where we will succeed and where we will fail, how the players' mentality will alter. In this respect the following episode seems very significant to me.

FOOTBALL REQUIRES COMPETENCE

Everyone has noticed the great improvement in Igor Konovalov, the attacker of Moscow Dynamo whom I've already mentioned. People ask: 'What has happened to you?' And he answers: 'I got married. It's time to take life seriously.'

I liked the answer of this twenty-year-old man. Finally the normal human stimuli have started working in our football.

Public Opinion Polls in the USSR

The All-Union Centre of Public Opinion Studies, which was established last year and is headed by the prominent Soviet sociologist Academician Tatyana Zaslavskaya, has conducted its first public opinion polls. Some of the results of these polls are as follows.

Pressing social and economic problems

Answering the question 'Which of the problems facing society most negatively effects your personal life?', 55 per cent of those polled indicated the poor supply of consumer goods. Every other person questioned also mentioned difficulties in procuring foodstuffs and complained of injustices in the distribution of benefits. When asked to name the most acute problem, the majority listed it as housing.

The frequency of the responses has divided the problems into two clear groups. The first group (it heads the list) comprises the lack of consumer goods, lack of foodstuffs, the housing problem, low living standards, ecology and social injustice. The second group (the bottom part of the list) includes the domination of bureaucracy, difficulties in education and raising the younger generation, poor health service and low pensions.

The pollsters believe that the priorities were such because the first group is composed of those which are 'nearest' to people's daily life, while the second group includes the problems considered by people to be 'distant' prospects. Crudely put, the population is more concerned about the solution of immediate problems (where to live, what to eat, what to wear) than about the fate of the aged and the future of their children.

What are the specific 'sore points' that hamper a resolution of social and economic problems?

As regards food, the main problems were listed as the lack of food products (52 per cent of respondents), the high prices of cooperative products (40 per cent) and the widespread use of 'blat' – connections, cheating and speculation in trade practices (33 per cent). In the area of housing the major concerns were the long (many years) waiting lists for a flat – 70 per cent followed by unfair practices in the distribution of flats and the low quality of construction work – 43 and 37 per cent respectively. The acuteness of the ecological problem is closely connected with air pollution in the cities – 69 per cent, the pollution of rivers, lakes and seas – 54 per cent, and with the growing radiation level in urban areas – 42 per cent.

Elections: a new style

To get an idea of the political atmosphere during the election campaign, people were asked to evaluate perestroika's progress. 27 per cent see the main achievements of perestroika as 'glasnost and true information in the press'. 13–19 per cent mentioned the questions of economic reform as a most important aspect, while only 13 per cent pointed to the multicandidate elections and a mere 8 per cent mentioned the changes in the structure of the highest state bodies.

Only 4 per cent blame perestroika for the economic difficulties, the majority (57 per cent) opinion is that the 'economic difficulties are the result of the mistakes of the past.' 18 per cent believe that 'the difficulties are the inevitable consequences of Socialism as an economic system.'

The poll has shown that 82 per cent were 'familiar' or 'partially familiar' with the new method for nominating candidates for People's Deputies of the USSR. 48 per cent rated the efficiency of the new procedure for candidates' nominations as positive, 12 per cent as negative and 39 per cent said it was difficult to judge.

The attitude of the population to the various forms of participation in the political process was also voiced in answers to a question about the impact of different kinds of public activity on governmental decisions. 49 per cent named publications in the press, radio and TV appearances, 38 per cent participation in mass public opinion polls, 14 per cent involvement in the elections of people's deputies.

Leasing in the non-agricultural sector of the economy

90 per cent of leaseholders viewed leases positively. When questioned about how the shift to leasing had allowed them independence of the ministries, 88 per cent responded that it had given them the right to spend the funds assigned for the development of production, science and technology; 80 per cent said it was the right to determine wages for the workers of their enterprises; 30 per cent said it was the ability to determine the foundation for promising production programmes.

The question 'What are the main difficulties in the operation of your enterprise under the new economic conditions?' received the following responses from leaseholders: 40 per cent named the absence of a wholesale market in material resources; 47 per cent the discrepancy between the new economic conditions and established economic practices and regulations which are still in force; 29 per cent the absence of an institutionalized, legal status for the operation of enterprises under the new economic conditions.

Problems and prospects of school development

73 per cent of the teachers who were polled believed that the secondary school system was in deep crisis and required fundamental restructuring. The parents who were polled linked school problems primarily with its 'poor financial state' (39 per cent). The relationship between teachers and pupils are not all that simple. While 61 per cent of the teachers claimed that they were ready to discuss any topic with pupils, only 43 per cent of the pupils responded that teachers indeed discuss acute problems with them; 16 per cent replied that they had had discussions concerning the ethnic question; 13 per cent problems of sex; 21 per cent the actions of the highest leadership of the country.

Many teachers suggest 'giving senior high school pupils the opportunity to choose representatives' in order to broaden the content of school education (64 per cent of respondents), 'an expansion of the network of special classes and schools' (35 per cent) and 'the introduction of new subjects at pupils' request' (23 per cent).

Public opinion on the election of managers

20 per cent of the workers polled and 35 per cent of shop foremen believed that there will be serious negative consequences if managers are elected. Ordinary workers realize, however, that the opponents of elections will not report to direct bans. The danger of turning elections into a mere show was voiced by 65 to 75 per cent of the respondents.

When analysing the methods to overcome the difficulties and obstacles inherent in the election of managers, the respondents focused their attention on the need to provide independence for ordinary workers in the election of managers (36 to 47 per cent); an enhancement of workers' involvement in the affairs of the enterprise (34 to 47 per cent); and the need to keep the workers better informed (35 to 51 per cent).

Armenia: Lessons for All
(On the Problems and Tasks for Ensuring the Adequate Quality of Construction)

What lessons imperative to the rebuilding of the devastated Armenian cities have been learned from the earthquake?

Valery Serov, Chairman of Gosstroy (State Construction Committee) of the USSR answers this question.

The tragedy of Armenia, which was severely damaged by the earthquake, has grieved our country, and has produced an unprecedented wave of solidarity and sympathy throughout the world.

After the first painful shock had passed, the time came for sober assessments and conclusions. It became increasingly clear that it was not only nature that had caused such large-scale disaster and tremendous loss of human life, but people themselves were also to be blamed. Some neglected their duty and conscience, honesty and responsibility, others merely resigned themselves to these people as to an inevitable evil.

There is a widespread opinion, expressed by some prominent Armenian construction experts and supported by experts from other constituent republics, that seismic mistakes accounted for approximately 20 per cent of the serious discrepancy between the strength of the tremors and their destructive consequences. Nine-tenths of Armenia lies within a 9-point zone, but the overwhelming majority of buildings were constructed to withstand tremors of up to 7 points.

Part of the responsibility must also be borne by Armenians who light-heartedly ignored the requirements for durability in favour of home-made designs. In the remodelling of their houses, these people displayed a dangerous inventiveness that turned their homes into deadly traps. Some 30 per cent of the responsibility can be attributed to design errors and inadequate standards. The *ad hoc* expert commission thoroughly analysed the technical documentation used during the construction of all the destroyed buildings and will bring legal charges against those responsible for substandard work. Another 30 per cent of the blame can be placed on some construction workers, their obviously shoddy work and sometimes even theft. Eye-witnesses who visited the most severely hit areas say that some seemingly intact prefabricated panels broke into pieces when struck only lightly with a hand . . . Certainly it is not only 'black humour' which accounts for the Armenian anecdote about the cement which at a court trial presents the alibi that it never was at the scene of the crime!

The above-mentioned factors appreciably aggravated the problems caused by the quake. At present the most acute problem is, of course, housing for the population of the devastated areas. The task is tremendous. Within two years it will be necessary to restore and rebuild houses with a total floor-space of four million square metres, as well as public, cultural, trade and service facilities. It should not be forgotten that the construction industry was also severely damaged, and more than twelve construction enterprises completely destroyed.

No matter how bitter it is to speak about and recognize these drawbacks, failures and even abuses, it must be done in order to guarantee that they are not repeated; to guarantee, to the best of our abilities, that the population is provided with safe, reliable and comfortable homes. In so doing, one should proceed from an understanding of the present situation – that is, we are not capable of building houses fit for the twenty-first century and, therefore, should build them so that it will be easier for our children to modify them to correspond to the standards of comfort at their own time. The main conclusions we must draw are as follows.

It is imperative that we stop treating the serious notion of durability light-heartedly. A niggardly approach to construction must be forever abandoned as a thing of the past, typical of the time of 'economic economy', when top priority was not given to quality, comfort or functional qualities, but to cheapness.

After heated debates in Armenia, it was decided to concentrate on monolithic house construction because it had proved to be most reliable in the disaster-struck areas. Home-made stone-cubes will be widely used. Frameless construction with prefabricated panels will also be allowed. A common finishing style made possible by the use of local materials will help to avoid architectural eclecticism, because aesthetics is an important element for evaluating the quality of construction.

As to the number of floors, it was decided to be cautious and to build three- or four-storeyed houses in towns and one- and two-storeyed houses in the countryside. The projects of would-be Armenian settlements are being discussed at farmers' meetings and at work collectives with thoroughness and attention to detail. The wide use of light concrete and mobile concrete-mixers as well as concrete-mixers with gravitational and forced systems are to be a precondition for high-quality construction work. Flexible steel frameworks will be replaced by rigid ones and reinforced concrete girders will give way to light metal structures.

It should also not be forgotten that alongside new housing construction there is the ongoing process of the capital repair of houses which suffered from the earthquake but were not destroyed, the reinforcement of intact dwellings throughout Armenia and the implementation of the All-Union Programme 'Housing 2000'. All other factors considered, the human factor is, of course, the decisive one in implementing the large-scale and extremely complex plans for rapid and high-quality construction. The pain from incurable losses is likely to change many people's attitude towards their work. Perestroika, of all the aspects of our life and Soviet society, also aims to overcome the harmful alienation of the people from the results of their work, to form the social, economic and moral conditions under which only honest and conscientious work, and a high sense of personal responsibility, will accommodate the interests of both individuals and society.

Putting aside the peculiarities of the specific seismic and geological conditions in Armenia, it is becoming clear that the lessons and conclusions from, as well as the considerations about, the tragedy should be learned by all Soviet people in whatever part of the country they live and work.

A Chronology of Perestroika
(July 1988 to July 1989)

28 August 1988 The USSR began its planned elimination of middle-range missiles as provided for by the INF Treaty. Three SS-20 missiles were destroyed by demolition on the Kapustin Yar testing ground.
30 September 1988 The plenary meeting of the CPSU Central Committee considered proposals to reorganize the Party apparatus, discussed personnel questions and accepted the request of Andrei Gromyko, Chairman of the Presidium of the USSR Supreme Soviet, to be relieved of his duties and allowed to retire.
1 October 1988 A special session of the USSR Supreme Soviet elected Mikhail Gorbachev head of the Soviet State and made other governmental changes.
5 November 1988 At the ceremonial meeting to mark the 71st anniversary of the Great October Socialist Revolution, Nikolai Slyunkov, secretary of the CPSU Central Committee, gave a programmatic report 'To Release the Constructive Forces of Socialism'.
18 to 20 November 1988 Mikhail Gorbachev visited India, marking the realization of the principles of new political thinking as outlined in the Delhi Declaration.
29 November to 2 December 1988 A special session of the USSR Supreme Soviet heard Mikhail Gorbachev's report, 'Towards Full Power for the Soviets and Building a Socialist Rule-of-law State', and adopted the laws on the elections of People's Deputies and changes and additions to the Constitution of the USSR.
1 to 4 December 1988 Four armed bandits took 30 schoolchildren and their teacher hostage in the city of Ordzhenikidze and fled to Tel-Aviv in a plane which was given to them on their

demand. The Israeli government demonstrated goodwill in combating terrorism in the air; without delay it extradited to the Soviet authorities the criminals, plane, money and valuables extorted by them.

7 December 1988 Mikhail Gorbachev spoke at the 43rd Session of the UN General Assembly putting forward new Soviet initiatives on the reduction of armed forces and armaments. This gave a new impetus to disarmament.

7 December 1988 A severe earthquake hit Armenia, killing a large number of people and causing an unprecedented wave of international solidarity and sympathy.

30 December 1988 The end of a four-month-long criminal trial involving high-ranking officials of the Ministry of the Interior, including Yuri Churbanov, the former First Deputy Minister of the Interior of the USSR and Leonid Brezhnev's son-in-law. The sentence passed by the Military Collegium of the USSR Supreme Court provoked a mixed reaction in the Soviet public. Some people were dissatisfied with the 'leniency of punishment' for the criminals.

31 December 1988 In his New Year Address to the Soviet people Mikhail Gorbachev stressed that the year of 1988 had been marked by large-scale work to restructure the USSR's economy and an improvement in international relations. He called on his countrymen to take resolute steps to deal with the heavy burden of unresolved problems for the benefit of the Motherland and the world.

10 January 1989 A plenary meeting of the CPSU Central Committee, unprecedented in the history of the Party, considered the question of the nomination of candidates for People's Deputies of the USSR on the Party ticket. It also issued an Appeal, 'To the Party and the Soviet People', which became the CPSU's political platform for the elections.

12 January 1989 Growing ethnic tension in Nagorny Karabakh forced the USSR Supreme Soviet to issue a decree on introducing Special Rule in the territory. All governmental functions in this autonomous region of the Azerbaijan SSR were taken over by the Committee of Special Rule directly subordinate to the highest bodies of State power and administration of the USSR.

A CHRONOLOGY OF PERESTROIKA

12 to 19 January 1989 The All-Union census of the population of the USSR provided a collective profile of the nearly 300 million people at the present stage of perestroika.

15 February 1989 The last Soviet soldier left Afghanistan. The Soviet Union scrupulously implemented the Geneva Accords relating to a peaceful settlement of the long conflict in that country and the region as a whole.

11 March 1989 Public organizations which were given 750 – one-third – of all the seats at the Congress of People's Deputies began electing their deputies.

15 March 1989 A plenary meeting of the CPSU Central Committee heard Mikhail Gorbachev's report, 'On the Agrarian Policy of the CPSU under Present Conditions', and adopted a programme for radical changes in the countryside. One hundred People's Deputies were elected on the Party ticket, which signifies the profound changes which are taking place in Party life during the course of political reform.

26 March 1989 Elections of People's Deputies of the USSR. For the first time in many years not voting mechanically, but truly electing the 1,500 most deserved Soviet representatives, the Soviet people made a big step towards democratic forms of free choice and politicizing of the masses.

2 April 1989 The first Soviet-Irish summit meeting in Shannon began a series of talks which Mikhail Gorbachev conducted with the leaders of Ireland, Cuba and Great Britain. Their outcome vividly showed that new political thinking has been gaining momentum and is winning credence with the world public.

9 April 1989 Sixteen people were killed in front of Government House in Tbilisi during actions aimed at stopping public disorder. According to Eduard Shevardnadze, a Politburo member who arrived in the Georgian capital, the decision to use units of the regular army had elements of haste and led to a change in the republic's leadership.

25 April 1989 A plenary meeting of the CPSU Central Committee gave a political assessment of the current stage of perestroika in the light of the elections which, as a matter of fact, had become a popular referendum supporting the renewal of society. The retirement of 110 members and alternative members of the CPSU Central Committee was viewed by many in the USSR and abroad as a positive step for perestroika.

28 April 1989   TASS circulated the proposal of the Party Control Committee attached to the CPSU Central Committee that the well-known publicist writer Roy Medvedev be reinstated in the CPSU. He was expelled from the Party in 1969 for writing the book *Let History Judge*, which investigated the nature and consequences of Stalin's personality cult.

7 May 1989   The press published a report on a session of the Collegium of the KGB which adopted decisions that provide for a wide range of practical measures to enhance glasnost in the activities of the agency and its troops.

15 to 18 May 1989   The first visit of a Soviet leader to China since 1959. Mikhail Gorbachev's talks in Beijing, which normalized Sino-Soviet State and Party relations, became a remarkable event of our times. Assessing their importance for the fate of the world, newspapermen termed this event 'a bridge over the precipice'.

24 May 1989   TASS reported that the Presidium of the USSR Supreme Soviet accepted the request of the prominent Soviet theatre director Yuri Lyubimov for restoration of his Soviet citizenship, which had been revoked without sufficient grounds during Brezhnev's term in office.

25 May to 9 June 1989   The first Congress of People's Deputies of the USSR opened. It is evidence of the unprecedented upsurge of social and political activity of the masses and awakening of their civic self-consciousness which was set in motion by the intellectual initiative of the Communist Party of the Soviet Union. The Congress elected Mikhail Gorbachev Chairman of the Supreme Soviet of the USSR, formed the Supreme Soviet and Constitutional Commission, and discussed a number of important questions. This unique forum issued an Appeal to the Peoples of the World calling for a large-scale exchange of ideas and people, cultural and spiritual values, contacts, dialogues at all levels, mutually acceptable compromises for preserving peace on Earth and for the well-being and progress of all mankind.

7 June 1989   The first joint session of the chambers of the

USSR Supreme Soviet appointed Nikolai Ryzhkov to the post of head of the Soviet Government.

12 to 15 June 1989 First foreign trip by Mikhail Gorbachev as the newly elected head of the Soviet State. This official visit to the Federal Republic of Germany opened, in the opinion of foreign commentators, a new chapter in European and world politics.

23 June 1989 The Union of USSR Lawyers was established. Its priority tasks are to promote democratization and glasnost in the legislative activities of the State and to foster a constitutional regime in the country.

25 June 1989 The press published a decree of the Congress of People's Deputies, 'On the Guidelines for the Domestic and Foreign Policies of the USSR', which means that, expressing the will of the people, the Congress takes over full state power of the country.

2 July 1989 Mikhail Gorbachev appeared on Central TV and raised the issue of elaborating and implementing a package of measures to normalize and harmonize ethnic relations in the Soviet Federation.

4 August 1989 The first session of the new Supreme Soviet of the USSR elected by the Congress of People's Deputies ended. It showed that an appropriate form had been found for a standing body of the USSR's highest legislative and controlling power that can put into practice and broaden the course outlined by the Congress. For the first time in the post-Lenin period the Soviet people have a government whose members had been scrutinized by the Deputies in the committees, commissions and at the sessions of the Supreme Soviet. Not all the candidates for ministerial positions passed this test: nine candidates, among them a contender for a Deputy Premier's post, were not confirmed for the posts of ministers and chairmen of State committees. The session, which concentrated on economic and social problems, approved changes in the existing Law on State Enterprise, thus stimulating the progress of economic reforms. It also passed a law on Urgent Measures for Improving Pension Provision and Social Insurance of the Population. The work of the Supreme Soviet's Commission on Privileges and Benefits provoke keen interest on the part of the Soviet public. Some specific recommendations of the Commission concerning the restoration of justice are already being carried out. A decree on Resolute Measures for Stepping Up the Fight Against Crime was also welcomed by all strata of Soviet society.

As regards foreign policy, the Supreme Soviet issued an Appeal to the US Congress to start a moratorium on nuclear weapons and to stop nuclear tests. It also ratified three international treaties signed by the USSR.

Bibliography

M. S. Gorbachev, *Perestroika and the New Thinking for Our Country and the World* (Moscow, Politizdat, 1987). Also published by Harper and Row in 40 languages, this work of great theoretical and practical importance has occupied a prominent place among political bestsellers. It is circulated in more than 100 countries with a total print-run exceeding 3.5 million copies.

M. S. Gorbachev, *On the Guidelines for Domestic and Foreign Policies of the USSR* (Moscow, Politizdat, 1989). The report and the closing speech delivered by the Chairman of the Supreme Soviet of the USSR at the Congress of People's Deputies of the USSR, which mapped out the general aims and goals of the renewal process in the Soviet Union.

N. I. Ryzhkov, *On the Programme of the Future Government of the USSR* (Moscow, Politizdat, 1989). The report and the closing speech by the head of the Soviet Government at the Congress of People's Deputies on the practical implementation of perestroika in the Soviet Union.

No Other Way (Moscow, Progress Publishers, 1988). A collection of articles written by prominent Soviet scholars, writers and journalists, edited by Yuri Afanasiev, which contains reflections on the future of perestroika and our country's past and present. The authors express various viewpoints; therefore this collection is a notable example of glasnost, democracy and pluralism in action.

'Speaking Frankly: Writers' Notes on Ethnic Relations', Moscow, *Khudozhestvennaye Literatura*, 1989. Famous men of letters representing a broad ethnic spectrum of the population of our multilanguage country openly share their opinions on the most acute problems facing Soviet society today.

'Not to Forget Man', *Komsomolskaya Pravda*, 31 December 1988. Interview on economic issues with Boris Eltsin, a former minister, now member of the Supreme Soviet.

'By the Force of Example, by the Force of Persuasion', *Pravda*, 20 February 1989. Detailed and frank answers to readers' questions given by Prof. A. Kapto (Doc. of Phil.), head of the newly established Ideological Department of the CPSU Central Committee.

'The Ecology of the Human Spirit', *Sovetskaya Kultura*, 23 March 1989. A profound dialogue full of humanism between Academician Dmitri Likhachev and Metropolitan Pitirim of Volokolamsk and Yuriev on major social, cultural and spiritual problems of modern life.

'The Intellectual Dignity of the Party', *Pravda*, 23 May 1989. A fundamental theoretical study by V. Legostaev of some important questions of the inner life of the Party, an encouragement to begin discussion about the future of the Party within the Party itself and the Party press.

BIBLIOGRAPHY

I. Klyamkin, 'Why it is So Difficult to Speak the Truth: Selected Passages from the Medical History of One Illness', *Novy Mir*, no. 2, 1989. In an attempt to find the answer to the causes of some acute problems of our society, the well-known journalist endeavours to look at our country's history with open eyes and without bias.

A. Nikolaev, 'Plunder', *Smena*, nos 18–19, 1988. A true story of the rapacious plunder of the priceless cultural heritage of the Soviet people by Stalin.

I. Shafarevitch, 'Rusofobia', *Nash Sovremennik*, no. 6, 1989. An article that provoked a mixed reaction in society and could be viewed as an example of the clash of opinions and heated debates that swept learned magazines.

Z. Yuriev, 'Home-made, Half-baked Omerta', *Smena*, no. 5, 1989. This exposure of the use of doping by Soviet athletes demonstrates how 'no-entry zones' and 'forbidden themes' are being eliminated in our press.

S. Antonov, 'Ravines', *Druzhba Narodov*, no. 1, 1988. A story about collectivization in the USSR, a most tragic event in the life of our huge country.

F. Burlatsky, 'After Stalin: Notes on the Political Thaw', *Novy Mir*, no. 10, 1988. A breathtaking narrative of the most vexed and ambiguous period in the modern history of the USSR, written by a well-known journalist who found himself in the very midst of the political and ideological work carried out by the 'apparatus'.

D. Volkogonov, 'Triumph and Tragedy: A Political Portrait of Josef. V. Stalin', *Oktyabr*, nos 10–12, 1988; 7–10, 1989. Probably the first attempt at an in-depth and unbiased analysis of the nature of the phenomenon of Stalin.

V. Grossman, 'Forever Flows', *Oktyabr*, no. 6, 1989. Another narrative by a famous Soviet writer about the fate of people during Stalin's rule. Of special importance is the philosophical and social commentary to it, *Lenin and Stalin* written by G. Vodolazov, that deals with the nature of 'the leader of all peoples's' personality cult.

A. M. Larina, 'The Unforgettable', *Znamya*, nos 10–12, 1988. Invaluable evidence by Nikolai Bukharin's wife of the dramatic events in the life of that prominent state and Party leader, and of the stormy and contradictory period in the history of the Communist Party and the Soviet state.

V. Nabokov, *Lolita*, Biblioteka Zhurnala Inostrannaya Literatura, Moscow, Izvestiya, 1989. The publication of this novel, which was a great success in the West and whose publication in the USSR seemed totally unrealistic only two or three years ago, is a most convincing proof of the dynamic changes in culture carried out by the State.

A. Naiman, 'Stories about Anna Akhmatova', *Novy Mir*, nos 1–2, 1989. One of the first in-depth studies of the talented Soviet woman poet who was anathematized and consigned to oblivion by Stalin's hirelings. This publication fills another 'blank spot' in Soviet literature and helps to restore historical justice towards an outstanding figure in Soviet culture who has made a tremendous input into the spiritual enrichment of the people.

G. Orwell, '1984', *Novy Mir*, nos 2–4, 1989. The translation into Russian and publication of the novel which had been denounced in the USSR as an anti-Soviet pasquinade, caused great interest on the part of the Soviet public which rose to fight the distortions of Socialism that occurred in the hard times of Stalin's rule and stagnation.

V. Pikul, 'It has Been a Honour for Me', *Nash Sovremennik*, nos 9–12, 1988. This new work by the well-known author of historical novels is the frank account of a Russian General Headquarters officer who served in the Russian army till the first years of World War II.

BIBLIOGRAPHY

Y. Poters, 'The Fish Do not Know Their Children', *Druzhba Narodov*, no. 3, 1988. An emotional novel by a prominent Lithuanian writer about the uneasy fates of his fellow-countrymen who were forcefully driven from their land in the time of Stalin's repression and the brotherly sympathy and help they received from the Siberians.

L. Razgon, 'An Eye-Witness Account', *Yunost*, no. 5, 1988; 1–2, 1989. The well-known writer who suffered all the hardships and deprivations which befell the victims of Stalin's repression machine recalls those hard times in the history of our people.

A. Hort, 'The Fitter Elizabeth', *Yunost*, no. 7, 1989. Satirical writers are ingenious in finding the most unusual plots to enhance the expository force of their works. This is also true of this story, written by a well-known Soviet author, which deals with a situation in which the world-renowned movie star Liz Taylor became . . . a team-leader in a Soviet work collective.

S. Kaledin, 'Construction Battalion', *Novy Mir*, no. 4, 1989. A frank, sometimes even shocking, narrative about the routine of the army construction troops, which caused a stormy public reaction and protests on the part of some servicemen.

L. Gabyshev, 'Odylan: or the Air of Freedom', *Novy Mir*, nos 6–7, 1989. A story, much of it autobiographical, about the world of a juvenile delinquents' colony full of humiliation and cruelty. It is one of those works written with talent which will help Soviet society to be firmly set on its road to the establishment of a real rule-of-law state.

E. Bogdanov, 'A Risk Group', *Druzhba Narodov*, nos 6–7, 1989. A highly social portrait of Moscow morals and manners which, as a matter of fact, may characterize any city in our country. This is an elucidating suspense story that carries the reader away with its graphic and rich language and a clearly outlined detective plot, although its main merit is a passionate call for humanism and kindness in relationships between people.

S. Lipkin, 'A Ten-Day Period', *Druzhba Narodov*, nos 5–6, 1989. A chronicle-type story, vivid and unusual, which considerably helps the understanding of the essence and causes of suddenly unleashed tensions in ethnic relations.

A. Tvardovsky, 'From the Working Notebooks', *Znamya*, nos 7–9, 1989. Basically this is a diary of the outstanding poet which reveals his sophisticated spiritual world at those uneasy times when he lived and wrote.

A. Polyakov, 'Apofigei', *Yunost*, no. 5, 1989. An ironic and very sad story about the moral degradation of a man who embarked upon the road of conformism for the sake of immediate benefits.

G. Vishnevskaya, 'Solzhenitsyn and Rostropovich', *Yunost*, nos. 6–7, 1989. Recollections of a direct participant in the events that brought together the fates of these talented creative individuals and which tragically affected the course of their lives.

Index

Abalkin, Leonid, 17
Abkhasia, 107, 117
Academy of Sciences: *see under* science
Afghanistan, 10, 49, 51, 53-4, 301
Aganbegyan, Abel G., 140, 143-57
agrarian policy, 4, 301
agriculture, 1, 3, 4, 7, 149, 154, 161, 168, 175, 185, 246
  fertilisers, 272
  prices, 151;
  see also collectives
AIDS virus, 84-5, 205
Aleksin, Anatolii, 130-1
Algeria: earthquake, 198-9
Alma-Ata, 101, 113, 115, 225
Andropov, Yuri, 169
Angara, River, 254, 268
APK (Agro-Industrial Complex), 4
'apparatus' (Party), 162, 169, 172-4, 177
Aral Sea, 257-8, 262, 267
Armenia, 12, 70, 112-4, 117-8, 155, 170
  earthquake, 198, 201-6, 295-7, 300
arms race, 59-61, 85, 94
Artisimovich, 187
astronomy 185-6, 190, 194
Azerbaijan, 5, 12, 70, 108, 114, 116-7, 300

Baikal, Lake, 254-7, 265, 268, 270-1
Baltic, 4, 101-2, 106, 109-12;
  see also Estonia; Latvia; Lithuania
banks, 151, 155
beauty contest, 2
Berdiayev, N. A., 234-6, 249
Bessmertnykh, Alexander, A., 41-64
'blat', 292
Blokhin, Oleg, 280-2, 284
Bodin, Jean, 88
bourgeoisie, 90, 134, 215
Bratsk Hydel, 259
Brezhnev, Leonid, 166, 169
Bromlei, Julian, V., 99-119
'Buran' space vehicle, 193
Bush, George, 64, 204
Byelorussia, 102, 108, 115

capitalism, 31, 36-7, 88-92, 94-5, 102
Caribbean crisis (1962), 48, 60, 85
Chekhov, Mikhail, 242

chemical science, 184, 187, 189
Chernenko, Konstantin, 169
Chernobyl disaster, 62, 85, 257
Chetverikov, Nikolai N., 121-37
China, 302
Chislenko, Igor, 280-3
Christianity, 102, 213-5, 222, 228;
  see also Russian Orthodox Church;
  Seventh Day Adventist Church
Churbanov, Yuri, 300
churches: *see* religion
cinema, 239
Citizenship, Law on, 112
CMEA: *see* Council for Mutual Economic Assistance
collectives, 3, 105, 107, 157, 161, 166, 170, 174-6, 246
Comecon: *see* Council for Mutual Economic Assistance
communication, international, 83
Communist Party of the Soviet Union, 25-7, 89, 104, 126, 131, 299, 300-2
computers, 186, 193-4
confrontation, 89, 91-2
Congress of People's Deputies, 2-4, 31, 68, 71-5, 107, 161, 175, 301-3
Constitutional Supervision, Committee for, 168
consumer goods, 150, 165, 291
conversion (for military production), 3
convertible currency, 3, 32, 147-9, 156-7
cooperatives, 30, 34, 149, 151, 171, 175-6
Council for Mutual Economic Assistance, 146, 157
CPSU: *see* Communist Party of the Soviet Union
crime, 4-5, 9, 14-5, 74, 83, 128, 299-300, 304
culture, 1, 33, 40, 233-49
currency, 3, 32, 154, 156-7;
  see also convertible currency
Customs Tariff, 153-4
Czechoslovakia, 282

decentralization, 150, 165-6
democratization, 1, 6, 25-8, 35, 68-9, 75, 110, 125, 134-5, 161, 163, 173-4, 181, 227, 278, 301, 303

INDEX

Deputies: *see* People's Deputies
détente, 89
diplomacy, 2, 9–10, 53
disarmament, 85, 300
disaster medicine, 198–207
Dostoyevsky, Fyodor, 163, 258
drama: *see* theatre
Dynamo Moscow, 280–6, 289–90

earthquakes: *see under* Algeria; Armenia; Peru
ecology, 1, 83, 94, 111, 137, 154, 191–2, 255–72, 291–2
Ecology and Peace Association, 271–2
economic reform, 3–6, 29–32, 292, 300
economy, 143–77
education, 33, 226, 293–4
election, 34, 301
electoral reform, 68–71, 174, 292
electric power, 254, 267, 272
Engels, Friedrich, 233
enterprises, 5–6, 150–2, 175, 293;
  see also State Enterprises, Law on
environment: *see* ecology
Estonia, 109, 114, 117
ethnic communities, 102
ethnic relations, 27–8, 40, 72, 101–19, 293, 303
European Community, 52, 154
exports, 143–7, 152, 154, 157

farming; *see* agriculture; collectives
Fiasco of Futurology, The, 94
Five-Year Plan (1991–5), 157
folk medicine, 15–6
foodstuffs, 291–2
football, 273–90
  Union of Football Leagues, 278
  World Cup, 281, 288
forecast, political, 77
forecasting, scientific, 152
foreign policy, 4, 43–64
  balances of forces and interests, 50, 59, 63
  diversity of today's world, 51–2
  realism in considering the past, 46, 49–50
foreign trade, 142–5, 150, 152–4
  harmonized system, 153–4
free enterprise zones, 1, 154
freedom of conscience, 213–4, 216, 222, 224–7
Frolov, Ivan, 8
Fyodorov, Svyatoslav, 205–6

Galbraith, John K., 94
GATT: *see* General Agreement on Tariffs and Trade
Gdlyan, Telman, 14–5
General Agreement on Tariffs and Trade, 103–4
Georgia, 103, 112, 114–5, 117, 301
German Federal Republic, 303
glasnost, 8–9, 23, 34–5, 40, 110, 123–5, 129, 130–6, 173, 192, 198, 278, 283, 292, 302–3
globalization, 82–3, 88, 93
Gogol, Nikolai V., 239
Gorbachev, Mikhail S., 2, 46, 55, 58, 62, 132, 155, 169, 173, 192, 299, 300–3, 305
Gromyko, Andrei, 293
Gumilev, Lev, 235, 238

harmonized trade, 153–4
health: *see* medicine
Homo sovieticus, 8
housing, 291–2
  action and lessons after Armenia earthquake, 296–7
human interests and values, 77, 86, 97
human rights, 40, 73, 94

Ilizarov, Gavriil, 13–4
imports, 144–6, 150, 153
India, 299
industry, 145–6, 150–2, 154, 164–5, 173, 185
interdependence, 81–2, 87, 143, 145
International Court of Justice, 87
International Monetary Fund, 148, 155
International Relations, Institute of, 9
internationalization, 36, 40, 81–2, 87, 97, 194
  to alleviate major disasters, 202
Ireland, 301
Israel, 299, 300
Ivanov, Ivan D., 141–57
Izvestia, 133

joint-stock companies, 30–1, 175
joint ventures, 6, 146–7, 149, 153, 176, 269
journalism: *see* mass media; press

Kamentsev, Vladimir, 142–3
Kapitsa, Peter, 184, 187, 194
Karakalpakia, 262
Kasyan, Nikolai, 15–6
Katun Hydel, 271
Kazakhstan, 108–9, 113–4
Kennedy, John F., 48, 61
KGB (Komitet Gosudarstvennoi Bezopasnosti – State Security Committee), 302
Kharkov, 174
Khlebnikov, Velimir, 236–7, 244
Khrushchev, Nikita S., 48, 166, 246–7, 266
Kirghizia, 114, 117
Kisin, Evgeni, 10–11
Korolenko, Vladimir G., 214–5
Korotich, Vitali, 9, 174
Kosygin, Alexei, 166
Kudryavtsev, Vladimir N., 65–78
Kulakov, Mikhail P., 217–28

Landau, Lev, 188, 194
languages, 102–3, 117–8

310

INDEX

laser, 185
Latvia, 109, 117
law, 65, 73–6
  international, 82–4, 86
  Law on Citizenship, 112
  Law on State Enterprises, 76, 152, 303
  Law on the Freedom of Conscience, 226–7
  Law on the Press and Mass Media, 35–6, 129
  religion and law, 222–3, 225–7
  Union of USSR Lawyers, 303;
  see also rule-of-law state
League of Nations, 86
leasing, 3, 7, 149, 175–6, 293
Lenin, Vladimir I., 29, 32, 37–9, 49, 103–4, 133, 135, 162–3, 183, 233, 245
Leninakan: *see* Armenia: earthquake
'Lenkom' (theatre), 247
Let History Judge, 11, 302
Ligachev, Egor, 15
literature, 35, 254
Literaturnaya Gazeta, 123, 133, 181
Lithuania, 114
Lobanovsky, Valery, 286, 288–9
Lokhonosov, Victor, 130
Lysenko, Trofim, 186
Lyubimov, Youri, 247, 302

Machiavelli, Niccolò, 43
Management Consultation and Managers' Training Centre, 177
managers, 6, 67, 161–77
  Association of Young Managers, 176–7
  election, 294
manual therapy, 16
market mechanism, 31–2
Marxism, 37–8, 40, 97, 162, 233
mass media, 16–7, 34–6, 82, 123–37, 223;
  see also press; television
media: *see* mass media
medicine, 13–6, 84–5, 195–207
Medvedev, Roy, 11–2, 302
Medvedev, Vadim A., 21–40
mercy, 2, 77, 224, 227
Meyerhold, Vsevolod E., 236–7, 239–48
Middle East, 54
militarism, 84, 93
military production, 3, 59, 85, 150–1, 184, 206–7
missiles: *see* nuclear weapons
modernization, 145–6
Molotov, Vyacheslav M., 48–9
mondialism: *see* 'world government'
money market, 153
morals, 2, 40, 227, 292
Moscow: research institutes, 190
Moscow News, 125, 181
music, 10–1, 15

Nagorny Karabakh, 5, 12–3, 101, 113, 118, 300

nationalism, 28, 101–3, 106, 110, 134
NATO: *see* North Atlantic Treaty Organization
Nature, State Committee for, 256
North Atlantic Treaty Organization, 53, 85
Novosibirsk Academic Township, 155, 189
nuclear energy, 154, 272
nuclear weapons, 52, 57–62, 82–3, 85–6, 181, 192, 299, 304

Ogonyok, 9, 174
Orthodox Church: *see* Russian Orthodox Church

Party
  allegiance, 184
  Conference (19th), 24
  relations with voluntary sector, 26
  role, 24–6, 34, 162–4, 233
Pauls, Raymond, 15
peaceful coexistence, 51, 85
People's Deputies, 3–4, 68, 71–4, 161, 174, 182, 234, 257, 292–3, 299–301;
  see also Congress of People's Deputies
people's diplomacy, 2
perestroika
  bibliography, 307
  chronology, 299
  effect on rival political systems, 89, 92
  ideology, 23–40
  public opinion, 292
  transnational character, 45–6
  two main achievements, 136
Peru: earthquake, 198–9
philosophy, 8
Phobos mission, 181, 194
physics, 185–7
pluralism, 2, 23, 34–5, 129–30, 135, 149, 163
political reform, 24, 67–78, 299–301
political sciences, 79
pollution, 256, 269, 292;
  see also ecology
Popov, Gavriil Kh., 159–77
popular front, 4
population
  census, 301
  ethnic communities, 102–3
Pravda, 125, 218
press, 8–9, 35, 123–4, 126–7, 130, 135–7, 215, 292
  Law on the Press and Mass Media, 35–6
pricing, 151, 164
professionalism in sport, 2, 278, 283–6
proletariat, 90
property, 2, 29, 149, 162
public opinion, 1, 23, 34, 124
  All-Union Centre of Public Opinion Studies, 291
  polls, 291–4
Pugacheva, Alla, 15

311

INDEX

Rasputin, Valentin G., 253–72, 279
Reagan, Ronald, 58
regional aid, 84
regional conflicts, 53–6
religion, 102–3, 118, 213–28
rule-of-law state, 5, 23–4, 32, 36, 40, 71, 73, 75, 77, 299
Russia (Federated Republic), 4, 70, 102
Russian Orthodox Church, 102, 217
Ryzhkov, Nikolai, 303

Sagdeev, Roald Z., 181–94
Sakharov, Andrei, 181–2
Schultz, George, 43
science, 105, 154, 183–207
   Academy of Sciences, 70, 181, 185, 187, 189–92
   research, 184, 186–8, 190–4
   social, 78, 97
   State Committee for Science and Technology, 185
Scientific Socialism, 11, 56
security, international, 53, 56, 58
   state: *see* KGB
Semenov, Nikolai, 184, 187, 189
Seventh Day Adventist Church, 212–6, 218–20, 223–5, 228
Shakhnazarov, Georgi Kh., 79–98
Sheverdnadze, Eduard, 43–4, 46, 301
Siberia, 103, 141, 168, 254, 260, 262, 268, 270
Sklifosovsky Research Institute of Emergency Medical Care, 196, 200, 202, 205
Slyunkov, Nikolai, 299
Sochi, 167
social insurance, 303
social science, 78, 97
Socialism
   basic benefits, 95–6
   humanistic nature, 39–40
   poles apart from capitalism, 94
   process characteristic of all countries, 96
   reassessed, 37–40
   Scientific, 11, 96
Socio-Ecological Union, 271
Solzhenitsin, Alexander I., 268
Soukhanova, Julia, 2
sovereignty, 87–8
Sovesskaya Cultura, 133
Soviet, local, 3
Soviet federation, 72
Soviet manager, 6
'Sovremennik' (theatre), 247
space research, 181, 185, 192–4
Special Rule, 5, 300

sport, 273–90
Sputnik, 185
Stalinism, 48, 96, 104, 133, 183–4, 227, 238, 245–6, 302
Stalinist Repression, Memorial to the Memory of the Victims of, 2, 9
standardization, 154
Stanislavsky, Konstantin S., 234–6, 239–43, 245–8
Starodubtsev, Vladimir, 7
State Enterprises, Law on, 76, 152, 303
Supreme Soviet (of the USSR), 68, 72–4, 76, 105, 272, 299–300, 302–3
   Chairman elected, 302

'Taganka' (theatre), 243, 247
TASS, 121, 302
Tatars, 101, 106, 112
Tbilisi, 101, 301
television, 1–2, 35, 124, 128, 233, 303
Teryaev, Vladislav G., 195–207
theatre, 231–49
transportation, international, 83, 154
TV-bridge, 1–2
Tyumen, 270

Ufa pipeline disaster, 203–6
Ukraine, 102, 106, 113, 115
United Nations, 83, 84, 87, 155, 300
United States, 43–4, 52–3, 57–62, 85, 151, 172–3, 304
Uzbek case, 14
Uzbekistan, 101–2, 113–5, 117, 262

Vasiliev, Ivan, 131
Vasilyevich, Anatoli, 214–5
Vega mission, 181, 194
Vernadsky, V. I., 226
Voice of Truth, The, 218
Volga, River, 257, 260–2, 264–5, 271
Vorontsov, Yuli, 9–10
Vysitsky, Vladimir, 247

Warsaw Pact, 53, 85
Washington, George, 44
water development/resources, 259–68;
   see also pollution
'world government', 86–8
writers: *see* literature; press

Yakuts, 114
Yashin, Lev, 273–90
Yeltsin, Boris, 168
Youtkevich, Sergei, 247

Zakharov, Mark A., 233–49
Zaslavskaya, Tatyana, 291